1980s Project Studies/Council on Foreign Relations

STUDIES AVAILABLE

ENHANCING GLOBAL HUMAN RIGHTS
Studies by Jorge I. Domínguez, Nigel S. Rodley, Bryce Wood, and Richard Falk

OIL POLITICS IN THE 1980s:
Patterns of International Cooperation
Øystein Noreng

SIX BILLION PEOPLE:
Demographic Dilemmas and World Politics
Studies by Georges Tapinos and Phyllis T. Piotrow

THE MIDDLE EAST IN THE COMING DECADE:
From Wellhead to Well-being?
Studies by John Waterbury and Ragaei El Mallakh

REDUCING GLOBAL INEQUITIES
Studies by W. Howard Wriggins and Gunnar Adler-Karlsson

RICH AND POOR NATIONS IN THE WORLD ECONOMY
Studies by Albert Fishlow, Carlos F. Díaz-Alejandro, Richard R. Fagen, and Roger D. Hansen

CONTROLLING FUTURE ARMS TRADE
Studies by Anne Hessing Cahn and Joseph J. Kruzel, Peter M. Dawkins, and Jacques Huntzinger

DIVERSITY AND DEVELOPMENT IN SOUTHEAST ASIA:
The Coming Decade
Studies by Guy J. Pauker, Frank H. Golay, and Cynthia H. Enloe

NUCLEAR WEAPONS AND WORLD POLITICS:
Alternatives for the Future
Studies by David C. Gompert, Michael Mandelbaum, Richard L. Garwin, and John H. Burton

CHINA'S FUTURE:

Foreign Policy and Economic Development in the Post-Mao Era

Studies by Allen S. Whiting and by Robert F. Dernberger

ALTERNATIVES TO MONETARY DISORDER

Studies by Fred Hirsch and Michael W. Doyle and by Edward L. Morse

NUCLEAR PROLIFERATION:

Motivations, Capabilities, and Strategies for Control

Studies by Ted Greenwood and by Harold A. Feiveson and Theodore B. Taylor

INTERNATIONAL DISASTER RELIEF:

Toward a Responsive System

Stephen Green

STUDIES FORTHCOMING

The 1980s Project will comprise about 30 volumes. Most will contain independent but related studies concerning issues of potentially great importance in the next decade and beyond, such as resource management, human rights, population studies, and relations between the developing and developed societies, among many others. Additionally, a number of volumes will be devoted to particular regions of the world, concentrating especially on political and economic development trends outside the industrialized West.

Enhancing Global Human Rights

Enhancing Global Human Rights

JORGE I. DOMÍNGUEZ

NIGEL S. RODLEY

BRYCE WOOD

RICHARD FALK

Introduction by Richard H. Ullman

1980s Project/Council on Foreign Relations

McGRAW-HILL BOOK COMPANY
New York   St. Louis   San Francisco
Auckland   Bogotá   Düsseldorf   Johannesburg   London   Madrid
Mexico   Montreal   New Delhi   Panama   Paris   São Paulo
Singapore   Sydney   Tokyo   Toronto

The Council on Foreign Relations, Inc. is a nonprofit and nonpartisan organization devoted to promoting improved understanding of international affairs through the free exchange of ideas. Its membership of about 1,700 persons throughout the United States is made up of individuals with special interest and experience in international affairs. The Council has no affiliation with and receives no funding from the United States government.

The Council publishes the journal *Foreign Affairs* and, from time to time, books and monographs which in the judgment of the Council's Committee on Studies are responsible treatments of significant international topics worthy of presentation to the public. The 1980s Project is a research effort of the Council; as such, 1980s Project Studies have been similarly reviewed through procedures of the Committee on Studies. As in the case of all Council publications, statements of fact and expressions of opinion contained in 1980s Project Studies are the sole responsibility of their authors.

The editors of this book were Susan Hall, Amy Litt, Michael Schwarz, and Thomas E. Wallin for the Council on Foreign Relations. Thomas Quinn and Michael Hennelly were the editors for McGraw-Hill Book Company. Christopher Simon was the designer and Teresa Leaden supervised the production. This book was set in Times Roman by Offset Composition Services, Inc.

Printed and bound by R. R. Donnelley & Sons.

341.481
E 58

Library of Congress Cataloging in Publication Data
Main entry under title:

Enhancing global human rights.

(1980s Project/Council on Foreign Relations)
Bibliography: p.
Includes index.
1. Civil rights—Addresses, essays, lectures.
I. Domínguez, Jorge I. II. Series: Council on Foreign Relations. 1980s Project/Council on Foreign Relations.
JC571.E683   341.48'1   78–13002
ISBN 0–07–017397–4
ISBN 0–07–017398–2 pbk.

1 2 3 4 5 6 7 8 9 RRDRRD 7 9 8 3 2 1 0 9

Contents

Foreword: The 1980s Project   ix

HUMAN RIGHTS: TOWARD INTERNATIONAL ACTION
  Richard H. Ullman   1

ASSESSING HUMAN RIGHTS CONDITIONS
  Jorge I. Domínguez

  Introduction   21

  1. International Human Rights Norms   25

  2. Case Studies   49

  3. Four Cross-National Human Rights Issue Areas   87

  4. Conclusion   103

MONITORING HUMAN RIGHTS VIOLATIONS IN THE 1980s
  Nigel S. Rodley   117

HUMAN RIGHTS ISSUES IN LATIN AMERICA
  Bryce Wood

  Introduction   155

  1. The Latin American Scene   159

  2. The International Scene   173

  3. Latin American Issues: The Outlook   199

CONTENTS

RESPONDING TO SEVERE VIOLATIONS

Richard Falk

Introduction   *207*

1. Types of Severe Violations   *215*

2. What Can Be Done about Severe Violations?   *231*

3. Future Prospects and Speculations   *247*

Selected Bibliography   259
Index   261
About the Authors   269

Foreword: The 1980s Project

These studies of the emerging international sensitivity to violations of human rights, of the spectrum of potential violations, and
of procedures that might be put in train to reduce or eliminate
them, are part of a stream of studies commissioned by the 1980s
Project of the Council on Foreign Relations. Each 1980s Project
study analyzes an issue or set of issues that is likely to be of
international concern during the coming decade or two.

The ambitious purpose of the 1980s Project is to examine
important political and economic problems not only individually
but in relationship to one another. Some studies or books produced by the Project will primarily emphasize the interrelation-
ship of issues. In the case of other, more specifically focused
studies, a considerable effort has been made to write, review, and
criticize them in the context of more general Project work. Each
Project study is thus capable of standing on its own: at the same
time it has been shaped by a broader perspective.

The 1980s Project had its origin in the widely held recognition
that many of the assumptions, policies, and institutions that have
characterized international relations during the past 30 years are
inadequate to the demands of today and the foreseeable demands
of the period between now and 1990 or so. Over the course of the
next decade, substantial adaptation of institutions and behavior
will be needed to respond to the changed circumstances of the
1980s and beyond. The Project seeks to identify those future
conditions and the kinds of adaptation they might require. It is not

the Project's purpose to arrive at a single or exclusive set of goals. Nor does it focus upon the foreign policy or national interests of the United States alone. Instead, it seeks to identify goals that are compatible with the perceived interests of most states, despite differences in ideology and in level of economic development.

The published products of the Project are aimed at a broad readership, including policy makers and potential policy makers and those who would influence the policy-making process, but are confined to no single nation or region. The authors of Project studies were therefore asked to remain mindful of interests broader than those of any one society and to take fully into account the likely realities of domestic politics in the principal societies involved. All those who have worked on the Project, however, have tried not to be captives of the status quo; they have sought to question the inevitability of existing patterns of thought and behavior that restrain desirable change and to look for ways in which those patterns might in time be altered or their consequences mitigated.

The 1980s Project is at once a series of separate attacks upon a number of urgent and potentially urgent international problems and also a collective effort, involving a substantial number of persons in the United States and abroad, to bring those separate approaches to bear upon one another and to suggest the kinds of choices that might be made among them. The Project involves more than 300 participants. A small central staff and a steering Coordinating Group have worked to define the questions and to assess the compatibility of policy prescriptions. Nearly 100 authors, from more than a dozen countries, have been at work on separate studies. Ten working groups of specialists and generalists have been convened to subject the Project's studies to critical scrutiny and to help in the process of identifying interrelationships among them.

The 1980s Project is the largest single research and studies effort the Council on Foreign Relations has undertaken in its 55-year history, comparable in conception only to a major study of the postwar world, the War and Peace Studies, undertaken by the Council during the Second World War. At that time, the impetus of the effort was the discontinuity caused by worldwide conflict and the visible and inescapable need to rethink, replace, and supplement many of the features of the international system that had prevailed before the war. The discontinuities in today's world are less obvious and, even when occasionally quite visible—as in the abandonment of gold convertibility and fixed monetary parities—only briefly command the spotlight of public attention. That new institutions and patterns of behavior are needed in many areas is widely acknowledged, but the sense of need is less urgent—existing institutions have not for the most part dramatically failed and collapsed. The tendency, therefore, is to make do with outmoded arrangements and to improvise rather than to undertake a basic analysis of the problems that lie before us and of the demands that those problems will place upon all nations.

The 1980s Project is based upon the belief that serious effort and integrated forethought can contribute—indeed, are indispensable—to progress in the next decade toward a more humane, peaceful, productive, and just world. And it rests upon the hope that participants in its deliberations and readers of Project publications—whether or not they agree with an author's point of view—may be helped to think more informedly about the opportunities and the dangers that lie ahead and the consequences of various possible courses of future action.

The 1980s Project has been made possible by generous grants from the Ford Foundation, the Lilly Endowment, the Andrew W. Mellon Foundation, the Rockefeller Foundation, and the German Marshall Fund of the United States. Neither the Council on Foreign Relations nor any of those foundations is responsible for statements of fact and expressions of opinion contained in publications of the 1980s Project; they are the sole responsibility of the individual authors under whose names they appear. But the Council on Foreign Relations and the staff of the 1980s Project take great pleasure in placing those publications before a wide readership both in the United States and abroad.

1980s PROJECT WORKING GROUPS

During 1975 and 1976, ten Working Groups met to explore major international issues and to subject initial drafts of 1980s Project studies to critical review. Those who chaired Project Working Groups were:

Cyrus R. Vance, Working Group on Nuclear Weapons and Other Weapons of Mass Destruction

Leslie H. Gelb, Working Group on Armed Conflict

Roger Fisher, Working Group on Transnational Violence and Subversion

Rev. Theodore M. Hesburgh, Working Group on Human Rights

Joseph S. Nye, Jr., Working Group on the Political Economy of North-South Relations

Harold Van B. Cleveland, Working Group on Macroeconomic Policies and International Monetary Relations

Lawrence C. McQuade, Working Group on Principles of International Trade

William Diebold, Jr., Working Group on Multinational Enterprises

Eugene B. Skolnikoff, Working Group on the Environment, the Global Commons, and Economic Growth

Miriam Camps, Working Group on Industrial Policy

1980s PROJECT STAFF

Persons who have held senior professional positions on the staff of the 1980s Project for all or part of its duration are:

Miriam Camps	*Catherine Gwin*
William Diebold, Jr.	*Roger D. Hansen*
Tom J. Farer	*Edward L. Morse*
David C. Gompert	*Richard H. Ullman*

Richard H. Ullman was Director of the 1980s Project from its inception in 1974 until July 1977, when he became Chairman of the Project Coordinating Group. Edward L. Morse was Executive Director from July 1977 until June 1978. At that time, Catherine Gwin, 1980s Project Fellow since 1976, took over as Executive Director.

PROJECT COORDINATING GROUP

The Coordinating Group of the 1980s had a central advisory role in the work of the Project. Its members as of June 30, 1978, were:

Carlos F. Díaz-Alejandro
Richard A. Falk
Tom J. Farer
Edward K. Hamilton
Stanley Hoffman
Gordon J. MacDonald
Bruce K. MacLaury

Bayless Manning
Theodore R. Marmor
Ali Mazrui
Michael O'Neill
Stephen Stamas
Fritz Stern
Allen S. Whiting

Until they entered government service, other members included:

W. Michael Blumenthal
Richard N. Cooper
Samuel P. Huntington

Joseph S. Nye, Jr.
Marshall D. Shulman

COMMITTEE ON STUDIES

The Committee on Studies of the Board of Directors of the Council on Foreign Relations is the governing body of the 1980s Project. The Committee's members as of June 30, 1978, were:

Barry E. Carter
Robert A. Charpie
Stanley Hoffmann
Henry A. Kissinger
Walter J. Levy

Robert E. Osgood
Stephen Stamas
Paul A. Volcker
Marina v. N. Whitman

James A. Perkins (Chairman)

Enhancing Global Human Rights

Introduction: Human Rights— Toward International Action

Richard H. Ullman

No time is ever really good for human rights. Those with power will always find persuasive reasons to silence, coerce, or otherwise deprive those without it. But some times are worse than others. Whether the 1980s will be among those periods, or whether they will be better, depends upon which is the stronger of two conflicting tendencies. On the one hand, the constituency for human rights—the number of concerned persons worldwide— is clearly growing, as claims for international equity are simultaneously being reflected in claims for domestic justice. On the other hand, as governments feel increasingly hard pressed in their efforts to cope with burgeoning populations, they are more likely to direct repressive power against those who disagree with their goals or their means of achieving them.

Although history is filled with examples of rulers who gratuitously injured those within their grasp—frivolous or sadistic execution, torture and bodily or mental injury of all sorts, and prolonged incarceration have been found to greater or lesser degrees in virtually all societies at all times—governments rarely indulge casually in egregious violations of human rights. Rather, they do so because they fear that otherwise they cannot continue to hold power, or they fear that they will be deflected from the pursuit of programs that they judge to be in their own interests (as individuals or as representatives of a class) or in the interests

1

of their entire societies. The less the pressure on governments and the more modest the programs they attempt to pursue, the easier it is for rulers to respect the personal integrity and dignity of the ruled.

Relative affluence may not be a sufficient condition to assure respect for human rights—there are societies, such as Brazil, where growing affluence has been accompanied by a drastic increase in official repression—but there are many who would argue that it is virtually a necessary condition. When resources are scarce, when there are too many mouths to feed, when governments feel impelled either by circumstance or by doctrine (or both) to pursue programs of great austerity, then opposition grows. Opponents may simply be persons who will try to divert resources for their own use or to benefit their clan, their tribe, or their class. Or they may be persons who wish to speak out against and organize against governmental resource allocations they consider to be wrong. Regimes that for one reason or another feel hard pressed lash out to assure adherence to rules or to stifle dissent.

In turn, repressive actions often generate more opposition from opponents, now even more determined, who may counter official repression with terror. And terror, in its turn, gives rise to more widespread and indiscriminate official repression. In such circumstances, even governments profoundly committed to the protection of human rights, such as the government of the United Kingdom in the contemporary case of Ulster, may come near a descent into the depths that have so much marked our century. At the other end of the scale are the governments of least-advantaged nations that are simply unable to cope with the overwhelming human problems they face every day. They may allow a minority to hoard resources needed throughout a society or permit widespread communal violence by one group against others. This may occur either because as governments they are powerless to prevent such depredations, or because they themselves are representative of only a portion of their population and, indeed, often consider the remainder (whether it be a minority or a majority) to be congenitally inferior and therefore not deserving of protection.

The 1980s are likely to see an intensification of trends that

2

could lead governments increasingly to violate human rights. One is the rising curve of population and all of the problems exacerbated by population growth: shortages of foodstuffs, uncontrolled expansion of urban regions and the consequent crowding of countless millions into slumlike conditions of living, increased pressure on nonrenewable resources such as fossil fuels, and the like. Population growth will continue since the leveling off that many demographers now predict will not take place until some years into the next century.[1] New energy technologies will not yet be operational in the 1980s and therefore the costs of all sorts of activities, ranging from fertilizing crops to housing persons, will continue to increase and pressures on many governments will seem correspondingly higher. One traditional safety valve—widespread migration across national frontiers by persons seeking better conditions—will largely disappear as governments become more active at barring entry and, in some instances, at preventing departure.

Another trend is that of technological progress that steadily enhances the ability of the state to spy upon and bring repressive force against targeted individuals and groups, without at the same time bringing about a comparable enhancement of the ability of those targeted to resist or erode the exercise of state authority. The advance of technology will also seem to pose new and different threats to governments. For example, increased use of nuclear fission as an energy source may drastically increase the amount of plutonium in circulation. The inordinate hazards to life that plutonium would pose, either as a chemical poison or as the fissionable core of nuclear weapons, comprise just one of the technologically generated threats that may cause governments to feel that public safety depends upon the use of surveillance techniques that increasingly impinge upon the lives of individuals. Yet the same wave of technological progress that brings nuclear energy makes possible far-reaching surveillance techniques, employable not only by the governments of advanced, industrialized states but also by those of less developed societies: the intelligence services of countries like Iran or Brazil will be able to purchase the same sort of sophisticated, computer-based surveillance and monitoring systems as those employed by the Soviet KGB or, for that matter, by the American FBI.

3

And just as police forces will be more able to monitor movements of persons and gain access to their most private communications, so will they also increasingly be able to take direct action against them—for example, by means of behavior-distorting chemicals and other techniques unknown to previous generations.

For all these reasons, the 1980s may be a gloomy decade for those concerned with human rights. At the same time, the ranks of persons, worldwide, who feel deep concern about violations of human rights are likely to grow. The communications revolution that has made the surveillance of persons easier also makes it possible for persons in many societies to be more aware of the existence of barbarism elsewhere. The television-watching public around the world cannot be unaware of terror and counterterror in Argentina and Ulster, of the murder of large numbers of real or imagined opponents by Uganda's Idi Amin, of the refusal of the government of Ethiopia to acknowledge the existence of famine in parts of its country and therefore to allow international relief organizations to operate, or of the suppression of dissidents in the Soviet Union or South Korea. The common humanity of the victims everywhere is a fact now more graphically engraved on the consciousness of all who are prepared to give the victims even a fractional part of their attention.

To some degree, and in some places, walls to national sovereignty are becoming more permeable so that persons in one society are prepared to assume some responsibility for preventing violations of human rights in other societies. This is particularly the case in Western Europe. Most of the Western European states have subscribed to the European Convention on Human Rights, which is monitored by an investigatory European Human Rights Commission and enforced by a European Human Rights Court. These institutions comprise a highly effective monitoring and enforcement system. The broad-based public concern over human rights that underlies them extends to European states that have not subscribed, as both the Franco regime in Spain and the Greek junta of the colonels could have attested. There is in Europe a widespread feeling that the common culture linking European societies to one another should not permit serious violations of human rights and that citizens of one national society

4

have a presumptive right to know about, comment upon, censure, and even exert sanctions against violations of human rights in other European countries.

The European human rights machinery has been primarily concerned with what are sometimes called the traditional civil or political rights. These are the rights enumerated in some of the first 10 amendments to the Constitution of the United States, and they have to do with the relationship between governmental authority and individuals or groups under that authority. Running through them is an underlying assumption of a natural juxtaposition between state and person and of the right of the person to be safeguarded against unusual, arbitrary, or over-reaching acts of state authority. At the center of this concept of human rights are the rights of free speech and of peaceful assembly and the presumption that so long as persons are allowed to speak out freely against governmental authority and to come together with others to organize opposition to that authority, those rights whose violation entails more drastic consequences—rights of the person against summary execution, torture, or unwarranted detention—would perforce be safeguarded.

Alongside this conception of rights, with its emphasis on political processes, there is another conception sometimes labeled "human needs." Broadly speaking, "human needs" include those aspects of existence necessary to secure the basic development of the person: adequate nutrition, housing, medical care, and education. Contemporary listings of human rights, such as the Universal Declaration on Human Rights, include these basic needs as human rights alongside the traditional civil and political rights mentioned above. Those who emphasize these basic needs contend that their assurance or deprivation is just as much a subject for and a result of state policy as is the assurance or deprivation of traditional civil and political rights. When, either through negligence or through deliberate acts of policy, governments deny the basic needs of persons living within the territory they control, they violate their human rights just as surely as they violate the human rights of political opponents whom they muzzle or jail. Often, motivations underlying these different kinds of deprivations merge. For example, in times of hardship

5

governments allocate foodstuffs so as to reward their political friends and punish their enemies. The same has sometimes been true in times of natural disaster when relief supplies have flowed to those groups, communities, or regions that have supported the particular central government in power and away from its enemies.[2] Governments can choose to pursue economic policies designed to emphasize the task of meeting the basic needs of the least advantaged members of the society. But other economic strategies may have an opposite effect, disproportionately rewarding those already better off and hurting or not substantially helping the poor.

There is no hierarchical relationship between civil and political liberties and human needs. Some observers would agree with Bertolt Brecht's memorable observation, *Erst kommt das Fressen, dann kommt die Moral*. ("First feed your face, then talk morality.") Others would hold that the classical liberal's emphasis on free speech is the key to the enjoyment of all other values, for only where there is broad political participation and where dissent may be freely expressed will those at the bottom of a social order be able to affect the fundamental allocational decisions that will determine whether or not human needs are met.

Not surprisingly, given considerations such as these, recent years have seen increasingly widespread recognition of the difficulty of drawing a distinction between "human rights" and "human needs." Within the West there is also a growing recognition that to some degree the misery of the least advantaged states has been exacerbated by actions and policies on the part of the advanced, industrialized, market-economy states, and that the latter have a responsibility to contribute to the alleviation of human needs in poor countries. There is thus a growing recognition of the legitimacy of demands for resource transfers from rich to poor countries and for structural changes in the world economy to assure that such resource transfers occur on a regular and continuing, rather than on an ad hoc basis. There is also an increasing awareness that special measures are necessary to meet needs created by special circumstances, such as natural or human-caused disasters. New attention has therefore been paid to mechanisms to provide international measures of disaster relief under the auspices of the United Nations Disaster Relief Organization or the UN's High Commissioner for Refugees.[3]

Human needs and human rights have necessarily been a central concern of the 1980s Project. It is a truism, yet one often lost from sight, that human beings are the irreducible minimum at the center of all the phenomena explored by social studies. All the policy measures delineated in the 1980s Project have an ultimate effect upon human beings, even though the human core is often lost from sight amidst abstract phrases like "maintaining nuclear deterrence," "reforming the international monetary system," "implementing global industrial policies," "damping armed conflicts," and the like. All of these actions are taken in the name of welfare—the welfare of national societies or of "global society," but ultimately the welfare of individual human beings. The 1980s Project, of course, commissioned studies directly related to meeting human needs.[4] Those in the present volume focus mainly upon "human rights," but they also indicate how artificial is the distinction between "rights" and "needs." There is a universal need for each human being to be secure in his or her own person. Such security consists of assurances against arbitrary acts of violence or brutality on the part of government. But it also consists of assurances of adequate nutrition, housing, medical care, and education.

The studies in this volume explore three aspects of the seamless web of human rights. First is the problem of defining human rights and of devising operationally useful indicators by means of which the behavior of governments in protecting or violating them might be assessed. Second is the problem of actually making use of these indicators, or others, in monitoring the actions of governments worldwide—the issue of *who* should do the monitoring and *how* it should be done. Third is the problem of acting upon the information provided by monitors: once it has been determined that a given government is guilty of egregious violations of the human rights of persons living under its authority, how can concerned parties—individuals, governments, and international organizations—cause it to modify its behavior?

Each of these problems raises formidable difficulties. Far from

7

least among them is the initial task of defining human rights in a world of many cultures and conflicting ideologies. Even among members of the same cultural grouping, there are frequently differences of opinion between elites and "average" members on the weights they would assign to different human rights or needs. In fact, there may be considerable agreement across national frontiers among elites; in some instances the existence of transnational elite networks, such as professional associations, cultural organizations, joint scientific endeavors, and so forth, may also affect mass perceptions. Another aspect of the task of devising indicators of standards of human rights is to frame them in such a way as to make possible both static comparisons across societies—snapshots of human rights behavior at any given instant—and dynamic comparison: the measurement of change, either improvement or retrogression, within a single society. For those concerned with human rights on a day-to-day, practical basis, it may be less relevant that country A is more restrictive than country B in allowing dissenters to make known their views or less egalitarian than country C in providing health services to rural regions, than that the new government of country A is less restrictive of dissent or more egalitarian regarding medical care than was its predecessor.

Jorge Domínguez's study in this volume is an impressive effort to develop operationally relevant intersocietal indicators for assessing human rights behavior on the part of governments. It is nevertheless only partially successful. In order to isolate indicators that would be at the same time comprehensive, mutually exclusive, and significant across ideological and cultural boundaries, Domínguez makes use of the eightfold set of value categories first suggested some three decades ago by Harold Lasswell and Abraham Kaplan—*power, respect, rectitude, affection, wealth, well-being, skills,* and *enlightenment.* Although Domínguez goes considerably further than Lasswell and Kaplan in defining these values in operational terms in order to reduce them to behavioral patterns measurable by impartial observers, he does so with some degree of arbitrariness. The value categories themselves remain somewhat abstract and their behavioral attributes rather arbitrary. These deficiencies would not matter, it can be argued, if widespread, crosscultural agreement can be achieved on the basis of this or, for that matter, any other set of value categories. But in so highly politicized a realm as human rights, crosscultural agreement will always be extraordinarily difficult to reach. To the extent that agreement is achieved because the values distinguished are abstract, controversy will then shift to the behavioral attributes assigned to make the values operational, and the task of arriving at "practical," "objective" indicators will not be made easier.

Domínguez's essay makes clear that he is aware that the value categories he has suggested may not be fully satisfactory. At the same time, he demonstrates persuasively that they are more satisfactory than other sets of categories now being used by other analysts. He is aware also of another deficiency: the scheme he proposes is more useful for making comparisons over time of conditions within one society than it is for making comparisons among several societies at a single instant. Thus, to cite the cases he himself explores, it is easier to chart progress (or its absence) over time in Mexico or Cuba than it is to compare Mexico and Cuba at any given moment. Finally, Domínguez deliberately abjures suggesting any hierarchical relationship among the value categories he employs. Rectitude and its behavioral attributes may or may not be more fundamental to the establishment of desirable conditions of living than power or well-being and their behavioral attributes. Observers may differ, in part guided by culturally induced preferences. Domínguez does not disclose what his own preferences are; he argues instead that *all* the value categories are, to greater or lesser degrees, important. Disclosure and consensus may or may not be necessary for the effective operation of any internationally based monitoring system whose purpose is to apply the value categories to the measurement of actual behavior. But both a hierarchy of preferences and consensus about that hierarchy would certainly be necessary before outsiders can take effective action to induce a government to modify its behavior in any significant way.

Effective action and how to take it is the theme of the other studies in this volume: the indices of human rights that Domínguez develops are obviously relevant only if there exist agencies to employ them and to publicize findings based upon them and mechanisms to bring pressure to bear against governments that violate generally accepted standards of human decency. Some such agencies already exist. The network of European institutions for receiving complaints regarding violations of human rights and for enforcing commonly held standards has already been mentioned. In the Western Hemisphere, the Inter-American Human Rights Commission—described in detail in Bryce Wood's contribution to this volume—struggles valiantly, with inadequate resources and against a climate of governmental hostility, to monitor and to publicize violations. On the global level, however, the UN human rights machinery has become so politicized as to be almost completely ineffective for either monitoring or for enforcement.

Monitoring and publicizing is the particular concern of Nigel Rodley's study. As he makes clear, with the exception of the European Commission, most of the effective monitoring that now takes place is done by private nongovernmental organizations, with Amnesty International as perhaps the preeminent example. With few exceptions, these organizations keep track only of violations of civil and political rights—Amnesty International, indeed, confines itself to securing the release of political prisoners—and do not concern themselves with deprivation of the basic human needs discussed by Domínguez. They do so because, like pressure groups on the domestic level, they cannot afford to dissipate their energies by focusing on a broad spectrum of issues, and they make what amounts to the tacit judgment that a simultaneous focus on basic needs would cost them political support within the Western democratic societies from which they draw their sustenance. Yet it may be argued, as Domínguez does by inference and Rodley does explicitly, that it is precisely their concentration on civil and political liberties that makes organizations like Amnesty International or the International Commission of Jurists seem to citizens of poor countries like political agents of the industrialized West; they feel the pain only of the tortured and not of the starving. To establish their credibility, even their *bona fides,* within the societies whose abuses of civil and political liberties they pinpoint, the monitoring organizations should call attention to deprivations of human needs as well.

Rodley makes clear that such a shift in focus should not be

10

expected of the existing nongovernmental monitoring organizations. But he holds up the prospect that if these various separate organizations can be tied more closely together, the confederation of agencies that emerged might gradually adopt a wider focus. And he puts forward a design for a new, broad-based monitoring agency whose mandate would include the whole spectrum of human rights within its purview. So far as basic needs are concerned, the agency's task need not be difficult. Much work has already been done by international bodies such as the International Labor Organization, the World Bank, the UN Development Program, and the World Health Organization to develop indices of adequacy in such areas as nutrition, housing, health care, and education. Rodley's new agency would find that much of the groundwork for assessing societal performance in these areas has been done and that appraisals will become routinely available. While technical disputes may exist concerning whether a particular index accurately describes a minimum standard of needs of life, there is little dispute over what specific needs are regarded as basic. One important function that the new agency might play would be to catalyze international agreement on these levels.

While there may be differences among technicians and experts regarding indicators for assessing governmental performance in meeting basic needs, controversy over civil and political rights will be much more widespread and also much more intense. That controversy, indeed, is the new agency's raison d'être, and it would surely spend most of its time and resources addressing the issues under dispute. But the only way it would be able to command general respect for its reporting in these more contentious areas would be to indicate that its concern extends equally to basic needs.

Concern with the entire length of the civil rights/basic needs continuum is a characteristic of Richard Falk's work in this volume. His assigned task was to suggest ways in which the international community might respond to the most severe violations of human rights. It is hardly surprising that Falk is more confident of the community's ability to define than to act against those violations. But it is noteworthy that his own list of the most severe types of offenses against human rights includes not only deliberate refusal by governments to satisfy the basic needs of members of their own society but also what he calls "ecocide"— actions by man, either instigated by government or implicitly sanctioned by governmental failure to prevent them, that substantially degrade the quality of the natural environment upon which all life depends.

Falk is one of the most penetrating critics of the current state-centered organization of the international system. He is deeply offended that the mere existence of a state frontier should alter profoundly the ways in which persons on either side of it live their lives and relate to governing authorities. Territoriality— state sovereignty throughout a demarcated territorial space—is, in effect, too often the refuge of racists, bigots, or just plain scoundrels. So long as the territorial state remains the centerpiece of political organization, Falk says, the international community can do nothing to prevent and little to remedy even the most egregious violations of human rights by governments. He posits, moreover, that the 1980s will see the growing prevalence of what he calls "hard states," in which governments beset by rising domestic demands seek fairly successfully to insulate themselves from outside pressures in order to follow increasingly repressive internal policies.

Yet a more optimistic forecast is also possible. So long as the state system continues more or less unchanged, what Falk calls "depraved states," like Idi Amin's Uganda or John Vorster's South Africa, will continue to exist within it. And they will not be susceptible to outside pressures short of efforts that threaten the very survival of their governments. But other states where there is today considerable repression and disregard for human rights—the Shah's Iran, Brezhnev's Soviet Union, Marcos's Philippines, Pinochet's Chile, or Park's South Korea, to name only a few of many possible examples—may be more susceptible to outside influences that may cause them to moderate their behavior. Even in the existing state system, the effect of modern communications is such as to increase substantially awareness of human rights abuses compared to half a decade ago. The

12

insulation that many governments wish is available only at a prohibitive price.

Rulers are also aware that their countries' abilities to attract outside investment and financial support may decline with unfavorable publicity. In the past this has often worked the other way: repressive regimes have been looked upon as "good for business." But this bias may be changing under the influence of widespread publicity and effective national and transnational lobbying in the industrialized democracies by persons and organizations committed to humanitarian purposes. Thus, in the 1980s, the Amins and the Vorsters may well remain more or less unreachable by external suasion. But the Pahlavis, the Brezhnevs, the Marcoses, the Pinochets, and the Parks may feel it necessary to be much less repressive than they have been in the 1970s. And the Amins and Vorsters—against whom, as Falk acknowledges, already a substantial consensus is building—may be the targets of concerted and effective international action that goes beyond mere suasion.

One straw in the wind is the increasing effectiveness of the Inter-American Human Rights Commission that Bryce Wood discusses in this volume. Although still relatively toothless compared to the European human rights machinery, the IAHRC has gained much in stature and in access over the past decade. Equally important, it has inspired Nigeria and other African states to press for a human rights commission for the Organization of African Unity (OAU). One of the OAU's central purposes is to shield African states from outside intervention. Now some Africans are saying that a concomitant of this noninterventionary norm is that they must themselves work to rid Africa of regimes that bring disgrace upon it. In 1977 Nigeria sponsored a UN General Assembly resolution calling upon all regional organizations to set up machinery to promote human rights. If the OAU now proceeds to do so, the Association of Southeast Asian Nations (ASEAN) may well follow its example. Such machinery cannot in itself give rise to dramatic changes. It is effective in Western Europe because political systems there are open and democratic and because Western Europe has seen substantial erosion of the barriers of sovereignty in other areas as well. It will be less effective—but not ineffective—within the various regions of the developing world.

No matter how effective regional institutions may be in calling attention to serious abuses of human rights, during the 1980s and beyond the task of bringing palpable pressure to bear against offenders will still fall almost entirely to nation-states. And such pressure as there is will likely be economic, not military. The international system's prevailing norm against military intervention, although often violated, is still sufficiently strong so that only in the most exceptional circumstances, such as rescuing foreign hostages, is it likely to be overridden to enforce the system's less strong norms concerning human rights.

Economic pressure can be resisted, even with force, but generally it does not raise the same specters of counterintervention and escalation that are present whenever military force is used. Yet in many instances, and provided it is used with determination, economic pressure may cause offending regimes to ameliorate their behavior. If economic sanctions are employed, the central roles will invariably fall to the industrialized democratic states, particularly the large ones—the United States, Japan, the German Federal Republic, Britain, France, and Italy. Their position is so central to the workings of the international economic system that whether or not sanctions will succeed or fail depends largely on them. Only when a human rights violator is closely linked to one of the two major Communist states, the Soviet Union or China, is the situation different. But if it is desired to bring pressure against Uganda, South Africa, Argentina, South Korea, or the Philippines (to list only a few examples), it is the industrialized democracies that hold the levers.

Moreover, in these instances the industrialized democracies do not have the luxury of "opting out." In the case of Uganda, for instance, the brutal regime of President Idi Amin Dada is entirely dependent upon Western purchases of Uganda's coffee crop for the foreign exchange with which he pays his army and police. Thus if Western states continue to import Ugandan coffee they in effect acquiesce in the continuation of Amin's rule. States with smaller economies, such as other African states, cannot exert decisive economic leverage on Uganda. Because their leverage is less, they enjoy the moral luxury of knowing that their decisions will not be of crucial importance to whether Amin remains or falls.[5]

The case of Uganda is perhaps special because it is so totally dependent upon the West and because pressure would be so painless for the West to apply. South Africa raises problems of a different nature. There is no question but that its close economic ties to the West—substantial trade and large Western investments—have provided much of the economic growth and consequent prosperity that have prevented the country's minority white population from losing confidence in the policies of its elected leadership. Richard Falk argues that only "direct large-scale military intervention would mount the kind of external leverage necessary to topple the [Pretoria] regime." That may indeed be the case. Yet severe economic pressure might possibly cause the regime to modify its racist policies. And by doing nothing to interfere with the existing economic arrangement, Western societies acquiesce in the continuation of those policies. Unlike the case of Uganda, however, applying economic pressure against South Africa would scarcely be painless for the West. The pattern of interdependence is pronounced.

As the world's largest national economy, the United States necessarily would play a crucially important role in applying any economic sanctions against human rights violators. Without American participation, economic sanctions against virtually any violating regime cannot be effective. Bryce Wood's essay in this volume discusses the importance and the complexity of the economic links between the United States and the republics of Latin America. Yet Wood draws back from recommending that Washington use its economic leverage to cause other governments in the Hemisphere to improve their treatment of their own citizens. His reluctance stems from skepticism that even considerable pressure would produce the desired changes—they might, indeed, only cause the target regimes to become more repressive—and from a reluctance to blur the traditional distinction between "economic" and "political" spheres that has been a fundamental feature of the liberal international economic system as it has developed since 1945. Both concerns are justifiable. The United States has an immense stake in an international economy where barriers to market-generated flows are minimal. And when pressure is applied to other societies, results are never entirely predictable.

But Wood also acknowledges the central role that both official and private United States actions have had in shaping patterns of political development in Latin America. North American private investments have been important stakes in Latin American politics; and conservative oligarchies that have enriched themselves through these investments have maintained their grip on power with the help of official United States assistance to their military and police forces. Tacit approval by Washington has meant much to Latin American regimes. When it is visibly withdrawn, the hands of opposition leaders are strengthened. Spurred by widespread congressional sentiment, the administration of President Jimmy Carter sharply curtailed United States assistance of all kinds to the most repressive Latin American governments and forbade U.S. firms to sell arms and other equipment even to their police forces. Because the aid programs were relatively small and because military and police equipment is often available from other supplies, these measures may be thought of as only "symbolic politics." Yet they had real effects. Some Latin governments released political prisoners and refrained from taking others.

A central question for the 1980s is whether the United States and other liberal democratic societies can effectively use their weight in the international system to bring about genuine and lasting improvement in respect for human rights elsewhere. In the case of the United States, much will depend upon whether a concern for human rights abroad extends beyond the President and policy-level officials in Washington to the entire government and to American society as a whole. Contacts with other societies take place at countless points, the interaction of innumerable private persons as well as officials. If American businessmen abroad or (to name only one category of officials) members of military missions wink at Washington's concern about human rights, their counterparts in other societies will do so too.

Furthermore, the United States and other Western societies will not appear credible when they express a concern for political and civil liberties elsewhere unless they put equal weight upon meeting basic human needs as well. That will mean taking seriously the substance (if not the rhetoric) of claims for a new international economic order during the 1980s, an economic order that will divert a greater share of global resources to the poorest countries. Yet it is also important that any commitment to help other societies meet basic human needs should be undertaken for its own sake—because there are so many needs to be met—and not for any possible leverage it will give the industrialized democracies in affecting civil and political liberties in other societies.

For the 1980s, at least, there is likely to be little erosion of the barriers of sovereignty that are the fundamental structural feature of the modern international system. And behind those barriers, many governments will continue to abuse the populations they control. This is not to say that the concern of outsiders and the pressure that other governments exert cannot make a difference. Obviously they affect decisions at the margin. And marginal decisions—to spare a prisoner's life, to refrain from torturing another, to release a third—are of vital importance. The human rights monitoring institution suggested by Nigel Rodley, the indicators for cross-societal comparison proposed by Jorge Domínguez, the strengthened inter-American human rights machinery urged by Bryce Wood, and the panoply of measures detailed by Richard Falk are all designed to help concerned outsiders affect state decisions at the margin. And sometimes they might provide ways to move governments to make more profound changes. Yet Richard Falk is right to remind us, as he does at the conclusion of his contribution to this volume, that the effort for fundamental change in the ways in which governments treat those they govern "is virtually synonymous with the quest for the next world order system."

NOTES

1.   See Georges Tapinos and Phyllis T. Piotrow, *Six Billion People: Demographic Dilemmas and World Politics* (New York: McGraw-Hill for the Council on Foreign Relations, 1978).

2.   For a discussion of the political manipulation of relief resources, see Stephen Green, *International Disaster Relief: Toward a Responsive System* (New York: McGraw-Hill for the Council on Foreign Relations, 1977), pp. 59–64.

3.   Ibid., pp. 65–76.

4.   See W. Howard Wriggins and Gunner Adler-Karlsson, *Reducing Global Inequities* (New York: McGraw-Hill for the Council on Foreign Relations, 1978).

5.   See Richard H. Ullman, "Human Rights and Economic Power: The United States Versus Idi Amin," *Foreign Affairs,* April 1978, pp. 529–543.

Assessing Human Rights Conditions

Jorge I. Domínguez

Introduction

Suppose the United States Congress required human rights impact statements linked to foreign assistance programs or arms sales. What shape would they take? Suppose the World Bank, the regional development banks, or major foreign assistance donors became interested in considering human rights criteria as an ordinary input into their decision-making systems, even if not a controlling or overriding factor. What criteria would be selected? How would one relate conceptual criteria to the real world? Suppose, in honor of George Orwell, a new international monitoring institution were launched in 1984 to look over human rights conditions worldwide. What would it monitor? How would it make judgments?

These questions belong to the future, but one neither too distant nor undesirable. The answers to all of these questions require a systematic basis for assessment and comparison. Perhaps the best approach would be through the use of indices, which are relatively objective efforts to assess a particular condition. Once the assessment of a condition is made, the indices can then be

NOTE: My research and writing has been made possible by the Transnational Relations Program of the Center for International Affairs at Harvard University, and by the 1980s Project of the Council on Foreign Relations. I am grateful to both. I am also grateful to the participants in the Working Group on Human Rights at the Council for their insights, comments, and criticisms, both directly on my paper and on the larger topic, which served to enrich my own understanding.

used to determine whether the condition is good or bad, and whether it is getting better or worse. Indices are part of our thinking whenever we say that something is improving or deteriorating. They are desirable because they facilitate comparisons across time and events, and because they facilitate action.

Many persons would agree that even a single case of torture or political imprisonment is morally unacceptable. For the sake of political action, however, it is often necessary to demonstrate that a single event is part of a pattern. Governments and political leaders, when faced with one or two cases, tend to dismiss them as exceptions that their laws and their goodwill can prevent from recurring. Thus, effective action on behalf of human rights requires a demonstration not just that there is a rotten apple in the barrel, but that the barrel is rotten, too. Establishing the existence of patterns requires the development of indices that help answer the following questions: What were the prior conditions? How have things changed? How much have they changed?

A call for the development of indices to assess human rights conditions is, of course, not new.[1] The efforts of international intergovernmental organizations in the twentieth century have often included the collection and publication of a great deal of pertinent quantitative information. However, three recent trends make a renewed call for indices somewhat different from those in the past. First, the efforts of international organizations to collect and publish data have expanded considerably in recent years, facilitating the task of monitoring human rights conditions. Second, scholars have supplemented those efforts in the one area where international organizations perform poorly: Information is now being collected systematically on political and social conditions that many governments would rather not publicize. International nongovernmental organizations, notably Amnesty International, have also advanced considerably the possibility of monitoring by collecting and publishing information concerning prisoners of conscience. Third, there is a sense of new urgency about the need for indices. Some of the evidence reviewed in this essay suggests that the deprivation of certain human rights has increased in recent years: The spread of torture is the most striking example. In a number of countries, constituencies have developed, possibly larger than those in the past, which seek to pressure governments and private and public international organizations to act on behalf of human rights. Thus, the development of indices to assess human rights conditions is now not only necessary, but also possible and urgent.

The pages that follow set forth my ideas for a comprehensive index of human rights. The reader should remember that this essay is primarily intended as an illustration of the possibilities for such an index. It is meant to be suggestive, not authoritative. A full-blown presentation of the data—accompanied by explanations of the ways in which each indicator offers information pertinent to an assessment of each value or condition embodied by the index—would be possible on the basis of the methodology I suggest below. However, such a study would be massive and would certainly exceed the resources of any one author. More important, such a tome would obscure in a thicket of data the immediate need for and possibility of a comprehensive human rights index. I hope the publication of this more modest study will serve three goals: to facilitate policies that are not yet law within national governments; to facilitate decisions that have not yet been made by international organizations; and to show how international human rights monitoring institutions that have not yet been founded might actually go about their work. In this sense, this essay is academic. Nonetheless, the gap between today's world and one in which the procedures suggested in the following pages might be used may not be so broad as many persons suspect. Indeed, some existing national and international institutions such as U.S. AID, or the World Bank group of financial institutions, could already make use of some of these procedures. If they did, it would be at least a beginning.

23

ONE

International Human Rights Norms

The concern with human rights in the world today stems from the perception widely shared with Rousseau that man, though born free, is everywhere in chains. The wish to break the restraints that have set boundaries to human belief and behavior recently has been gathering force. It was articulated as a widely subscribed international norm only with the United Nations' Universal Declaration of Human Rights. The text and spirit of this declaration are widely known in their essentials, and there is no need to repeat them. The bulk of the document's assertions address formal civil and political liberties, which are familiar to readers of constitutional documents inspired by the American and French revolutions. The Universal Declaration is emphatic and detailed in its chronicling of such classic human rights as freedom of expression, information, association, religious belief and practice; a freely functioning judicial process and court system; equality before law and government; and so forth. But the Universal Declaration—as a document of the twentieth, not the eighteenth, century—includes topics less commonly understood by the United States public to fall under the rubric of human rights. Here we stress those aspects of the Universal Declaration that are typically not emphasized in the United States.

The United States Declaration of Independence asserts the precedence of "life" over "liberty"; but not until the twentieth century did national and international documents begin to declare that the right to "life" has social and economic implications that go beyond a narrow definition of civil and political rights. Article 25 of the Universal Declaration states that "everyone has the right to a standard of living adequate for the health and well-being of himself and his family, including food, clothing, housing and medical care and necessary social services, and the right to security in the event of unemployment, sickness, disability, widowhood, old age or other lack of livelihood in circumstances beyond his control." Similarly, Article 22 asserts that "everyone . . . has the right to social security and is entitled to realization . . . of the economic, social and cultural rights indispensable for his dignity and the free development of his personality." Article 24 says that "everyone has the right to rest and leisure, including reasonable limitation of working hours and periodic holidays with pay." Article 26 asserts the right to free elementary, and possibly other, education. Article 27 states that "everyone has the right freely to participate in the cultural life of the community, to enjoy the arts and to share in scientific advancement and its benefits." Thus, the Universal Declaration is also emphatic, though less detailed, in asserting the importance of certain social and economic factors as human rights.

It is also instructive to consider a constitutional document that has never been honored in important respects for a substantial period of time: the Soviet Constitution of 1936, known as the "Stalin Constitution." This document reminds us of the often cosmic gap between formal norm and actual practice—a problem not peculiar, by any means, to the Soviet Union. And it highlights the way in which many nations share norms at a formal level. This sharing of norms helps to make possible, though not faultless, a cross-ideological and cross-cultural assessment of human rights. Also, it suggests that the advancement of human rights lies not with additional or national documents, but with compliance and enforcement. Thus, Article 125 of the Soviet Constitution of 1936 says that "the citizens of the U.S.S.R. are guaranteed by law: a) freedom of speech; b) freedom of press; c) freedom of assembly, including the holding of mass meetings; d) freedom of street processions and demonstrations." Article

126 guarantees the right "to unite in public organizations." Article 127 guarantees the "inviolability of the person. No person may be placed under arrest except by decision of a court or with the sanction of a prosecutor." Article 128 notes that "the inviolability of the homes of citizens and privacy of correspondence are protected by law." These formal norms, then, are not unique to the constitutions of the North Atlantic; it is, in principle, possible to speak of a worldwide consensus on formal human rights norms.

AN INDEX OF HUMAN RIGHTS CONDITIONS

Characteristics of an Operational Framework

Human rights should be understood to encompass the notions set forth in the Universal Declaration, which include civil and political as well as economic and social rights. Although the Universal Declaration provides useful normative guidelines for an index, it is not a framework that can easily be used to assess actual *human rights conditions*—a shorthand term that refers to the degree to which actual political, social, and economic conditions are consistent with the norms articulated by the Universal Declaration. Such an index of human rights conditions should have several characteristics:

1. It should reflect the norms of the Universal Declaration, which means it should include not only the right to free speech, for instance, but also the right to live and to have basic human necessities. These are norms to which states have consented formally.[2]
2. It should be flexible enough to admit the possibility that most human rights goals of the Universal Declaration may be achieved simultaneously. Although it is beyond the scope of this essay to determine whether some types of states are more likely than others to achieve the norms of the Universal Declaration, certain data does point to an association between

27

high levels of political and civil liberties and high social and economic standards of living.[3] The experiences of some two to three dozen countries—in Western Europe, North America, Japan, and some older parts of the British Commonwealth—suggest that in the long run it may be possible to achieve all major goals in the Universal Declaration. Yet most nations today show a substantial sacrifice of some aspects of the Universal Declaration for the sake of others. Relatively few of these nations have come close to matching the achievement of the above-mentioned, far smaller group on any number of significant criteria. More time, however, may change this judgment. All that is asserted here is that these norms can be achieved; their simultaneous achievement is neither necessary nor inevitable.

3. The index should achieve the actual values that social science surveys have identified as being shared by people of different cultures and ideologies.[4] Even though a purely empirical definition of important values based primarily on such surveys would emphasize social and economic human rights far more than civil and political ones, this essay will retain its concern with all the themes of the Universal Declaration for three reasons: The values given greater weight according to social science surveys may change with changing conditions; the formal set of international norms stresses civil and political rights a great deal more than do the social science surveys; and those rights appear to be very important in shaping the quality of individual social and economic life.

4. An operational framework should be politically prudent and plausible on an international scale. The chief advantage of a framework linked to the Universal Declaration is precisely the relative universality of formal adherence to the Declaration. The study and assessment of human rights is linked inextricably to deeply held values. Judgments are made enormously difficult by ideological and cultural variation. Thus the existence of a document setting norms for human rights to which many states have consented, even if fewer have honored, aids any attempt to make assessments with cross-cultural and cross-ideological applicability. The framework

28

should also be consistent with recent emphases by developing countries on economic and social issues, as summarized in the documents of the New International Economic Order. This international consensus, however fragile, facilitates the building of broad political coalitions on behalf of human rights.

5. Though informed by universal and timeless values, the index must facilitate cross-national and cross-ideological comparisons in order to set minimal standards, sensitive to changing times and situations, for governments to meet and surpass.

6. The index should facilitate an international effort to monitor human rights conditions in many countries. Since monitoring often depends on publicity and discussion, the index should consist of terms and procedures that are intelligible to public officials and to an educated international public. These terms and procedures should also be related to the work of social scientists, who are among the main producers of information pertinent to worldwide monitoring of human rights, and whose work is essential to replicate, validate, or refute findings.

There are a number of problems inherent in attempts to apply an index to different situations that no existing or foreseeable index can solve. First, there is the problem of getting valid and reliable data. There is a necessary and unavoidable loss in normative and conceptual richness in any transition from discussions of the concepts of human rights to analyses that use "hard" data to assess human rights conditions. One way to reduce this loss is to investigate different sorts of conditions ("indicators") in assessing each category of human rights through the device of "values" that will serve as a "bridge" between the rights embodied in the Universal Declaration and the actual human rights conditions that the index is intended to evaluate. Although these values are a conceptual link between the data and the norms, no amount of analysis should mitigate a necessary skepticism toward the ability of any data satisfactorily to make operational any of the concepts normally used to define human rights. But even though it is very difficult to assess concepts by means of quantitative indices, an operational approach is essential if concepts that do reflect conditions are to be grounded and tested.

29

Some of the cells in an operational matrix can be filled with relatively precise quantitative information for a number of years. Certain kinds of economic or educational information, for example, are easily available. Some cells, on the other hand, cannot be filled with adequate quantitative information for more than a few countries, if any. This, unfortunately, is especially true for civil liberties. In general, relatively few countries practice systematic, deliberate statistical fraud over a sustained period. But many governments do not publish unflattering data; and all governments, to one degree or another, face technical problems in data gathering, even in the population census. Of the statistical data regularly published, population data (including educational data) tend to be more accurate than aggregate economic estimates; all data are less reliable for rural areas and ethnic minorities than for urban areas and majorities; and data on political and civil liberties (with some exceptions) tend to be the most judgmental—even if presented in numerical form—and least reliable.

A second problem is the unequal availability of information. Some countries supply a great deal of information concerning their social blights precisely because their governments and people are deeply concerned and are trying to do something to remove these blights. Others, however, withhold information to conceal social ills. Thus, the availability or absence of information does not necessarily correlate with good or bad conditions.

A third difficulty is that some categories may not mean precisely the same thing from country to country. Thus a political prisoner in country A might be considered a common criminal in country B; since the same can be said for a broad array of issues, cross-national comparisons are extraordinarily difficult.

Yet a fourth difficulty is that all values are not alike. Genocide has a different moral standing than literacy reduction. Because much attention is devoted to this problem in subsequent pages, not much else needs to be said here. But even when assessing a single value, one should not confuse the *level* of performance with its direction or *rate* of change over time. For instance, if the rate of torture declines in Chile under military rule, that is an improvement; if one Irish Republican Army (IRA) bomber

30

is tortured in the United Kingdom, where such practices are rare and severely punished, that is deterioration. More attention needs to be paid in these political cases to levels.

Despite all these problems, which lead to an unavoidable loss of conceptual richness as one shifts from norms to data, the indices remain necessary and useful. We constantly use indices of some sort, though not always consciously, in our thinking. When judgments are made, it is by means of an implicit ordinal scale: something is better than something else. Operational indices are also desirable because they make possible comparisons, decision making, and action. But indices do only that. They cannot replace norms; they exemplify and test them, albeit inadequately. Though they form the bases for sensible and efficient judgments, they are not a substitute for judgment. This essay is not a plea for mad preoccupation with numbers, but it does rest on the conviction that quantitative empirical research is useful and necessary in order to make judgments about human rights, and that making our implicit scales explicit is preferable to hiding behind imprecise terminology.

AVAILABLE FORMULATIONS

Alternative existing efforts to make operational a conception of human rights fail to meet one or more of the criteria already outlined. Perhaps the most thorough effort to report qualitative information about liberty in numerical form has been Freedom House's Comparative Survey of Freedom, under the direction of Raymond D. Gastil.[5] This survey is focused explicitly and exclusively on political and civil rights. The key elements in the survey's political rights component are the degree and kind of political opposition: Can opposition groups compete in and win elections? The key element in the civil rights component is freedom of the press. However, data about these two elements are rarely available in quantitative form. The most that can be said is that there is more or less of each, and that the trend is up or down. These are useful judgments that lend themselves to an ordinal scale. In fact, though, it is disputable that much is gained by assigning such numbers—other than the ability to make a

31

quick visual inspection of a table at the risk of inferring a false precision. Though Freedom House has never explicitly suggested that its survey measures what matters and excludes what does not, its texts, maps, and press releases tend to assume that the survey provides a complete description of the relevant human rights. This tendency is aggravated in the United States by the practice of identifying the term "human rights" exclusively with civil and political rights. The Freedom House Survey also incurs a danger in saying that only under nonauthoritarian governments is there freedom of any kind or respect for human rights. To put it differently, to advance the cause of human rights, one should be able to recognize that certain human rights may be well protected in nondemocratic political systems. This is normatively desirable, empirically accurate, and politically prudent; it would facilitate the building of worldwide support for the advancement of human rights even among peoples who disagree fundamentally on ideological questions. The Freedom House Survey and related works[6] are needed for particular kinds of political assessment, but they are too narrow to provide a framework for general human rights assessment, and too closely linked with particular political systems to enable people from different countries, with minimally shared values, to act in concert.

A rather different alternative formulation has been presented by Argentina's Bariloche Institute.[7] The Bariloche group has identified a number of *needs* without satisfaction of which human beings are in one way or another impaired or become ill. These needs, it is claimed, are universal. Bariloche does not, however, include the "modes of enjoyment" that are part of the matrix used in the index below. The Bariloche Institute's authors have also argued that human beings tend to satisfy needs along a hierarchical scale, though the hierarchy of needs may be different from the hierarchy of aspirations. This assumption of hierarchies has led those authors to concentrate on four basic needs: food, health care, housing, and education. The Bariloche Institute's work, therefore, stresses a set of values quite different from those emphasized by Freedom House. Freedom House's liberties are absent from the Bariloche listing. The Bariloche Institute's emphasis on needs departs substantially from the stress on rights

32

of the Universal Declaration. This is a crucial normative difference that makes building a worldwide coalition on human rights difficult. The Bariloche Institute has been concerned primarily with meeting the basic needs of people whose needs are still unmet and for whom civil and political rights are of less pressing importance; it has paid less attention to the concerns of those who have met basic human needs and who wish to stress rights that they do not have or that may be in jeopardy. The Bariloche Institute's hierarchical assumptions are also less open than a broader index would be to the possibility of a simultaneous advance on all human rights fronts.

In sum, the alternative formulations of ways to assess human rights conditions are less than satisfactory. First, they are normatively biased to stress certain questions more than others and thus are much less likely than a comprehensive index to aid the building of worldwide coalitions to support and advance human rights. Therefore they are less desirable on political grounds. They do not provide for sufficient consideration of all human rights. They have hierarchical assumptions that are not always consistent with some empirical findings about the ways in which change occurs. They are inconsistent with international norms. Though the issues stressed by the alternative formulations are implied to be cultural universals, in fact they are of greater importance for certain nations, ideologies, and cultural traditions than for others. These existing alternative frameworks, therefore, are less open to a variety of value stresses and rankings, and are thus less flexible than a comprehensive framework would be.

THE MODIFIED LASSWELL-KAPLAN FRAMEWORK

A useful framework for evaluating human rights conditions is provided by the eight basic values of social life identified by Harold Lasswell and Abraham Kaplan:[8] power, respect, rectitude, wealth, well-being, enlightenment, skill, and affection. Lasswell and Kaplan identified these values on the basis of theoretical and empirical studies in social science. The values represent an attempt to synthesize the results from a variety of

33

scholarly works based upon surveys, observations, or the mass media analyzing people's responses concerning their hopes and fears. In addition to these eight "basic values," the modified framework will include four "modes of enjoyment"—security, growth, equality, and liberty—which are necessary both to facilitate measurement and to reflect more accurately the norms of the Universal Declaration.[9]

The modes of enjoyment cut across all the articles of the Universal Declaration. *Security* is the expectation that the current level of enjoyment of human rights will at least not deteriorate. Security involves both the persistence of minimal general conditions (for example, no increase in the numbers of political prisoners, or in the severity of their treatment) and a person's physical security to enjoy these conditions. However, few persons would be satisfied if told that there will be "security" in the continuation of illiteracy or of severe restrictions upon expression. Implicit in the Universal Declaration is the hope that conditions will improve—that there will be growth, not simply continuity, in the enjoyment of certain human rights conditions, and that the abilities of individuals and societies to cope with their problems will grow. Thus, to single out *growth* as the second mode of enjoyment calls attention to the need to increase individual and collective abilities to enhance human rights.

Indicators of relative security and growth help us to know "how much human rights," and "how much more or less over the course of time." Indicators of the third mode of enjoyment, *equality* of both opportunity and result, help us to know the extent to which human rights are available to, and enjoyed by, all people—a central concern of the Universal Declaration. And indicators of the fourth mode, *liberty,* measure the relative freedom of persons to develop and act in accordance with their own personalities.

The combination of these four modes of enjoyment and the eight basic human rights values forms a 32-cell matrix that is shown in Table 1. Each cell is a "container" of various facets of life. In order to decide what belongs in each, certain decisions—necessarily somewhat arbitrary—must be made. I have tried to decide which specific indicators to use for each cell on the basis of

TABLE 1

	Security	Growth	Equality	Liberty
Enlightenment				
Skill				
Well-being				
Respect				
Affection				
Rectitude				
Wealth				
Power				

the norms outlined in the Universal Declaration, supplemented by the available empirical data.

Enlightenment involves knowledge, insight, and access to information. It is closely related to *skill,* but the latter means proficiency in any pursuit—an art, a craft, a trade, or a profession. In daily life, the exercise of the right to enlightenment entails reading and writing, speaking and listening, and expressing one's opinions and learning from the opinions of others. The matrix cell for equality of enlightenment indicates, for example, whether there are equal educational opportunities for urban and rural residents, different social classes, racial or religious groups, women and men. These distinctions are, in fact, the ones commonly used to assess relative equality in the enjoyment of particular values. Liberty of enlightenment, however, is more difficult to quantify. One indicator might be the relative availability of channels for education other than those of the state (private or religious schools, for example). Others that involve a greater exercise of judgment on the part of the evaluator might be the degree to which mass media are subject to censorship, or the degree to which teaching is either forcibly biased or constrained. At issue throughout is the degree to which there is a free flow of information within a given society.

Well-being includes health and personal safety. Rates of death, and the incidence of starvation, malnutrition, and disease, are measurements of the rights to life and to health. The normative

35

judgment that these are rights to be enjoyed equally by everyone stresses once again the distributional issues—susceptible to relatively easy quantification—already noted. One indicator of personal safety or security is the rate for any given nation (or smaller social unit) of crimes of violence against persons. Indicators of security of well-being are the relative availability of health-service personnel, hospital facilities, police officers, etc. Well-being is one of the values most frequently tested in public opinion surveys. Few governments admit to deficiencies in their commitment to enhancing well-being, but their performances vary considerably.

Affection encompasses love, friendship, and loyalty. In the Universal Declaration, affection receives expression through those articles emphasizing the role of the family. But the Declaration also acknowledges the importance of the bonds of sentiment between the individual and the larger community, including the nation. Affection merges, as a basic value, with *respect*, which refers to the dignity, honor, recognition, prestige, or reputation of both individuals and groups. Disregard of this value is at the heart of a great many disputes in social life, for it is "respect groups"—differentiated according to their race, color, sex, language, and national or social origin—that often are most clearly deprived of their human rights. The linkages between affection and respect as basic values are most apparent in the instance of women, the largest single respect group for whose human rights the Universal Declaration expresses concern; their role in the family, especially motherhood, is also the object of solicitude. A woman's right freely to choose a life-style and to be considered a fully productive person, not simply a dependent or a sex object, and the degree to which her physical dignity is acknowledged, particularly in security against rape, are often critical indicators of more general aspects of respect and affection within a society. The participation of women in the labor force and in political institutions, their access to birth control and other family planning facilities (and a cultural milieu that permits choices about family size), and access as well to day-care facilities, so that they can enjoy their right of motherhood without having to sacrifice other rights, are all important indi-

36

cators. In assessing the performance of a society with regard to the values of affection and respect, it is important to take into account the nature of interpersonal relationships and authority patterns within the family. These are revealed through anthropological studies, opinion surveys, and the like. This information is also needed to interpret divorce statistics for a given society: In some male-dominated societies, where divorce is readily available to men but not to women, they indicate a threat to family stability (and therefore to the value of affection), while in other societies they are an indicator of the increased liberty of women.

The value of respect is reflected in the Universal Declaration's concern to protect the rights of privacy, rest, and leisure. These may come into conflict with efforts by governments to politicize all aspects of life, including leisure-time activities. Similarly, governmental efforts that introduce political concerns into the criteria by which marriage partners select each other, or to induce persons into formal marriage because of ideological concerns, threaten rights adumbrated in the Universal Declaration. These are difficult to quantify, although public opinion surveys and the relation of the marriage rate to government policies may shed some light on the enjoyment of these rights. The degree to which the rights of ethnic, racial, religious, and other minorities are protected can be evaluated through indicators of income, education, employment, participation in government and politics, and participation in group associations and other communal, cultural, and fraternal activities.

Rectitude comprises the moral values of virtue, goodness, and righteousness, often made concrete through adherence to various world views, ideologies, and religious beliefs. It also encompasses the citizen's right to expect fairness and nondiscrimination, not only in the realm of belief but also in other areas, from his or her government. Although similar to respect, rectitude emphasizes freedom of belief, freedom to form one's own conscience, and freedom of religion from state interference. It also emphasizes "right" behavior on the part of the organs of the state. Adherence to this value is difficult to assess quantitatively, and many judgments concerning societal performance must necessarily be impressionistic. On the specific issue of religious beliefs and practices, indicators must address questions such as: Can religious organizations minister to their members? Are these abilities affected positively or negatively, or to the benefit or detriment of another religion, by governmental action? Can religious practices be carried out in public? Does the state place barriers in the path of those who aspire to be religious leaders?

Wealth is income and property, including goods and services. The Universal Declaration raises three different issues related to wealth. First, there is a concern for the standard of living of the poorest members of a society, measured not only in ability to acquire goods but also in degree of access to services such as education and medical care. A second issue is the right to hold property, explicitly guaranteed in the Declaration. Governmental regulations that unduly limit this individual right, or its exercise "in association with others," may run afoul of the Declaration. Finally, the Declaration aims at protecting the right of the worker to work, and his or her freedom from slavery. The Declaration upholds freedom from unemployment as well as a worker's right to "just" wages. The rights of trade unions to protect workers' interest, and not merely for governmental convenience, are also explicitly cited. Quantitative indicators regarding societal performance on just about every aspect of wealth are readily available for most countries.

Power is participation in decisions affecting one's life; more generally it involves an individual's or an institution's capacity to influence decisions or outcomes while resisting substantial changes in one's own beliefs, structures, and behavior. Power is at the heart of the Universal Declaration. Many of the articles supportive of other values also touch on power: The Universal Declaration is particularly concerned with how governments exercise their power to shape other values and modes of enjoyment. Articles 1 and 2 stress the centrality of the individual, without regard to membership in respect groups, in the Declaration's understanding of basic human rights. Articles 4 and 5 condemn slavery and torture, which are both related to liberty but overlap with power and other values. Articles 7 through 9 stress judicial rights, including not only freedom from arbitrary arrest but also equality before the law. These are measurable quantitatively, at least in part, through the rates of political imprisonment per total population; the proportion of indictments or convictions across income, education, ethnic, or racial groups; and similar measures. Articles 10 and 11 stress the security of the person before law enforcement agencies, partly measured by the above indicators, partly also by trends in the arrest rates. Article 12's concern with the right to privacy, and Article 20's with freedom of association, can be measured partly by the government's efforts to control social, economic, and political mass organizations, and to include or exclude persons in their membership; similarly, governmental measures to limit privacy or leisure, through formal or informal pressures, run afoul of Articles 12 and 24, and can be measured in part because these statistics are often reported (see the Cuban case study later in this essay). Article 13, on freedom of internal and international migration, can be measured quantitatively from statistical yearbooks and census data. Freedom of asylum (Article 14) must be judged qualitatively; Articles 15 through 19 limit the government's power over enlightenment, respect, affection, rectitude, and wealth. Article 21 underwrites the concern for elections. Elections are inherently quantitative, and are so treated in the case studies; however, procedural guarantees of free and competitive elections must be judged qualitatively, and such is also done in the case studies. Rights of legislative assemblies to free deliberation are also implied. Articles 28 through 30, once again, restrain the power of the state in order to ensure individual liberty and security.

There is a paradox in the Declaration concerning the growth of power. Its central focus is its stress on the limitation of governmental abuse. Yet the demands for the enhancement of human rights in respect to such values as well-being and skill are difficult to achieve without growth of governmental power. This is not the only paradox in the Declaration, but it is probably the one that is most difficult to resolve. The impressive growth of governmental power, documented in the Cuban and Mexican case studies later in this essay, not only facilitated improved performance on some human rights but also arguably led to political authoritarianism. I cannot settle this issue; but readers should

39

be forewarned that the growth of power identified in the country case studies should not be cause for rejoicing, but for a closer look at the costs and benefits of such an outcome.

In sum, the modified Lasswell-Kaplan framework is a procedure to simplify and to operationalize the Universal Declaration. The framework recombines the articles in the Declaration, and reduces their overlap into fewer reasonably distinct intellectual containers. In order to fill the container with quantitative indices, however, there is need to return to the Declaration itself. Indicators are selected according to the suggestions of the articles of the Declaration. The Declaration does not weigh some articles over others; the problem of weighing, however, is discussed in the next section on alternative empirical applications of the modified Lasswell-Kaplan framework.

The structure of the matrix of values just outlined is consistent with previous themes. First, because it is tied to the Universal Declaration, as well as to the empirical and theoretical works of scholars, it is normatively and intellectually fairly comprehensive. Second, it is open to empirical testing, and to the possibility that advances may be made among all human rights; that is, that positive quantitative correlations may be found. Third, it attempts to be consistent with the actual preferences of individuals throughout the world, and does not make the prior claim (of varying validity across cultures and ideologies) that some rights are by their nature superior to others. The value matrix leaves that hierarchical ranking, if or when it is necessary, to individuals and peoples to decide; the value matrix, therefore, is intellectually flexible and permissive. Fourth, it is consistent with formally declared international norms. A possible objection to the value matrix is that it assumes cultural universals, namely, that all peoples value the same things. The charge is not valid; the value matrix is open to decisions made in the context of particular cultures, or ideologies, to rank certain values above others. The value matrix, therefore, is preferable to culture-bound approaches precisely because it can be used both by those who assume cultural universals and those who do not. Fifth, this operational framework has already facilitated cross-national comparisons; it has been applied to many countries.[10] It can continue to be used to set minimal cross-national standards of performance. Sixth, though the operational framework was designed by social scientists for their own work, its concepts are intelligible to others and reflect the themes of the Universal Declaration in summarized and more operational ways.

ALTERNATIVE EMPIRICAL APPLICATIONS

The assessment of human rights conditions requires that citizens, public officials, scholars, and governmental or nongovernmental organizations concerned with human rights should map out the entire spectrum of performance in human rights conditions for any one country where these conditions are being assessed. Such a comprehensive mapping does not require that one make all values equal or neglect some at the expense of others; it does require sensitivity to many values and an openness to different value rankings. Comprehensive human rights case studies are required to do this. Critical areas can be identified; admirable trends can be praised; regrettable or damnable ones can stand out; costs and benefits of public policies can be evaluated. Use of the value matrix does not make all countries appear homogeneous; on the contrary, it brings out elements of similarity and of contrast. The stress should be on the full range of the matrix, not on a single aggregate score; an aggregate score would obscure violations of certain human rights in countries that have a mixed record. Comprehensive case studies, however, are laborious and time-consuming. Particular users of the value matrix—for political, ideological, or cultural reasons—may be more interested in some values than in others. This will result in a ranking of value preferences, and the necessarily differential weighing of value performances. The value matrix is flexible; it can be used by those who rank values and performances differently; its flexibility (resulting from the absence of a prior assumption about value hierarchies) is indeed one of its chief strengths. This section surveys possible alternative rankings.

41

TABLE 2

	Growth	Equality	Liberty	Security
Enlightenment	Bariloche	Bariloche	Freedom House	Both
Skill	Bariloche	Bariloche	Freedom House	Both
Well-being	Bariloche	Bariloche		Bariloche
Respect	Freedom House	Freedom House	Freedom House	Freedom House
Affection			Freedom House	Freedom House
Rectitude	Freedom House	Freedom House	Freedom House	Freedom House
Wealth	Bariloche	Bariloche	Freedom House	Both
Power	Freedom House	Freedom House	Freedom House	Freedom House

The accompanying Table 2 illustrates how the concerns of Freedom House and the Bariloche Institute would fit the value matrix. In general, the Bariloche Institute appears to be concerned chiefly with growth, equality, and security in enlightenment, skill, well-being, and wealth. Freedom House, on the other hand, is principally concerned with growth, equality, liberty, and security in the areas of power, rectitude, and respect; it is also concerned with issues of liberty and security with regard to enlightenment, skill, affection, and wealth. There is little overlap in their concerns. Each approach alone is not sufficiently comprehensive or sensitive to the general performance in all human rights. In contrast, efforts should be made to uncover the full range of human rights conditions, not just the state of those human rights one cherishes the most.

Suppose, alternatively, that the criterion for selection of values and measurement of performance were international acceptability. It may be argued that some elements are more likely to secure general agreement and therefore to receive remedial action by national governments than others. Thus, one should emphasize a relatively short list of values for this purpose. If the short list is to secure agreement among *governments* on the grounds of likely implementation, the past and probable performance of countries suggests that certain "growth values" would be emphasized: enlightenment, skill, well-being, wealth, and power (see the case studies on Cuba and Mexico). Though the performance of the world's governments on all but the last indicator has been slower than many deem desirable, it is certainly more impressive than performance on any other short list of values. Although some governments may make commitments to equality, security, and liberty, or to respect, affection, and rectitude, no other short list seems equally likely to gain the support of governments worldwide. On the other hand, if the short list is to secure agreement among the peoples of the world through some mechanism yet to be invented, it is likely that such a list would resemble closely that of the Bariloche Institute. And if one believes that a short list of rights should include matters that are ordinarily discussed as human rights in the United States—and which are a part of the Universal Declaration—such as freedom from torture and execution, freedom from indefinite political incarceration, freedom to leave and to reenter one's country, or freedom from racial or ethnic discrimination, then the criteria of international feasibility and consensus would have to be abandoned. There is no evidence that these are the values that most peoples or most governments put at the top of their lists; and there is evidence that improved performance has been far more feasible and successful in other values than in these. Thus, if one cherishes liberal values, and one seeks to persuade others to do the same, political prudence requires that any short list for concerted international action should also include some of the basic needs that the Bariloche Institute (and others) have identified, and which are a part of the Universal Declaration.

Another effort may be to focus only on those problems caused by active, purposive, affirmative government policy. This is a useful way of devising a short list. It would include such items as political prisoners and torture. It would exclude issue areas that are beyond the immediate control of governments, even well-intentioned ones, because they lack the capacity to bring about changes, such as ethnic and racial discrimination and slavery (too ingrained in the society), a high infant mortality rate

43

(not enough health personnel and facilities), brutality (short of torture) toward prisoners, violations of domicile without personal property injury, and legal inequalities (long-standing practices). It would also exclude instances of governmental neglect that may worsen human rights conditions, such as decisions by governments not to acknowledge publicly the existence of an epidemic for fear of interrupting the tourist season or harming agricultural exports, or not to permit international disaster relief for famines. A strategy of narrowing the human rights agenda to purposive, affirmative governmental action would leave aside issues that many would consider of great importance.

Yet another approach is put forth in the accompanying study by Nigel Rodley of the institutional aspects of monitoring human rights violations in the 1980s. Rodley proposes to focus first on the rights whose derogation is not permitted under any circumstances under Article 4 of the International Covenant of Civil and Political Rights, which would include discrimination on the basis of race, color, sex, language, religion, or social origin; rights of life; freedom from torture and from slavery; and freedom of conscience and thought, as well as certain procedural legal rights. These are substantively important rights, drawn from an international document commanding wide formal adherence. However, the principal difficulty with this approach is that it excludes social and economic rights. Why should not freedom from induced malnutrition or from induced epidemics—caused by the state's failure to act or its delayed response in a critical situation—rank equally with freedom of conscience? Moreover, there is a political disadvantage in stressing a narrow set of rights instead of a broader one that would facilitate international coalition building. Finally, the non-derogable rights of the Covenant, important as they are, are not fully compatible with the actual value rankings found in worldwide surveys.

The value matrix can also be used to measure performance in regions. Like-minded countries in Western Europe, in Eastern Europe, in Latin America, or elsewhere may emphasize certain values. Just as the matrix lends itself to different value rankings for global purposes, so too it lends itself to similar rankings at the regional level. At this level, some values need not be stressed because existing conditions pose very limited problems (e.g., literacy in Europe); other concerns may not be stressed because political decisions have ruled them out (e.g., ownership of basic industry in Eastern Europe). Nevertheless, even at the regional level, those concerned with human rights should attempt to measure performance across the entire spectrum, leading to a comprehensive evaluation, even if action is necessarily or desirably limited to a few areas.

A PERSONAL NORMATIVE RECOMMENDATION

Although this index of human rights is intended to be flexible, and thus adaptable to the purposes of different users, it could be used most effectively if two criteria are employed. First, any organization concerned with human rights should not retreat from the Universal Declaration. A broad operational framework is necessary and desirable. Second, for the purposes of facilitating action and focusing on the principal issues in emergencies—and only for those purposes—the values within the framework should be ranked. This ranking would not mean disregard for lower-ranking values; it would mean a differential emphasis on actions to be undertaken while the monitoring of performance on all human rights in the Universal Declaration continued. Any ranking, however, must be an abbreviated summary of the core values of the Universal Declaration, including civil, political, social, and economic rights. Thus I would emphasize the intersection of the values of well-being and power. At the top of the hierarchy I would place concern for any identifiable government action that reduces a people's right to life and health. Attention would be focused not only on political massacres, arbitrary executions ordered by governments, and torture but also on governments whose identifiable actions aggravate famines and epidemics.

The intersection of these values cuts across the distinctions between civil and political rights, on the one hand, and social and economic rights, on the other. One of the nonderogable rights mentioned by Nigel Rodley—life—is highlighted but not limited to civil and political rights. This is not a short list; it is at the top of a hierarchy that deliberately and necessarily rests on a broad and comprehensive consideration of all rights in the Universal Declaration. It focuses not simply on purposive actions by governments, but also on identifiable government neglect. The weight of the past is not enough to place a government at the top of the "most wanted" list of violators. For example, a government would not necessarily be condemned if a nation's supply of health personnel were inadequate (although such shortages are increasingly regarded as grounds for condemnation); however, a government too proud to acknowledge a famine—thereby preventing emergency relief—would be acting in a way that identifiably violates the right to life.

The achievement of these rights is not necessarily feasible, but efforts to secure them are nonetheless essential. The values at the top of the hierarchy are both more selective and more wide-ranging than those identified in alternative formulations. Emphasis on the intersection of well-being and power values may elicit support because it reflects the principal concerns of the Universal Declaration. The approach is politically prudent; it facilitates international monitoring, and the building of coalitions, as well as the setting of minimal international standards and public discussions of human rights conditions. Specific focus on these rights does not mean implicit tolerance of slavery or ethnic discrimination, even though they do not affect the right to life in the same way that a massacre, torture, or an induced famine or pandemic would. Rather, it suggests that the right to life is preeminent. The list of values must be hierarchical rather than a "short list" precisely because the violation of rights beyond those directly affecting life and health remains—and should remain—intolerable.

There are two kinds of "consumers" for the index I suggest. First are governments and possibly intergovernmental organizations. The United States government, and probably most governments of the Organization for Economic Cooperation and Development (OECD) countries, have the capacity to collect the data needed to produce detailed studies. Recent United States legislation forbids aid to governments violating human rights and suggests that the need for international human rights assessment has arrived in the 1970s. Data organized in ways similar to that of the suggested index can be used to guide government policy not only in human rights, but also in other areas; data so organized would also facilitate legislative oversight of foreign policy in human rights areas. Such data should be released to enable nongovernmental organizations to incorporate it into their decision making and activities without having to bear the expense of producing the assessments themselves. Worldwide or regional intergovernmental organizations, however, are not likely to produce these assessments. They have the resources to do so, but are paralyzed by partisan politics or by neglect on the part of member countries. As is currently the case for nongovernmental organizations, it is not really practical to demand more now of global or regional intergovernmental organizations, even though strengthening them would still be desirable. A second type of consumer in the 1980s might be a new kind of nongovernmental organization, discussed elsewhere in this book. The principal recommendation of this essay for such an organization is that it have the capacity to produce comprehensive country and issue-area assessments.

TWO

Case Studies

Comprehensive case studies of individual nations permit an assessment of change within those countries. But they are insufficient: The meaning of performance in any one country, as it changes over time, can often be evaluated only with reference to the performance of some other country. Country case-study comparisons are therefore very desirable, though even more laborious than individual case studies. Another mode of analysis facilitating understanding of conditions in particular countries and pointing to areas of grievous violation is the study of worldwide trends in selected human rights issues. These issue-area studies can point out conditions in particular nations that might otherwise escape attention. Thus this and the following chapter of this essay include two country case studies and four issue-area case studies. The country case studies provide the historical and cultural context of the human rights performance of particular countries; the issue-area case studies help to specify what is, in fact, the international standard of performance. Both approaches are necessary. The issues to be investigated in Chapter 3 were selected according to the criteria outlined there and are derived from the framework discussed in the earlier parts of the essay. If an international monitoring mechanism is established, it should do both detailed country and issue-area case studies; this essay presents only samples of each. The Cuban and Mexican case studies seek to illustrate the entire value matrix; the issue-area case studies highlight the fundamental values of well-being, respect, and power, and the modes of enjoyment of growth, liberty, and security.

The following case studies of Cuba and Mexico illustrate how the matrix can be applied to particular countries, and how operational indicators are used within each category. These two countries were chosen—apart from the special competence of the author—for three reasons. First, they are important to the United States; they are its immediate neighbors. Second, substantial information is available on each, which permits a comprehensive case study without undue independent data-gathering. And third, their ideologies and political systems are different despite similarities in their cultural and historical heritages. Thus, studies of Mexico and Cuba illustrate the way in which the index can be applied to nations of differing ideologies. They do not, however, show how the index is suitable for countries of differing cultures; such an illustration would have required a third extended case study, which space did not permit. Limits of space and the demands of readability place an additional constraint. Although the value matrix should be used comprehensively, particularly for public policy making and judgment, the presentation of the cases here will be abbreviated; quantitative material will be presented only selectively; footnote citations will be given in full, however, so that it will be evident that comprehensive and quantitatively detailed country case studies could be put forth, if space permitted.[11]

CUBA

Enlightenment and Skill

One of the most impressive results of revolutionary rule in Cuba is the expansion of the scope and domain of the educational system. More people are now educated than ever before, including more adults. Education is now perceived to be relevant to a larger number of issues than ever before, from the running of the home to the running of the government. In the 1953 census, 23.6 percent of the population was illiterate. In the early 1970s the proportion of illiterates was under 5 percent of the adult population. The median level of education rose from the third to the sixth grade between 1964 and 1975. School enrollment (private and public) per 1,000 population almost doubled at the primary level and doubled at the secondary (general and vocational) level between 1958 and 1972. There was no change at the university level.[12]

Another important effect of the revolution on education has been the marked increase in the number of children from rural areas who attend school. Whereas before the revolution many of these children did not go to school, now their enrollment is more nearly proportionate to their actual share of the population. Similarly, the proportion of adults who try to pursue their education has increased due to less tacit discrimination according to class. The government has tried to reduce the economic obstacles to education by providing scholarships to tens of thousands of students at all levels. The enrollment in adult education schools for workers and peasants, which train the poorly skilled and unskilled, exceeded an annual average of more than 400,000 during the 1960s—five times the enrollment in 1960. In the early 1970s, however, there appears to have been a decline in the government's commitment to equal opportunity through scholarships and adult education, as adult enrollment has been just more than 200,000 per year.[13]

Since these patterns in enlightenment and skill have generally persisted since the revolution, they might be expected to continue in the future. However, the educational system is not likely to make any additional new strides toward egalitarianism, in part because the degree of egalitarianism is already quite high, and in part because fundamental government priorities have changed. In addition, Cuban education suffers from a lack of liberty; even scholars sympathetic to the Cuban revolution have noted that "the method of instruction could best be described as [a] catechistic-authoritarian, teacher-centered approach characterized by a single teacher talking at a class of passive students."[14] More generally, both the amount and variety of certain kinds of information available to the people have declined. The daily newspaper run per 1,000 population fell from 129 in 1956 to 78 in 1967, rising to 95 in 1972.[15] More importantly, the government main-

51

tains and defends a monopoly of information, and can block the flow of information it does not want. In contrast, press censorship was weak and porous in the 1950s when even Fidel Castro could publish attacks on the Batista government in some national daily newspapers and in the leading weekly news magazine.

Well-being

The record on well-being can be summarized simply: Political disruption caused several basic health indicators to deteriorate in the 1960s, but investment in public health resources during the 1960s finally led to a marked improvement in those indicators during the early 1970s. Although a variety of morbidity indicators supports this argument, the infant mortality rate should suffice to make the point. The rate of deaths per 1,000 babies in their first year had been declining in prerevolutionary Cuba. It was 33.0 in 1958, rising to 39.7 in 1962, dropping to just below 38 in 1963–1964, and rising to a peak of 48.2 in 1969, followed by a sharp decline to 27.5 in 1972.[16] These comparisons are unaffected by changes in the method of statistical reporting in the two periods—there were two reporting systems in the 1960s and conditions deteriorated under both.

The degree to which well-being may be expected to continue is less clear. The number of hospital beds per 1,000 population fell between 1958 and 1974; the number of medical doctors for every 10,000 people fell from 10.5 in 1958 to 7.5 in 1972, but rose (because of the large classes graduating from universities) to 11.1 in 1975. The lack of success in treating health problems such as tuberculosis and leprosy (as reflected in morbidity statistics) has been due partly to cutbacks of 20 to 60 percent in the number of hospital beds allocated to patients with those diseases.[17] Security of well-being has also improved because of more thorough law enforcement. The murder and robbery rates per 100,000 population fell from 3 and 106 in 1960 to 1 and 93 in 1967.[18]

Equality has also improved. All medical services are now free. There were many free public hospitals before the revolution, but the best medical care often required payment for private hospitals and health personnel. The revolution eliminated ability to pay as the criterion for access to quality medical care. The availability of medical services has increased in the 1970s, and has become distributed more evenly among classes no matter what services are required. The distribution of services among regions has also become more balanced, but marginally. The rural share of general hospital beds increased from 1958 (under 1 percent) to 8.1 percent in 1962, but it declined to just over 6 percent in 1972—still well above the prerevolutionary level. The proportion of medical doctors in the province of Havana increased in every census after 1899, reaching a high of 62.4 percent in 1955; but the proportion fell to 42 percent in 1972 (Havana's share of the 1970 population was 27 percent).[19] In sum, there has been a trend toward more equitable distribution of health services, but the chief emphasis on equality occurred in the early years of revolutionary rule. Except for the trends in the distribution of medical doctors, the commitment to egalitarianism in well-being, as in enlightenment and skill, has declined in the 1970s.

Respect and Affection

The record is mixed for two respect categories identified earlier: race relations and relations between men and women. There was no equality of result between blacks and whites in prerevolutionary Cuba—though there was less inequality than in the United States, and considerable equality of opportunity. Cuban blacks and mulattoes make up somewhat more than one-fourth of the population. Before the revolution, blacks and mulattoes were severely underrepresented among engineers and medical doctors, but overrepresented among unskilled workers and domestic servants. Blacks and mulattoes received substantially less pay than did whites for equal work in all income and occupational categories.[20] On March 22, 1959, the revolutionary government ended legal racial discrimination in Cuba. Those clubs and beaches that had been closed to nonwhites (and not all had been) were opened to everyone. But *legal* racial discrimination had in fact been a limited problem; the perseverance of the attitudes that gave rise to racial discrimination was more subtle, and quite serious. Yet the government has remained committed to full

53

equality of opportunity, regardless of color.[21] Unfortunately, although data on incomes and occupations were collected in 1970, none have been published since the revolution. Because blacks were disproportionately poor, they are likely to have benefited disproportionately from the improvement of the lot of the poor.

Because the revolutionary government claims to have solved the racial problem, writing about the problem has become subversive. Black intellectuals who think that the revolutionary government still practices racial discrimination have become exiles. Afro-Cuban writers, conscious of blackness as their distinguishing characteristic, have been in disfavor. Black solidarity organizations that flourished before the revolution have been banned. The intellectual, artistic, mutual aid, and labor societies run by blacks for blacks have been forced to disband. Visitors continue to be impressed by how much less tension exists in relations among races in Cuba than in the United States. But they also continue to report persistent racism, however subtle, in public and private life. Standards of status—in posters, newspapers, and beauty contests—remain white. Afro-Cuban religions, the object of solicitude as folklore—as an exotic remnant of a superstitious past, preserved in museums and ballet dances—do not enjoy the same respect and toleration accorded to Roman Catholicism, Protestantism (excluding small sects), and Judaism.[22]

Complaints about racial "tokenism" in revolutionary leadership and policies are illegal though legitimate. Only 9 percent of the 100 members of the Central Committee of the Communist Party of Cuba, appointed in 1965, were black and mulatto, the same proportion as in the Cuban Senate and the House of Representatives in 1945, with little change since then. Then, as now, this is about one-third of what would be expected from their share of the population, and suggests little impact by revolutionary rule in increasing the representation of blacks among the political elite.[23] Within the Cuban Armed Forces in the 1970s, there were disproportionately many blacks serving as troops, and disproportionately few officers—the result of both historical conditions and selective military service legislation.[24]

There are also differences—though not very large—between

blacks and whites regarding health. Data from public health surveys both before and after the revolution suggest that blacks are more vulnerable than whites to all sorts of diseases, probably because of their poverty (though a strict historical comparison of the two periods is impossible with the available evidence).[25] Blacks predominate in the incidence of parasitic disease, as well as tuberculosis, and in the number of accidents directly tied to poverty, far above what would be expected from their share of the population in each province. Only a few surveys show whites more vulnerable to diseases—and these deal specifically with illnesses such as heart disease and cancer that are typical of wealthier populations with longer life expectancies. Even here, however, blacks are disproportionately represented in several surveys.

Although there has been a modest growth in respect for Cuban blacks, as a result of mass opinion and government policies, the situation of blacks has changed only modestly. Most gains were made in the early years after the revolution. Yet the fact that blacks are not free to be concerned with issues especially pertinent to them or to associate politically with one another free from governmental control is the chief threat to the long-term, secure enjoyment of their modest gains, and a deterrent to greater equality.

The revolutionary record is also mixed in terms of the growth of respect for women as persons, not merely as sex objects or dependents, or the advancement of their equality with men. The proportion of women in the paid work force rose from 17.2 percent in 1953 to 26.8 percent in 1975.[26] This rather slow rate of incorporation into the paid work force hardly varied before and after the revolution, and can be attributed to underlying processes of modernization that were independent of government policies. Nonetheless, the government has sought to incorporate women into the work force through the Women's Federation. The most striking effort occurred in 1969, when cadres of the Women's Federation visited 400,000 women who did not work for pay, and who were not physically or mentally handicapped and had no small children or adolescents at home. As a result of this effort, the net increase of women working for pay was only

55

34,752.[27] Since many of the women who joined the paid work force in 1969 would have done so even without encouragement from the Women's Federation, that effort hardly enhanced the effects of modernization in putting more women to work. This finding underscores the substantial conservatism among Cuban women, and also suggests an important aspect of their liberty: They are free to be idle.

Cuban women now seem to have more freedom of choice in their personal relationships than they did before the revolution. The divorce rate (per 100 marriages) quadrupled from 1958 to 1972;[28] in 1972 one of every three marriages broke up. The Cuban family had been patriarchal and authoritarian; the divorce rate thus indicates increased freedom to break away from familial authoritarianism. Child care services are fairly widely available; however, the demand outstrips the supply, leading to relative overcrowding. Birth control devices are widely available. The government has recently codified and partially altered family legislation (duties relating to marriage, divorce, alimony, orphans, etc.) ; the new family code, and the thesis on women of the first party congress, have been discussed by millions of Cubans. The combination of legal change and codification, and a massive political education campaign on the role of women, suggest that the status of women is likely to improve further. Security for women means above all that they will continue to enjoy respect. Security thus results from a near-halving of the rate of rapes per 100,000 population (1960–1967).[29] The area in which women have made no gains is politics. In 1975, women accounted for only 5.4 percent of the full membership of the Central Committee of the Communist party (and in 1948, 4.4 percent of the membership in the House of Representatives); the women's share of the membership of the party fell slightly from 1963 to 1974. Their share in local government in Matanzas Province fell by three-quarters from 1967 to 1974. Unlike party elections, these local elections were open to the public, who, faced with men and women whose politics were the same, chose on one of the few available grounds: sex category.

Finally, changes in interpersonal and family attitudes have

been few. In surveys of Havana Province junior high school students in 1960 and 1965, women were more likely to report constraints on career decisions.[30] In a survey of high school and university students in 1962, less than four-tenths of the students agreed that men and women should have equal sexual freedom.[31] In a 1975 survey in the town of Batabanó (Havana Province) asking people to name the most important inventions of the century, the miniskirt ranked among the top three.[32] A carefully controlled small survey of divorced men and women in metropolitan Havana asked who *should* have authority in marriage (men, women, or both); six-tenths of the divorced men *and* women said the man alone.[33] In sum, many beliefs pertaining to the freedom of women in interpersonal relationships, to the role of women in society, and to the family remain very traditional.

Nonetheless, the condition of women in Cuba has generally improved during revolutionary rule, most strikingly in the governmental provision of social services for women, less so in the incorporation of women into the paid work force, and least so in politics. At the level of individual beliefs, change has been rather slow, although the government has tried to increase the rate. On the whole, liberty in Cuba appears most prevalent in the area of women's rights: The government respects women's decisions not to work; the divorce rate has increased in a country where a male-dominated wife was the norm; and the government has sought to redress the balance of rights and duties in the family. Unlike enlightenment, skill, and well-being, the condition of women changed most in the late 1960s and early 1970s.

These remarks also bear on the changes in Cuban family life as an indicator of affection. The security of family life has also been seriously challenged by the explosion of the divorce rate. And, though attitudes of parents toward their children have not changed much, children have been modifying their relationships toward their parents. Junior high school students were much more likely to want to pull away from their parents in 1965 than in 1960.[34] Though the government tolerates the divorce rate, it does not like it. The authorities have engaged in mass campaigns to stimulate formal marriages among people who have been living together. The success or failure of these campaigns is reflected in the marriage rate, which rises in conjunction with governmental efforts and declines when they subside.[35] But the government has apparently succeeded in increasing the marriage rate in the long run (see Universal Declaration, Art. 16).

The government has sought to emphasize another aspect of affection both in and beyond private life—that is, affection for the revolution and national symbols, somewhat at the expense of the right of freedom from interference with privacy and the right to leisure (Universal Declaration, Arts. 12, 24). For instance, it asks good revolutionaries to include political criteria in their choice of a marriage partner (Universal Declaration, Art. 16).[36] Unfortunately, there is no quantitative evidence to bring to bear on these questions, although all other evidence suggests that the government has had substantial success.

In sum, the value of affection, as indicated by government interference in private family life, probably exhibits the lowest degree of security and stability of any fundamental value in Cuba. The claims to liberty within the family, among spouses, and from children have rocked the Cuban family. The government has also impinged on private affection patterns, with the result of reducing freedom of choice. It has stimulated, to a degree yet to be measured, a growth of affection for revolutionary and national symbols, at the expense of rights to privacy and leisure.

Rectitude

Norms of rectitude, relegated to the private sphere before the revolution, have been centralized and politicized, away from individuals and churches, into the hands of party and government. Morality in Cuba is determined according to political, ideological, and revolutionary standards. Centralization and politicization have cut back the degree of equality, security, and liberty of those who dissent from the single, public, revolutionary standard of rectitude. Though there were honest officials before the revolution and there have been corrupt ones since, the degree of corruption among public officials seems to have declined substantially since the revolution.

The government, in an effort to reduce the influence of standards of rectitude that compete with its own, has crippled the Roman Catholic church. The number of Catholic priests dropped by two-thirds from 1960 to 1970, and the number of inhabitants per priest quadrupled to 33,700. Much of this shift resulted from deportation of priests.[37] However, Cuba was already a secular society before the revolution. Only a quarter of the Catholics, and only a sixth of those with a religious affiliation, regularly attended Sunday mass or their respective religious services; only one of every six couples was married in a church.[38] Though institutionalized Catholicism was weak, a quarter of the population formally consulted Spiritists, an eighth consulted Afro-Cuban religious authorities, and a quarter consulted astrologers regularly.[39] Thus, though secularism was dominant, between one-tenth and one-quarter of Cubans had religious beliefs, however unorthodox. The impact of the revolution on religious beliefs and practices has been modest. The degree of religiosity has changed very slightly from the 1950s. The years 1960 through 1962 were the ones of greatest state-church conflict; even after that period, the strength of the historic, bedrock religious minority had not been reduced. And in regions such as Bayamo, Oriente Province, Afro-Cuban religion remained strong after the revolution, though a bit less so than before, with over 40 percent believers.[40] Relations between state and the Roman Catholic and Protestant churches have been improving since the early 1960s.[41] Antireligious propaganda is less prevalent than in other Communist countries. The churches have lost their schools and other types of activities, but religious persecution—except against sects such as Jehovah's Witnesses, Gideonites, and some Pentecostal and Afro-Cuban sects—has declined.[42]

In sum, Cuba today is a secular society principally because it has always been so. There is still persecution of several thousand members of religious sects, but there is considerable toleration otherwise. Religious organizations, however, cannot comment on political issues, run schools or hospitals, or have religious events outside of church or temple premises. Religious liberty, security, equality, and growth have been stunted, but most efforts to curtail the established churches have subsided.

There has been a strong effort to centralize standards of rectitude, and to increase the number of people adhering to them. There has also been an increase in sexual puritanism, as the government seeks to shape private rectitude. The result is a society more conscious of, and more committed to, standards of rectitude than in the past, and where people appear to believe that the government, in fact, applies these standards uniformly.

Wealth

A variety of economic indicators declined substantially during the 1960s, taking account of rates of inflation and the growth of population.[43] Agricultural production per capita was below its 1952–1956 level every year between 1962 and 1973, except in 1970 when the large sugar crop caused a brief increase in production.[44] The performance of the Cuban economy until the early 1970s was dismal; in fact, 1970 was the worst year for the economy since the revolution.[45] But the economy recovered in the first half of the 1970s, largely because of economic reorganization and sharply rising prices of raw sugar. Industrial and agricultural production rebounded vigorously, except for sugar (which declined) in 1971–1972.[46] Agricultural production surpassed the levels it had reached in the 1960s, but not its prerevolutionary levels.[47] Gross material product grew in the first half of the 1970s, so that by the end of 1973 gross product per capita reached the level it had attained in the first year of revolutionary rule (1959).[48] Yet this rough equivalency does not take account of price inflation and indeed suggests that the annual growth in real per capita GNP in the 15 years following the revolution was probably trivial, possibly negative.

Since the revolution, however, the economy has been outstanding in its redistribution of benefits. Overt unemployment, which oscillated between 10 and 16.5 percent of the work force in 1959, was reduced to less than 2 percent by 1970.[49] However, because underemployment flourished, labor productivity actually declined. With increased labor efficiency in the early 1970s, spot or regional unemployment reappeared.[50] The government continues to support those who become unemployed as a consequence of efficiency drives until they are retrained for another job. Education, medical care, and day-care centers are provided free of charge; quality services are now available, for the first time, to every Cuban. Many recreational facilities are also provided free of charge. In the 1970s, however, some goods and services that previously had been free again cost money; the prices of others (electricity, long-distance transportation, and worker-canteen meals, for example) increased, sometimes sharply. Rationing was introduced in 1962 when the economy collapsed for the first time. It has always been a symbol of failures in economic growth but it has also guaranteed a fairer distribution of scarce goods. The ration card summarizes in symbol and fact the twin aspects of revolutionary economic performance: success in redistribution, failure in growth.

Though data on prerevolutionary income distribution are inadequate, there seems to be a greater equality of incomes now than before 1959. Wage scales were set (in the mid-1960s) ranging from 64 to 844 pesos per month. During the 1960s, however, the trend toward wage egalitarianism accelerated. The rate of wage increase in the 1960s was three to four times faster for the poorer wage earners, typically in agriculture, than for all wage earners. The relative advantage of the most highly paid wage earners (those in the field of electric power and petroleum derivatives) declined in the 1960s.[51] But while the general trends in the 1960s advanced equality, inegalitarian trends have resulted from the new policies to accelerate economic growth.[52] In the 1960s, and even more so in the 1970s, the elites have been able to obtain preferential access to certain highly limited goods and services. Yet Cuba remains a substantially more egalitarian society than it was before the revolution.

Security of wealth from crime shows two phases. The robbery and theft rates per 100,000 population fell from 106 and 379 in 1960 to 93 and 235 in 1967. The total number of crimes against property (with or without violence) was cut by almost three-quarters from 1959 to 1964. But most likely stimulated by the increasing shortages of consumer goods in the later 1960s, the number of crimes tripled again by 1968,[53] leading to a modest decline in the security of wealth. Even so, the net number of crimes was still lower in 1967 than in 1960.

There is very little liberty to acquire wealth in Cuba. Most private entrepreneurship is prohibited. Private peasant land ownership persists, accounting for a gradually dwindling share of agricultural activity and ownership. But the last bastions of non-farm private enterprise—petty trade and services—were socialized in 1968. An exception has been the legalization of private contracting for petty repair services in the mid-1970s, provided that the persons performing the services do so in their spare time and retain a regular job. The mobility of workers—on the job and from job to job—is closely regulated by the government, which keeps extensive records on every citizen. Workers cannot strike collectively; however, in 1970, some 400,000 workers (one-fifth of the work force) absented themselves from work on the same days,[54] apparently as a result of the accumulation of relatively spontaneous and uncoordinated individual decisions. This worker discontent was a reason for the broad policy changes in the early 1970s. The workers' illegal acts exemplify how the liberty to withhold one's labor can have great success and broad effects. The 1970 collective job action is an important limiting case, showing both the difficulty of autonomous collective job action and its possibilities.

The trade-off between security and liberty is exemplified best by the 1971 law against loafing, which guarantees a job to every able-bodied citizen and specifies a social duty to work. It punishes able-bodied males (but not females) who fail to work or absent themselves from work. It provides, on the one hand, for a citizen's claim on the state for jobs or for income supplements if a job is lost as a result of the introduction of labor-saving devices. On the other hand, this law makes a repeat of the 1970 collective job action more difficult, and it gives wide discretion to management, union leadership, and government to define loafing.[55]

Power

The power of the central government has grown, enabling the government to make impressive redistributions of social and economic resources and to achieve many desirable human rights conditions. Yet there is a trade-off between the growth of centralized power and the liberty and equality of individuals to exercise political power. A single ideology, endorsed by the central governing institutions, prevails. Despite twists and contradictions, the precepts of that ideology govern most of social life; people with contrary views are met most often with suspicion or (in an ever smaller minority of cases) with repression.

One measure of the decline of both liberty and equality of power is that party membership, which reached 2 percent of the population only in 1974,[56] has become a de facto requirement for the exercise of the growing power of the state. Thus power is concentrated among a small elite; blacks and women share little in the decision making. Restraints on criticism and competition, of course, further bolster the power of the state. Cuba has only one party, and its party and government have a monopoly over the mass media. There is no freedom of association to oppose the party and government. Although it would be inaccurate to describe the exercise of power by elites as merely reflecting the policies of Fidel Castro, it is nevertheless accurate that Castro is far more than *primus inter pares*. Political power, when he chooses to exercise it, rests decisively in his hands.

Restrictions on formal liberties are explicit in constitutional and legal documents, almost all of which reserve broad discretionary powers for the government. Yet these powers have increasingly been exercised with restraint and seem to be applied in full force only to political offenses. Citizens who commit minor crimes are treated rather lightly: Although three-fourths of the persons charged with misdemeanors in the Popular Tribunals of Havana Province were found guilty in 1972, four-tenths of the sentences were no more than public admonitions.[57]

Yet there has been little liberty to differ with the prevailing political ethos and there are still political prisoners. The numbers peaked near the time of the Bay of Pigs invasion in 1961 when tens of thousands of people were arrested, though most very briefly. However, many persons have received long prison sentences (by world standards) for committing political crimes. According to the official (and very conservative) government statistics, there were 259 political prisoners per 100,000 population in 1965 and 44 per 100,000 in 1974, 15 years after the revolution.[58]

What appear to be attempts to give individuals a sense of participation and some personal power in Cuban politics in fact largely symbolize a highly limited liberty. There has long been a degree of political bargaining in Cuba among factions within the Communist party and the government and among various organizations over policy issues.[59] But even these organizations, which have steadily increased their membership and influence, are ultimately controlled by the party. The party, for example, in fact appoints and removes leaders, and assigns tasks. The direct participation of their members in the policy-making process is more apparent than real. Nonetheless, the size of the membership is impressive: The Committees for the Defense of the Revolution included four-fifths of the adult population in its ranks in 1973; three-fourths of Cuba's adult women belonged to the Women's Federation in 1974; and more than 90 percent of the peasants, the workers, and the primary school students belonged respectively to the Peasants' Association, the Labor Confederation, and the Pioneers' Union.[60]

There were three other developments in the early 1970s that tended to increase liberty and equality of power. First, citizens are now legally able, and in fact encouraged, to contact public officials to complain about defective or inadequate goods and services. Public officials and the press are encouraged to act as ombudsmen for concrete, discrete local problems. Second, revolutionary rule has been formalized through the approval of a new constitution, new legal codes, and a new concern with the implementation of the laws ("socialist legality") to limit the broad discretionary powers of the central political elite. Legislators may or may not have much impact on actual legislation, but in any case they may act as national ombudsmen and facilitate links among middle- and local-level officials for purposes of lobbying. Third, some electoral competition has been introduced, although it is sharply restricted even in such apparently competitive elections as those for local government.[61] There has been more than one candidate per post, for instance, in most regional and local labor union elections since the mid-1960s. Yet the government's nomination and campaign procedures limit the meaning of electoral liberty and the impact of politics on national policy.[62] Candidates for government cannot nominate themselves, nor can opponents of the government associate with one another in order to suggest candidates. Instead, nominations are made by assemblies in which secret ballots are prohibited. Nominations for provincial and national assemblies are made by the party and its national organizations; the person chosen need not have been elected at the local level. In addition, only the party and its mass organizations are allowed to campaign. The candidates are forbidden not only to campaign but even to debate issues. Their appeal to the voters is dependent on campaign literature—a biography, study materials about the election, and a film on local government—that is produced by the government. Nominees whom the party dislikes are induced to withdraw because the party forewarns them of adverse material to be included in their biographies.

In sum, political centralization and its growth are the dominant characteristics of Cuban politics. The power of the central political elite has become quite secure. It is this high degree of political security, perhaps, that has led to the recent but modest trends limiting the degree of centralization. The emphasis on new political procedures such as socialist legality, for instance, has served to protect much of the population from the arbitrary power of the state. Nonetheless, even though the number of people who have power is increasing, power is still held quite unequally and exercised under great constraints. Virtually no issue, however private, is outside the scope of government, and no individual beyond its domain.

Summary

The following Table 3 is a gross "photograph" of the performance of revolutionary rule by the mid-1970s. The table does not show trends within the revolutionary period, although, in principle, a series of such tables could do so. It is a five-point scale, from $+ +$ to $- -$; NR means not relevant. Performance is particularly

TABLE 3
The Performance of the Cuban Political System: Summary

	Growth	Equality	Liberty	Security
Enlightenment	+ +	+ +	– –	+
Skill	+ +	+ +	–	+
Well-being	+	+	NR	+
Respect	+	+	–	+
Affection	–	NR	–	–
Rectitude	+	–	–	+
Wealth	–	+ +	–	+
Power	+ +	– –	– –	+ +

favorable in growth and equality of enlightenment, skill, and wealth; in growth and security of power holding; and in equality of wealth. Performance is unfavorable in issues pertaining to liberty.

MEXICO

Enlightenment and Skill

There has been a steady and impressive decline of the Mexican illiteracy rate over the long run. The rate of illiterates (population aged six years and over) fell from approximately 67 percent in 1930 to 28.3 percent in 1970.[63] The sharpest decline occurred during the period of very fast economic growth in the 1940s. The proportion of children enrolled in all primary schools per 1,000 population almost doubled from 1940 to 1970. Secondary school enrollment per 1,000 population tripled from 1959–1960 to 1970; academic secondary enrollment per 1,000 population almost tripled during the same period.[64] Within given age groups, people were better educated and skilled, although growth was not equal for all age groups.[65] Yet the tasks ahead remain formidable: The absolute number of illiterates actually grew somewhat in each decennial census (except 1950), reaching 11 million in 1970.[66]

As more and more youngsters were educated and many adults remained illiterate, the skills of the two age groups grew increasingly unequal. However, some indicators of inequality in the levels of skill and enlightenment among urban and rural populations have either stayed the same or narrowed. For instance, the rate of promotion in both urban and rural schools increased substantially from 1940 to 1970. Even though urban schools are still better than rural schools, education has improved throughout the nation and the gap between urban and rural primary schools has diminished. The percentage of urban children attending primary schools increased only slightly from 1940 to 1970, but that of rural children more than tripled in the same period.[67] Once again, more children from urban than rural areas went to school in 1970; while enrollments increased throughout the nation, the gains were spectacular in rural areas. The persistence of these patterns suggests that these trends are very likely to continue. And while public schools predominate in the educational system, private schools are not prohibited. In sum, very substantial growth in enlightenment and skill has been accompanied by an expectation of continued educational opportunity in public education, while retaining the option of schooling independent of government. But even though some inequalities have been reduced substantially, gross inequalities persist.

Well-being

There has been a long-term trend in the growth of well-being, as best shown by the decline in the infant mortality rate (deaths per 1,000 births). This rate, 207 for 1922–1929, was cut in half by the late 1940s and to 51.4 in 1973.[68] The general mortality and morbidity rates show the same trend.[69] Deaths are now caused less by parasitic and other contagious diseases, which have been controlled through mass public health measures, than by the degenerative diseases typical of more affluent populations (cancer, heart attack, etc.).

Nutrition is an indicator of both well-being and wealth. Data indicate the persistence of much nutritional inequality amidst overall growth in 1970. The per capita consumption of meat rose by one-third from 1930 to 1970.[70] However, while a fifth of the people in all households ate no meat at all in 1970, almost a fifth did so every day; in 1970, more than one-third of the people in all households never drank milk, while almost half did so every day.[71] Other indicators show that some inequality has been curbed. The proportion of persons over one year old who wore no shoes dropped from more than 25 percent in 1940 to less than 10 percent in 1970; shoes are now available throughout the country, in rural as well as urban states.[72] There is still much inequality of well-being. Many of the benefits of growth come to middle-income people who can purchase shoes, meat, and milk. It is likely, also, that the decline in the infant mortality rate, morbidity rates, and associated indicators is sharply class-bound. Though health care is available to the poor, access to steady quality care is linked to ability to pay. Class inequality, rather than geographic or regional inequality, is the chief problem. While the rural areas are still comparatively poorer, they are better off than they used to be.

Security of well-being appears to have increased for the population as a whole, although the data must be treated cautiously. But the degree of security of well-being is also sharply class-bound. The percentage of males indicted for crimes was more than halved from 1930 to 1970 in steady decennial declines (more than four-fifths of all indicted persons are male). The rate of increase of the absolute numbers of indicted males has been slower than the rate of increase of the population. It is unlikely that the Mexican judicial system is now less efficient than 40 years ago, or that the statistical coverage is now poorer. The passing of both the violent revolutionary decades and the abject mass poverty of the 1930s appears to have had a salutary effect on the crime rate. The general decline can be illustrated for specific crimes over both the long and the medium run. The percentage of males indicted for theft was halved from 1930 to 1970; the percentage for crimes against persons was cut by a fifth from 1960 to 1970, and for crimes against property by a quarter in that same period.[73] Finally, the hypothesis that the Depression may have been the historic peak (thus far) of the Mexican crime rate is supported by statistics on deaths by violence per 100,000 population, which rose by a quarter from 1903 to 1937 and was cut in half from that high point by 1964.[74] Crime and violence in Mexico, historically high, are less so today.

In sum, there has been substantial growth of well-being thanks to mortality reduction, and the results in security are positive because of crime rate declines. Performance is weakest in equality; despite some substantial gains, gross inequalities persist among social classes.

Respect and Affection

Issues of respect are posed by the role of Indians and of women in Mexican society; the role of women also opens up the general discussion of family life. The proportion of the Mexican population aged five years old and over that speaks Indian languages only fell steadily from 13 percent in 1910 to 2 percent in 1970. The proportion of the population able to speak an Indian language also fell to 8 percent in 1970. The absolute number of Indian monolinguals declined from about 1.2 million people in 1930 to about 860,000 in 1970; the proportion of bilinguals declined slightly from 1930 to 1960, but had increased again by 1970. Thus the absolute number of persons able to speak an Indian language remained about the same from 1930 to 1970—somewhat more than three million people.[75] The correspondence between social class and ability to speak Spanish is very high.[76] Language classification alone tends to understate the portion of the Mexican population with strong Indian cultural characteristics; in 1970, 13 percent of the population still wore Indian clothing and shoes.[77]

The politicians, the bureaucrats, the educators, and the philosophers of the Mexican revolution have debated at length not whether to assimilate the Indian into the dominant Spanish culture, but how to do so. There was virtual unanimity that linguistic and cultural assimilation was indispensable. Modernization and assimilation in Mexico have proceeded simultaneously; sometimes assimilation has occurred without modernization, but modernization without assimilation has been politically intolerable. There is no modern Indian elite in Mexico. National consolidation has been successful, but at the cost of the obliteration of the cultural past of the Indian peoples of Mexico. State symbols in Mexico incorporate and exalt the Indian past as a part of the symbols of a single state; but apart from that, Cortés has long since triumphed over Montezuma.[78] Anthropological studies support the broad outlines of this argument, too.[79]

Respect for women as persons with roles beyond family life has changed slowly. The proportion of women in the paid work force declined as a result of the revolution, to rise again only after 1930, accelerating during the 1940s; the share of women in the economically active population rose to 21 percent in 1970,[80] double the 1910 and triple the 1930 levels. The shift from an agricultural to a more industrial society, and the impact of the revolution, brought women back to the home; the absolute number of women working also declined. The accelerated pace of modernization, however, has finally led to dramatic increases in the number of women in the paid work force. Mexico was also slower than most Latin American countries in extending suffrage to women, which was fully achieved only by 1953. In 1958, Mexican women accounted for 6 percent of all national candidates for deputy and senator, and for 5 percent of all those elected.[81] And in a large survey in the late 1950s, half of the men expected fair treatment from government, but less than 40 percent of the women did. This differential ratio persisted at every level of education. It suggests that women were more likely to perceive governmental discrimination against them, probably on the basis of experience.[82]

Mexican women and men do not differ in their attitudes toward the family: they are equally conservative. This prevents the exercise of liberty in the family, subordinating women to men. For example, more than half of the women in a large survey in the late 1960s reported that it would be their husbands who would decide whether they would or would not work.[83] The liberty of the women was also restrained by the low rate of use of contraception, because big families acquired over many years kept them home and reduced their options in life. Only one-fourth of the women surveyed were practicing birth control, and only one-third had ever used any type of birth control. One important reason for the low use of contraception was simply that Mexican women wanted big families: Three-fourths of the women surveyed said that the ideal family should have six or more children. Mexican families surveyed (averaging between five and six children per couple) were big because they wanted many children. The major stated reason for the lack of use of contraception, however, was religious: Two-thirds of the women and a majority of men said they did not practice contraception because of religious reasons. Thus the limited social role of women results from cultural patterns; Mexican culture shapes women's attitudes so that many seem to choose not to choose; that is, they apparently prefer a life-style that allows only two roles: wife and mother. The lack of contraception indicated by the survey resulted not only in big families but also in abortion. Approximately one in eight pregnancies ended in abortion; three-fourths of the married women surveyed had had one or more abortions in their lifetime.[84] Equality between men and women has increased slowly in Mexico. The liberty of women is still restricted, for noncoercive or cultural reasons, though probably somewhat less than it has been. Women remain securely tied to the past. The rate of divorces among Mexicans per 100 marriages doubled from 1.3 in 1926 to 2.8 in 1970,[85] but its 1970 level still remained extraordinarily low, in absolute terms as well as below the world median. Beyond the survey evidence showing that future patterns may resemble present ones, a different indicator of security—the rate of indictments for rape—remained unchanged from 1940 to 1970.[86]

In sum, there has been a mixed pattern in the growth of respect for Indians and for women, and in their equality with non-Indians and men, respectively. The improvement, at best, has been very slow, and for Indians has had high cultural costs. While trends are expected to continue, Indians are not free to pursue their ethnic identity. Finally, a highly authoritarian family structure has changed little.

Rectitude

The Mexican revolution has not produced a secular ideology to serve as a basis for moral judgment. On the contrary, one of the most frequent charges against the successors to the Mexican revolution has been the practice of corruption in government. While it would be difficult to argue that there is more corruption since the revolution than before, it is equally difficult to argue that there is less.

The Mexican revolution unleashed a classic struggle between the Roman Catholic church and the state. The number of priests, unchanged from 1910 to 1926, fell by about 11 percent by 1940, the period of sharpest church-state conflict; the number of inhabitants per priest rose slightly from 1910 to 1926, and then by two-thirds to 5,088 in 1940. After 1940, government attacks on the church subsided; however, though the absolute number of priests doubled from 1940 to 1967, population grew faster, so that the number of inhabitants per priest increased slightly.[87] The Catholic hold on Mexicans remains strong. The proportion of persons married by the church had declined slowly in each decennial census since 1930, but it returned again to the 1930 level—83 percent—in 1970. The proportion of persons claiming to be Roman Catholic has declined trivially to 96.2 percent in 1970.[88]

Although legal restrictions on the Roman Catholic church dating from the peak of anticlericalism remain on the books and are enforced to a degree, the church in fact has considerable freedom to preach and to act: Most persons still adhere to sacraments such as baptism, marriage, and communion; four-fifths of the adult population go to communion at least occasionally.[89] A secular government has not stopped this. Curiously, the major problem for liberty in the exercise of moral values appears to be the preponderance of the Catholic church. Even if considerable self-restraint is exercised by the Catholic bishops, the church has a near-monopoly on religious symbolism; Catholic moral norms prevail by the sheer numerical weight and the relatively high religious loyalty of the Catholic people. Government deference to the Roman Catholic church has constrained in part the religious liberties of others.

Catholics in Mexico do not comprise a single religious-political subculture. A survey of the political attitudes of devout and less devout Mexican Catholics (the non-Catholics were too few for analysis) showed no differences between the two groups in general attitudes toward the state, the expectation of treatment from government bureaucracies, pride in nation, or similar variables. There was, however, a difference in party identification. All Catholics who identified themselves with a political party were overwhelmingly likely to do so with the ruling Institutional Revolutionary Party rather than with its chief opposition, the National Action Party, but regular churchgoers were twice as likely as nonchurchgoers to identify themselves with the opposition.[90] Thus religion did not establish a political subculture, but it did make for some partisan differences.

In sum, there has been no demonstrable change in the moral climate of Mexico. While liberty of moral belief and practice is fairly widespread, the weight of Roman Catholicism may limit informally the liberty of others. The pattern of equality among Catholics, non-Catholics, and the state, except for the 1925–1940 period, is not very different from the prerevolutionary period, and it does not appear likely to change.

Wealth

Perhaps the single best-known success story of the Mexican governments, before and after the revolution, has been sustained economic growth. Clark Reynolds has estimated that the compounded annual rate of growth of gross domestic product per capita in constant prices (1950) was 2.2 percent during the last prerevolutionary decade. It ground to a halt during the Depression of the 1930s. The 1940s showed the fastest real growth in twentieth-century Mexico, with a rate of 3.9 percent; subsequently the rates continued to be positive, though less spectacular: 3 percent from 1950 to 1960, and 2.7 percent from 1960 to 1965. Gross national product per capita in 1970 prices grew at an annual average rate of 3 percent from 1960 to 1970, and of 2 percent from 1970 to 1972.[91] Even though Mexico's rate of growth has slowed in recent years, the long-term pattern of economic growth is steady.

The economic security of the population has exhibited a more mixed pattern. Despite some severe technical statistical problems, it appears that real wages for unskilled labor at best remained the same from the depths of the Depression in the 1930s until the mid-1950s. Real wages for rural unskilled labor may have been halved between the mid-1930s and the mid-1940s; real wages for urban unskilled labor may have fallen by one-third. Real wages then rose steadily from the mid-1940s through the 1960s. Therefore, the takeoff of Mexican economic growth in the 1940s—the Alemán presidency, in particular—was characterized by a severe decline in the real wages of the Mexican poor and a probable increase in income inequality. The initial rise of the economy was characterized by a decline in real wages; only after the 1940s did real wages increase. The legal minimum daily wages in constant prices doubled from 1950 to 1964–1965 for both urban and rural wages.[92]

The pattern of economic equality is also mixed. The increase in real per capita gross domestic product, so impressive over the long run, at first benefited the rich only. The economic benefits of growth in Mexico have been shared more equally only in more recent years. Aggregate measures of income inequality appear to have worsened in the 1950s and early 1960s. In the early 1960s, Mexican aggregate income distribution was about 51 percent worse than in the United States. The share of income of the bottom 40 percent of income recipients fell from 1950 to 1963. The bottom 40 percent did not become absolutely poorer, because real wages rose during these years, but they lost a third of their relative share of income. The top 5 percent of income recipients lost a quarter of their income share from 1950 to 1963. Therefore, the great beneficiaries of Mexican economic growth— in terms of both absolute income and relative share of income— were the middle class. Within the middle class, however, the eighty-first to the ninety-fifth percentiles registered the most dramatic gains in share of income, from one-fifth in 1950 to one-third in 1963 (twice their population share).[93] In sum, income in Mexico has been redistributed from the upper class to the upper middle class, and from the lower class to the lower middle class, with the upper middle class (15 percent of the income receivers) coming out best of all.

There is a mixed pattern of economic liberty in Mexico. The policies of the successors to the revolution have reduced or eliminated the role of foreign enterprises in the exploitation of the subsoil and the soil. In the petroleum sector, for example, the 1938 state takeover under President Cárdenas has led to government ownership of all production and refining.[94] Agricultural ownership was modified through the agrarian reform legislation, especially under the Cárdenas presidency.[95] In 1961, Mexico reserved all new extractive and processing mining concessions for its nationals, and for corporations in which Mexican capital held a majority share. The "Mexicanization" of mining was virtually completed in 1972.[96] The 1944 Mexicanization decree, and subsequent legislation, have also empowered the Mexican government to monitor, regulate, and implement policies on the degree of foreign control over subsidiaries of multinational enterprises operating in Mexico. This legislation has been applied primarily to very large firms. Mexican owners had no, or trivial, equity participation in two-thirds of the subsidiaries of United States–based multinational enterprises in Mexico in the 1960s.[97] Therefore, though there are some important limitations to the activities of non-Mexican enterprises in Mexico, there has been considerable flexibility in policy implementation.

Given this substantial state regulation of foreign ownership, it is somewhat surprising that Mexican government expenditures were only one-sixth of gross domestic product in 1968–1969, ranking thirteenth of 18 Latin American countries, and at the bottom of the seven largest countries. However, Mexico ranked fourth of 19 Latin American countries in the share of the public sector in fixed investment in 1969 (40.8 percent).[98] One explanation is the very low level of military expenditures in Mexico. Of the 20 Latin American countries, Mexico ranked eighteenth lowest in military expenditures as a percent of gross national product in 1972. That share, approximately seven-tenths of one percent, has remained unchanged from 1963 through 1973. In contrast, Chile's rate under Presidents Allende and Frei was two and a half to three times the Mexican level, and Brazil's rate was even higher for a comparable period.[99] Freed from a high military burden, the Mexican state has concentrated its efforts on stimulating both public and private investment. Public institutions, such as Nacional Financiera, have played a major role in facilitating investment in cooperation with the private sector.[100] The

Mexican government has also become an entrepreneur in petroleum and electricity,[101] or a coparticipant in large economic enterprises such as steel.[102] Thus the Mexican government has carved out an important and, at times, decisive role for itself, but it leaves considerable leeway to the private business sector. Mexican businessmen have also successfully and autonomously lobbied through their national organizations to modify public policy in matters affecting business, even when the power and prestige of the president was at stake.[103]

The major limitation on economic liberty in Mexico appears in labor-management relations, specifically curtailing labor. Labor has benefited from growth since the early 1950s. These material benefits, however, were obtained largely at the expense of economic liberty. No strike can occur legally in Mexico without government authorization. From 1941 to 1958, strikers in federal industries exceeded 4 percent of the federal labor force only in the 1943–1945 period, which reflected the strains of World War II. From 1941 to 1958, real losses due to strikes exceeded 0.2 percent gross national product (1940 prices) in only one year (1.1 percent in 1944). Except during the period 1943–1944, the government never recognized more than one-fifth of all strike demands formally filed as legal strikes; from 1948 to 1958, legal strikes never exceeded 7 percent of all demands filed. Thus there is a considerable class-bound asymmetry in the exercise of economic liberty. Compared to the limitations on the right of labor to strike, the limitations on the economic liberty of business are mild. Autonomous collective bargaining, free from government intervention, does not really exist in Mexico. Compulsory arbitration before mixed labor-management boards, in which the government holds the preponderance of power, is the normal practice.[104]

In sum, economic growth is the success story of the Mexican revolution. Real standards of living, though they declined for the poor from the 1930s to the 1940s, have increased generally over the long term. Income inequalities widened, probably severely, in the 1940s, and slightly in the 1950s. Although all categories of income recipients have benefited in real terms over the long run, benefits have accrued disproportionately to the upper middle class. The persistence and widening of gross inequalities and the long-term deterioration of the relative share of income of the bottom 40 percent of the population suggest that Mexico's economic growth has deprived its citizens of certain human rights. The class characteristics of economic liberty lead to a similar judgment. The uncertain and changing priorities of the political elite regarding economic equality and liberty are not likely to reassure the Mexican working class. On the other hand, workers have received real benefits. Thus their expectations about the future—security—are mixed.

Power

The Mexican government has used its power to promote growth—of enlightenment, skill, wealth, well-being, and of power itself. The use of power to increase equality occurred primarily in the presidency of Lázaro Cárdenas in the late 1930s, and somewhat under President López Mateos (1958–1964). By Latin American standards, Mexico's degree of income inequality is average—hardly a great achievement for governments heir to a revolution. The achievements of the agrarian reform, too, were the result primarily of policies implemented in the 1930s, though some important policies were also implemented under President López Mateos. The power of the state in Mexico has grown over time as a result of the large-scale regulation of private enterprises, foreign-owned and national, including labor-management relations. The state plays an important role in investment, and it has become an entrepreneur through public enterprises.

Power in Mexico is also distributed unequally. The president has been the candidate of the Institutional Revolutionary Party (PRI), and of its predecessors with varying names, since the revolutionary decade. The official government party candidate has received no less than three-fourths of the votes in presidential elections, and since 1958, about 88 percent.[105] In elections for the Chamber of Deputies, though the PRI share of the votes has declined in each of the five elections between 1951 and 1973, its share was still three-fourths in 1973.[106] Until 1943, the national Congress approved all legislation unanimously. Until 1963, the proportion of votes cast against nonunanimous legislation never exceeded 6 percent of the membership of the Chamber of Deputies. The 1963 constitutional amendment created a form of modified proportional representation to guarantee minority party presence in the Chamber. Since the 1964 sessions, the PRI share of the Chamber has dropped to 82–84 percent.[107] Never has the president lost a bill in Congress. The chief formal national restraint on the power of the presidency has been the Supreme Court. From 1917 to 1960, the presidency was sued in the Supreme Court approximately 1,700 times, more often since 1940 than before. The Court has ruled for the claimant and against the presidency in approximately one-third of the cases.[108] The informal restraints on the power of the presidency—the limited pluralism of economic interest groups and a fairly competitive (though not entirely unaffected) press, among others—have probably been more important than the Court, though their weight is difficult to estimate. These restraints include the need to maintain a viable coalition and effective presidential power within a constitutional structure that allows the president a single six-year term. It is the office, not the incumbent, that has concentrated and disproportionate power in Mexico. This constitutional norm and practice facilitates the operation of informal restraints on incumbents and prevents dictatorial control by one man. The process by which presidential candidates are nominated is still rather obscure; its net effect appears to be the institutionalization of rule by a small elite.

As the president is powerful within the central government, the central government is powerful in relation to all other governmental units. The federal share of annual government expenditure has been more than 70 percent since 1923.[109] Though the hypothesis that benefits accrue to those who organize and participate politically to help themselves seems true in many countries, it must be strongly qualified in the case of Mexico. Data from 36 different communities in Mexico indicate that there is no statistically significant relationship between the degree of organizational capacity in a community and the degree of benefits received from the central government. The Mexican central government is sufficiently autonomous that it can choose whom to benefit, disregarding local organizational capabilities.[110] Thus the inequality of power resources is quite striking.

Power equality refers not only to the distribution of power capabilities but also to the equal treatment of citizens by power holders. Although the concept of equality before the law is difficult to quantify with the data at hand, there is evidence for substantial class equality in the courts' treatment of citizens indicted for crimes. In 1970–1971 there were 114,907 persons indicted before lower courts (*juzgados de primera instancia*); four-fifths of these were found guilty. Although the findings of guilt vary according to occupation and social status, there is no consistent class pattern to that variation. On the one hand, only 61.3 percent of all professional and technical people indicted were found guilty, while 86.6 percent of those employed in agriculture were found guilty; on the other hand, 82.8 percent of top administrative and managerial personnel were found guilty, as were only 76.9 percent of industrial workers.[111]

The degree of political liberty in Mexico is somewhat difficult to assess. One reason to classify Mexico as an authoritarian political system is that there is no liberty to dislodge the political elite, which has ruled the country for decades, and there is no liberty to stop its legislative policies once it has agreed upon a common program. However, the Mexican political elite is not always cohesive—in part because presidents change and differ from each other—and, therefore, it does not prevail regularly on key issues. There is, consequently, considerable room for political bargaining and compromise, and for pressure by autonomous interest groups. Because of the inequalities in wealth and enlightenment, this exercise of political liberty through lobbying enhances inegalitarian results.

There is some, though modest, electoral liberty in Mexico. Because the results of most national elections are foreordained, the voting turnout has typically been less than 55 percent and often under 50 percent of the population aged 20 or over. (The 1952 election was the last in which only males were allowed to vote.)[112] There is an organized, legal electoral opposition in Mexico. By the 1958 elections, the main opposition party, the National Action Party (PAN), was contesting most of the Senate and Deputy seats. By the end of the 1960s PAN officials ran the governments of 18 municipalities in many different states.[113] In

Mexico, one need not abstain since one can vote for an opposition that, in some limited instances, can win and govern. The extent of political liberty in Mexico is also shown in the government's response to open, possibly violent confrontations. The central government can prohibit any political organization or activity that challenges its authority, however modestly; this has not been done very often, though at times it has been decisive. The government relies primarily on co-optation, modest reforms, and if necessary, bribery and informally sanctioned violence to meet such challenges. Extralegal violence against government opponents has also been used sporadically.[114] These legal and extralegal procedures, therefore, restrain sharply the exercise of economic and political liberty.

University student protests also indicate some of the limits to the exercise of authoritarian power in Mexico. Through the 1960s, the grievances of university students were discussed in the press. Their protests have led to the resignations or dismissals of university officials, the Regent, and the Chief of Police of Mexico City, and the Attorney General of the Republic. A degree of opposition and competition, which had some effects on government decisions, was allowed even while repression was being exercised and even during some of the most serious challenges to the central government in 40 years, such as the student protests of 1968 and 1971.[115] Mexico is an authoritarian regime, but it is close to being a more competitive and open type of system. It may never get there, but it is inappropriate to class it with other authoritarian regimes (such as Chile since 1973) as if it were indistinguishable from them.

There are also political prisoners in Mexico.[116] At the time of the 1968 university student protest, it was claimed that there were 85 political prisoners who had been held for several years for the crime of "social dissolution." Those figures yield a rate of 0.2 political prisoners per 100,000 population. But by the end of 1968, apparently "thousands" of persons had been arrested, however briefly, during the university student protests of that summer and fall. If one assumes 10,000 arrests, that would make for about 22 arrests per 100,000 population. However, these are not all prisoners. A more accurate count comes from the numbers of prisoners who were held for at least a few days or weeks, and subsequently released. The *New York Times*, which followed those events (at about the time of the 1968 Olympics) very closely, reported a total of 471 prisoners released in three different amnesties in 1968. The maximum reported student claim of persons who had disappeared in early October was 300; these should be counted separately because, if released, the government would not want to acknowledge that they had been seized in secret. In the first half of 1971, the government and its opponents agreed that there were about 150 political prisoners still left from the 1968 protests; all but 26 of these were released by the end of the semester. Adding these three sums, there were about two political prisoners per 100,000 population in 1968; and 0.3 political prisoners per 100,000 population had been held for two and a half years, from the fall of 1968 to the spring of 1971. In addition, the modest guerrilla activity in Mexico in the 1960s and 1970s has led to localized repression, killings, and political imprisonment, mostly in rural areas, to an extent difficult to estimate, though it appears modest; the rate of political prisoners might double if all the numbers were known.

In sum, central power has grown in Mexico. The state is more competent and it has greater weight on the lives of its citizens. Power is held very unequally, and with important limits on political liberty. There is a limited pluralism in Mexico. Though Mexico has an authoritarian political system, the system is far less repressive than that of other authoritarian regimes. Power holders are secure, and those without power are not likely to get it.

Summary

Table 4 is a gross "photograph" of the performance of the Mexican political system in the mid-1970s. This table does not show trends through time. It is a five-point scale, from + + to − −; NR means not relevant. Performance is particularly favorable in the growth of enlightenment, skill, well-being, wealth, and power; power holders are secure. Performance is particularly weak in the equality of power holding, followed by equality of

TABLE 4
The Performance of the Mexican Political System: Summary

	Growth	Equality	Liberty	Security
Enlightenment	+ +	+ −	+	+
Skill	+ +	+ −	+	+
Well-being	+ +	+ −	NR	+
Respect	+ −	+ −	−	+
Affection	+ −	NR	−	+ −
Rectitude	+ −	+ −	+ −	+ −
Wealth	+ +	−	−	+ −
Power	+ +	−	−	+ +

wealth, and by the liberty of power, wealth, respect, and affection.

CROSS-COUNTRY COMPARISON

The preceding case analyses each compared the performance of a social system to its performance in earlier periods. The framework used for these analyses also can be adapted for a comparison of two (or more) cases. For cross-national and cross-ideological assessments of human rights conditions, some common standards—derived by comparing conditions among different countries—are necessary to assess human rights indicators, although fairness and political prudence recommend a stress on assessing each country's performance relative to its own past. Such standards, for instance, would facilitate evaluation of whether Mexico and Cuba are doing "well" or "poorly." Two cautions are in order. First, the Mexican governments have not faced an internationally hostile environment since the first half of the 1940s; the Cuban government faced a very hostile environment from 1960 to the early 1970s. Second, Cuba has long been a much more modernized society than Mexico, as some of the Cuban prerevolutionary data cited above make clear. Thus a comparison of the two countries at any given time will necessarily be biased in

82

favor of Cuba, while comparison across time favors Mexico, because it did not face such international obstacles. A valid comparison must assess the two countries' performances over time, not at any one time.

There is no substantial difference between Mexico and Cuba in their patterns of growth in literacy; primary schooling grew faster in Cuba than in Mexico; secondary-general schooling grew faster in Mexico than in Cuba. Growth in enlightenment and skill strongly characterized both social systems. However, the difference in class equality between the countries is magnified by the fact that in Mexico the ability to pay persists as one basis governing the quality of schooling, whereas in Cuba strong efforts have been made to reduce class inequalities in education. Although gross class inequalities remain in Mexican education, both countries have substantially reduced geographically based inequalities in enlightenment and skill. The Mexican government does not prevent establishing private schools; Cuba's does. There are expectations that these patterns will last.

The growth of well-being is more impressive in Mexico than in Cuba. This unorthodox conclusion can be explained by an important fact that is still rarely recognized: the large-scale exodus of health personnel in Cuba (the "blame" for which must be shared between those who chose to leave and the political system that led them to do so). Yet there is more equality of well-being according to class in Cuba than in Mexico, largely because ability to pay does not shape the access of the Cubans to medical care but does shape that of the Mexicans. Both countries have substantially reduced inequalities of well-being between rural and urban populations, although both remain beset by gross inequalities. Security is comparable in both countries; liberty is not relevant.

The Cuban government is more committed than the Mexican government to the growth and equality of respect for ethnic minorities and women. However, ethnic minorities in both countries have undergone some loss of cultural uniqueness, which seems more pronounced in Mexico. Both countries show a very slow pattern of incorporating women into the paid work force, and glacial change in the incorporation of women into politics.

There is also little liberty for respect groups (ethnic minorities and women) in both countries, although for different reasons: In Cuba, while the liberty of women has increased, there are very sharp limitations on the liberty of ethnic minorities to organize socially or politically; in Mexico the reasons are not political, but lie in the persistence of a very authoritarian family structure (though it has become perhaps a bit less so). In Mexico the liberty of ethnic minorities is also substantially restricted (though less so than in Cuba). These conditions seem less likely to change in Mexico than in Cuba.

The Cuban family has been adversely affected by the revolution. The number of families breaking up because of divorce has increased at an extraordinarily fast pace. The liberty of the family from government interference has declined because political and ideological criteria have been injected into marriage patterns. Individual attitudes toward the liberty of women remain traditional. The shifts of government policy regarding the family are no guarantee of security. Yet the authoritarian Mexican family, which allows very little liberty for any but its adult male members, is much more stable.

Since each revolution, sensitivity to rectitude has grown in the Cuban social system, but not in that of Mexico. In Mexico, there seems to be little tendency (except during the 1925–1940 period) for patterns of rectitude to change. The greater liberty for the Catholic church since the 1940s has not been matched by its greater toleration of individuals who have moral and religious standards that differ from its norms. In Cuba, there is substantial inequality between the government's preferred morality and religious or other nongovernmental moral standards. Although religious persecution has abated significantly since the early 1960s, some sects still suffer from it. There are sharp limitations on the exercise of religious freedom, especially outside church or temple walls. This pattern is expected to continue.

Economic growth has characterized Mexico since the 1930s, but its absence has characterized Cuba since the revolutionary government came to power. Though Cuban performance can be predominantly attributed to internal Cuban conditions, and especially to the catastrophic economic policies of the late 1960s, a hostile international environment accounted for much of the economic disruption, especially in the early 1960s. Cuba's economy grew substantially only in the early to mid-1970s. The distribution of wealth in Cuba, despite contrary trends in the 1970s, has become substantially egalitarian—vastly so in comparison to Mexico. Economic equality is the success story of the Cuban revolution. There are sharp limitations on the exercise of economic liberty in both countries, especially by the working class. Cuba and Mexico do not differ in stability: Both have experienced some changes in the 1970s.

Finally, the power of the state has grown greatly in both countries, though more in Cuba than in Mexico. Power is held unequally in both countries, though more unequally in Cuba than in Mexico. People who hold power are comparably secure in both countries. Restrictions on political liberty are a serious problem in both countries, but far more so in Cuba than in Mexico. Though the greater authoritarianism in Cuba than in Mexico predominantly stems from internal political conditions, these conditions have been partly shaped by a hostile international environment and a close association with the Soviet Union.

Most of Mexico's improvement has been in growth (except in rectitude, respect, and affection); most of Cuba's has been in equality (except in power and rectitude). The degree to which all of these values are likely to persist in the two countries is hard to distinguish because both social systems seem to be very stable. The extent to which geographically based inequalities have been reduced is also comparable. Even though in both social systems liberty has been sacrificed to achieve other goals, the loss of liberty has been more severe in Cuba than in Mexico. Authoritarian capitalism in Mexico has raised the standards of living of most people, though it has done so unequally; authoritarian socialism in Cuba has brought about a redistribution of wealth—even amidst economic stagnation—from the more to the less affluent population and a redistribution of enlightenment and skill, which have grown and been distributed more equally in Cuba than in Mexico. But the Cuban political elite has been more willing than the Mexican political elite to suspend political liberty and to impose lengthy prison terms on its political enemies.

THREE

Four Cross–National Human Rights Issue Areas

The development of time-sensitive country profiles is the most thorough method for the assessment of human rights conditions. It is also insufficient. A country may appear to be performing well relative to its own past on a particular indicator, but it may not be performing as well as the rest of the world. Alternatively, a country may not only be performing poorly on a particular indicator, e.g., political prisoners, but it may be performing even worse than most other countries. Since performance on most human rights issues changes from country to country, knowledge of a cross-national pattern of performance is necessary to judge a particular country's performance on a given issue. Comparisons of the overall performance of several countries and of the performance of many countries on a given issue are not mutually exclusive; on the contrary, they are mutually compatible and structured by the same framework. Assessing human rights should lead to action that is well informed by prior analysis, which requires both country and issue-area comparisons. Studies of particular issues can serve to spot problem countries; studies of a country's overall performance can explore the context of its performance on a given issue. "Issue-area" analysis may facilitate action by international organizations or governments by simplifying the problem; studies of overall performance within a country provide the perspective needed to modify the information available on a single issue and thus to restrain intemperate decisions to act. Profiles of individual countries are especially suitable for assessing change on values such as literacy, for which complete success is distant and rate and direction of change are the important indicators to measure. Issue-area analyses are especially suitable for assessing values for which any violation, at any time, is intolerable. Since even a little torture is not tolerable, a much less flexible standard can be applied.

This section focuses on four human rights issues: infant mortality, slavery, torture, and political prisoners. These issues have been selected somewhat arbitrarily, although each is part of the framework derived from the Universal Declaration and most persons would agree that they are important. Slavery, torture, and political imprisonment are highly important to persons primarily concerned with civil and political liberties; to those with a broader human rights agenda, infant mortality also is highly important. These issue areas show how data can be gathered to assess a country's performance on a particular value. Infant mortality is an indicator for well-being; political imprisonment is an indicator for individual liberty in the face of government power; the existence of torture is one of the most extreme indicators of the deprivation of both liberty and power and of security of individual respect; slavery was not discussed in the case studies because it does not exist in Mexico or Cuba; the existence of slavery indicates a deprivation that would appear in the matrix under liberty-respect and liberty-wealth (i.e., in employment under slave conditions).

Infant mortality and political imprisonment are more susceptible than slavery and torture to quantitative treatment. Nonetheless, the reliability of the data for both indicators can be questioned, especially in the case of political imprisonment, which requires the use of multiple sources of data. Torture seems at least susceptible to being quantified according to an ordinal scale, but information on slavery is such that scaling is extraordinarily difficult. Each issue also shows a different worldwide performance pattern over time. Worldwide performance on infant mortality and slavery has improved in the twentieth century; on torture, it has deteriorated; on political prisoners, the pattern seems to be cyclical. Infant mortality and torture are some of the values I would rank at the top of a hierarchy—values whose violation, if or when they result from identifiable government action (more clearly in all cases of torture, but only so in some infant mortality cases), is least acceptable to me.

If international monitoring of human rights were to exist, there would be both country case studies and issue-area case studies, related to each other by the use of a common operational framework.

INFANT MORTALITY

Worldwide performance during the twentieth century regarding infant mortality is, by and large, a success story in those countries for which data are available over a long period of time. The death rates per 1,000 babies in their first year are still far too high in many countries, and there are disparities among the rates of different countries. However, the worldwide tendency, especially in Europe, Asia, and the Americas, throughout this century has been unmistakably toward a reduction of infant mortality.[117] Yet this also means that a social system in which infant mortality has been reduced over time has had no more than ordinary success. If, however, a nation's infant mortality rate fails to decline, or increases, its performance has been unusually poor. The long-term pattern of decline is so statistically overwhelming that a presentation of the data would be boring, though heartwarming. Nevertheless, there are several instances in which regimes have performed very poorly.

The government of Rafael Trujillo of the Dominican Republic (1930–1961) is an example. Under the Trujillo regime, the infant mortality rate rose from 48.8 in 1935–1939, to 69.9 in 1940–1944, to 87.6 in 1945–1949, then dropped slightly to 79.7 in 1950–1954, and rose again to 83.5 in 1955–1959, and to 101.5 in 1960–1961. The result of a change in regimes was equally dramatic. The rate had dropped to 72.7 by 1965, to 50.1 by 1970, and to 38.6 by 1973.[118] The performance of the Trujillo regime is difficult to match statistically.

The Republic of South Africa has kept infant mortality statistics carefully separated by race since World War II. The infant mortality rate of the white South African population has dropped rather steadily from 37.0 in 1945–1949 to 21.0 in 1971; the rate for the Asiatic South African population also has dropped steadily from 74.6 in 1945–1949 to 35.6 in 1971. The black South African infant mortality rate dropped from 133.1 in 1945–1949 to 124.8 in 1960–1964, rose to 133.6 in 1969–1970, and fell to 122.2 in 1971. During the same period, the Asiatic infant mortality rate dropped 52 percent from a moderately high baseline; the white rate dropped 43 percent from a low baseline; and the black rate dropped only 8 percent from a very high baseline during a quarter of a century, with a low degree of pattern security.[119]

In sum, since the expectation on the basis of overall issue-area analysis is that infant mortality rates will decline steadily, social systems that do not exhibit a declining trend should be scrutinized closely. Year-to-year infant mortality rate shifts can vary upward or downward; however, if three-to-five-year averages fail to drop, especially in cases where the baseline is still high, the people in that country are experiencing substantial deprivation. High infant mortality rates can serve as a warning light for other serious problems. By the same token, though some of the poorer countries have inadequate facilities to gather statistics, some of the wealthier countries that do have adequate capacities fail to report their findings. The effort to gather pertinent data on a steady basis is also, of course, part of the need for human rights assessments.

SLAVERY

The low incidence of slavery worldwide in the twentieth century compared to previous centuries is also, by and large, another success story. Judgments regarding slavery, however, necessarily differ from those regarding infant mortality. High rates of infant mortality, while alarming, need not reflect badly on an incumbent government's performance provided there is substantial and rapid progress toward reduction; the presence of any slavery is intolerable according to prevailing international norms. Slavery is internationally illegal; few practices have been condemned more soundly in world agreements. Partly for this reason, in the United Nations slavery surveys most governments deny that slavery exists under their jurisdiction. Most reports on the persistence of slavery must rely on nongovernmental organizations, and especially on the London-based Anti-Slavery Society. Discussions of slavery suffer from the handicap that the governments most concerned with its eradication are those most likely to report its existence; governments least committed to eradication are most likely to cover it up. Therefore, the fact that a country may not be commonly acknowledged as having slavery does not necessarily mean that slavery is not practiced within its borders.

A study of contemporary slavery must focus on four different problems, each having as a common trait a clear lack of consent or the existence of coercion. The first involves the coercion of women into marriage, the arrangement of marriages against the consent of one of the partners, the coerced establishment and compulsory enforcement of harems, and the enforcement of these practices by social custom and, at times, by police power. These kinds of slavery have no terminal date. The governments of Australia, Chad, India, and the United Kingdom (the latter on behalf of Rhodesia, Hong Kong, and the New Hebrides) have reported this type of slavery, as have nongovernmental organizations in Cameroon, the Philippines, Uganda, and Zaire.[120]

The second type of slavery is the seizure of individuals against their consent, not necessarily for financial, political, or sexual reasons, to perform a wide variety of services without compensation and without limit of time. This type, of course, is closer to the traditional notion of slavery. The most grievous case of this sort of slavery has been reported in Saudi Arabia, where, in the mid-1960s, nongovernmental estimates placed the number of slaves at 250,000. Slavery of this sort was also imposed in Rwanda and northern Cameroon and by non-Indians on Indians in Brazil and Paraguay. Less clear cases existed in Mali and in the Federation of South Arabia in the mid-1960s. In the mid-1970s, cases were reported in El Salvador, Honduras, Guatemala, Nicaragua, and Equatorial Guinea, among others. Only the government of India has admitted the presence of this type of slavery in its territory, and it did so for the purpose of eradicating that slavery.[121]

The third type of slavery results from debt bondage; debtors who cannot pay their debts are seized as compensation for the unpaid debt, or surrender their children as payment. The fact that the debt may be considered paid after a certain amount of time can make this case of slavery less clear-cut. The government of India has reported this practice, particularly among tribal peoples. Comparable practices have been reported by nongovernmental organizations in Nepal and Bolivia.[122]

In countries where these three types of slavery exist, two criteria should be employed in assessing conditions: The first is the existence of a commitment to suppress slavery; the second is evidence of decline in the practice. Thus change in performance can be measured best in the case of governments that face up to the problem and report periodically on it. Of all the countries surveyed where at least one kind of slavery was reported, the one showing the clearest policies to suppress remaining instances of slavery was India, where the law, the police, and ransom payments were being used, albeit against considerable odds, to suppress slavery. However, several million Indians today still serve as bonded laborers.[123] More is known about slavery in India precisely because its government has made substantial efforts to suppress its practice. Some governments, such as those of the Philippines and Cameroon, often deny the existence of slavery under their jurisdictions, even though there are reliable reports that they take at least occasional steps to suppress it. Some local government officials in Cameroon, however, have used police power to force women who escaped from harems to return to them.[124] And even though the late King Faisal of Saudi Arabia freed his own slaves and committed funds to ransoming slaves, Saudi Arabia has remained one of the most extreme examples of the persistence of slavery.[125] The principal problems for human rights assessment stem from governments which neither recognize the persistence of slavery nor take any steps to suppress it.

The fourth type of slavery is forced labor of political prisoners; most documented cases have been in Eastern Europe, the Soviet

Union, and the People's Republic of China during the 1950s. However, many countries have had to resort to forced labor for varying periods in order to complete economic development projects and to punish "undisciplined" workers.[126] These conditions, however damnable, pertain more properly to a discussion of political prisoners and of freedom of labor. The other three types of slavery do not involve politics, and subjection occurs either without limit of time, as in the first two cases, or for a very long time, as in the case of debt bondage, the less clear-cut case of slavery.

TORTURE

A third issue, torture, is defined by Amnesty International, the most authoritative agency on the subject, as "the systematic and deliberate infliction of acute pain in any form by one person on another, or on a third person, in order to accomplish the purpose of the former against the will of the latter."[127] From the eighteenth to the beginning of the twentieth century, the reduction of the use of torture also appeared to be a success story. But during the second quarter of this century, torture reappeared in Europe and has subsequently spread like an epidemic. Amnesty International asserts that torture definitely increased from the late 1950s to the early 1970s, even after discounting for the spread of communications (which permits better reporting of cases of torture) and for the changing class composition of the subjects of torture (the better educated know how to complain more loudly and effectively).[128] Unlike slavery, torture is practiced widely and with increasing frequency. But as in slavery (and unlike the case of infant mortality), the existence of any torture has evoked strong international legal condemnation. A more disturbing implication is that technological change, which has helped to reduce the infant mortality rate and has probably contributed to reducing the perceived need for slave labor, may have facilitated the reemergence and spread of torture. Electricity leaves no visible marks. Psychology and pharmacology, as many of their victims

93

TABLE 5
Torture

Political System Response to Torture	"Mere" Brutality	Occasional, Selective, Time Limited	Administrative Practice	Adjunct to Massacres
Some concern	Colombia Mexico Grenada	India Chile pre-1973 Venezuela United Kingdom North Ireland Sri Lanka Pakistan post-1972 Peru post-1975 Cuba post-1971		
Permits discussion	Salvador Honduras Panama	Ecuador Peru 1970–1975 Spain	Argentina Brazil Philippines/ Marcos South Africa	
Represses discussion	U.S.S.R. Paraguay up to 1970 Haiti Poland	Paraguay after 1970	Greece 1967–1973 Morocco Uruguay Tunisia post-1968 Chile post-1973 Egypt Iran Syria South Korea Equatorial Guinea Bulgaria Cuba until 1971	Rwanda Burundi Indonesia Uganda/Amin

have discovered, can also be used effectively. The accompanying Table 5, which suggests the current scope and responses to torture, has been compiled from the 1973 *Report on Torture* and subsequent publications of Amnesty International.[129]

Table 5 embodies two ordinal variables that can be inferred from Amnesty International's qualitative discussion of torture.

It provides a quantitative basis, albeit modest and selective, to assess torture conditions. The classification of specific countries is primarily illustrative; the types of torture practiced by different governments do change and information on such practices is rarely fully reliable. But a quantitative index can classify torture according to the following definitions: First, there is "mere" brutality, which is not a systematic activity with a rational purpose and need not require or intend the breaking of the victim's will; second (and this category often overlaps with the first), there is the occasional use of torture against selected groups or for limited periods; third, torture may be an administrative routine governments use in dealing with opponents; finally, torture may be an adjunct to massacres of thousands of people. Perhaps no other practice is more contrary to prevailing international legal norms.

Table 5 also includes an evaluation of political systems' responses to torture. First, there may be some institutionalized concern in the political system. A government executive may initiate steps to investigate and suppress torture as did the United Kingdom in response to torture in Northern Ireland. Alternatively, reasonably autonomous parliaments and/or courts may investigate and suppress torture at least to some degree. Most of the countries in the upper row of the table fall within this second part of the first category. For example, in 1975 President Carlos Andrés Pérez of Venezuela supported judicial indictment and conviction of military intelligence torturers, who were sentenced to 21 years in prison; and after years of inaction, Peruvian courts indicted 12 policemen in 1975 on charges of practicing torture.[130] Second, a political system may permit nongovernmental institutions (such as political parties, mass media, or churches) to discuss publicly and condemn cases of torture, which could somewhat deter its practice. Third, a government might repress discussions of torture, and it might not allow government institutions to respond publicly and overtly to suppress the practice.

The table of torture shows a relationship between lower levels of torture (in frequency and intensity) and some institutionalized concern in the political system with suppressing torture; it also shows a relationship between higher levels of torture and conditions in which public discussions of torture are suppressed. Given the characteristics of political systems, international pressure may be most effective in curtailing torture in the countries in the upper left of the table. The governments along the bottom row are unlikely to pay much attention to international pressure, while the governments along the top two rows, and especially along the top row, may be quite sensitive to such pressures. Although a broad concern with human rights may suggest that the nations at the bottom right of the table are the most urgent areas for some action, a concern informed by pragmatic considerations of effectiveness is likely to focus on those countries whose governments are more susceptible to international pressure.

Not all countries in which torture is practiced are included in the table. That a nation is not mentioned may simply mean that no reliable information is available. Amnesty International says that Costa Rica was "the only Latin American country from which [it] has received no allegations of torture."[131] Amnesty International also found that "there are at the moment few states in Africa, whether independent or ruled by ethnic minorities or colonial powers, where torture has not been used over the past decade against internal political dissidents or suppressed racial or religious groups and few, if any, which are willing to investigate such practices."[132] Similarly, "few parts of Asia" are free from torture, though the countries of South Asia were typically found to have political systems that either permitted discussion of torture or were somewhat institutionally concerned.[133] Amnesty International found substantial numbers of political prisoners in Eastern Europe and the Sovet Union, but relatively few allegations of torture, except where brutality was practiced. Bulgaria was the only country in Eastern Europe for which evidence of torture as an administrative practice in the 1970s has become available.[134] In Western Europe, Amnesty International found that there was substantial torture in Greece from 1967 to 1973; some torture on the Iberian peninsula, under the now virtually dismantled authoritarian regimes; and torture (along with considerable concern on the part of the British government) in Northern Ireland.[135] In general, Europe, North America, Australia, and New Zealand had little or no torture.

POLITICAL PRISONERS

There are no worldwide trends for political prisoners: The number of political prisoners held is increasing in some societies and diminishing in others. Unlike the other three issues, for which quantitative data is either very good or very bad, estimates of the numbers of political prisoners in countries vary greatly depending on whether the source of information is the government or its opposition. Typically, governments have narrow definitions of political imprisonment; oppositions have broader definitions. Table 6 presents estimates of the rate of political prisoners per 100,000 population.[136] These selections are illustrative; absence from the list does not mean that a country has no political prisoners.

TABLE 6
Rate of Political Prisoners per 100,000 Population

	Number of political prisoners	Source*	Year	Rate
Albania	25,000–30,000	CE	1962	1,462–1,754
	16,000	Opp.	1966	838
Bulgaria	4,500	ICJ	1962	56
	1,170	AI	1975	13
East Germany	29,632	AI	1950	172
	12,000	AI	1960	74
	6,000–8,000	AI	1965	38–50
	18,383	AI, govt.	1972	108
Hungary	17,500	ICJ	1960	175
Rumania	40,000	AI	1950	242
	12,000	AI	1960	65
	7,674	Govt.	1960	42
	0	AI	1965	0
U.S.S.R.	10,000	AI	1975	4
Bangladesh	42,000	AI	1973	57
	21,000	AI	1974	28
India	17,843	Govt.	1975	3
	20,000–54,000	AI	1975	3–9

*CE: Council of Europe; Opp.: opposition; ICJ: International Commission of Jurists; AI: Amnesty International; Govt.: government; Tyson: Brady Tyson (see footnote 136); Thomas: Hugh Thomas (see footnote 136).

TABLE 6
Rate of Political Prisoners per 100,000 Population (Continued)

	Number of political prisoners	Source	Year	Rate
Indonesia	500,000	AI	1965	687
	116,000	AI	1971	98
	45,000	Govt.	1971	38
	70,000	AI	1972	58
	39,000	Govt.	1973	31
	50,000	Govt.	1975	38
	55,000	AI	1976	41
	31,000	U.S. govt.	1976	23
Nepal	200	AI	1975	1
Philippines	500–6,000	U.S. govt.	1976	1–14
Singapore	68	AI	1975	3
	40	AI	1976	2
Sri Lanka	18,000	AI	1971	141
	6,000	AI	1973	45
Chad	242	AI, govt.	1975	6
	0	AI, govt.	1976	0
Ghana	600	Opp.	1965	8
	1,400	Opp.	1965	18
	250	AI	1972	3
Ivory Coast	380	AI	1970	9
	190	AI	1974	4
	55	AI	1975	1
Malawi	500	Govt.	1966	12
	1,000–1,500	Opp.	1966	25–37
	1,000	AI	1974	20
Nigeria	50	AI, govt.	1975	0.1
Rhodesia (Africans only)	2,000	AI	1964	53
Zanzibar	1,000	Govt.	Jan, 1964	294
	2,500	Opp.	Jan, 1964	735
	110	Govt.	end 1964	32
	348	Opp.	end 1964	102
	1,000	AI	1974	244
Argentina	1,200	AI, govt.	1973	5
	4,537	Govt.	1976	16
	3,000	Govt.	1976	11
	5,000	Opp.	1977	18
Bolivia	2,000	ICJ	1971	40
	200	ICJ	1973	4

TABLE 6
Rate of Political Prisoners per 100,000 Population (Continued)

	Number of political prisoners	Source	Year	Rate
Brazil	12,000	Tyson	1970	13
	1,000	Tyson	1973	1
	1,500	AI	1975	1
	800	AI	1976	0.7
Chile	40,000	AI	Sept, 1973	391
	10,900	Govt.	Nov, 1973	107
	18,000	ICJ	end 1973	176
	9,000–10,000	ICJ	Mar, 1974	86–96
	6,000	Govt.	Mar, 1974	58
	7,000	AI	mid-1974	67
	4,027	Govt.	Oct, 1975	38
	5,000	Church	Dec, 1975	47
	317	Govt.	1976	3
	700–800	Red Cross	1976	6–7
	900	Opp.	1977	8
Cuba	100,000	Thomas	Apr, 1961	1,420
	20,000	Govt.	1965	259
	4,000	Govt.	1974	44
Honduras	100	AI	1976	3
Mexico	921	Govt., Opp.	1968	2
	150	Govt., Opp.	1971	0.3
	500	AI	1976	0.8
Nicaragua	500	AI	1976	23
Paraguay	150	AI	1966	7
	81	ICJ	1971	3
	500–1,200	AI	1974	19–47
	300	AI	1975	12
	338–450	AI	1976	12–16
Uruguay	6,000	AI	1975	196
	5,000	AI	1976	161
	2,000	Opp.	1977	63

The data on political prisoners show four different patterns of holding political prisoners. The first pattern, exemplified by the Eastern European countries, Cuba, and Indonesia, shows very high rates (above 100 per 100,000 population) in the early stages of consolidating a regime, followed by fairly high rates (above 40 per 100,000 population) for a decade, and often for longer periods. However, the tendency is to reduce the rate over time. There are exceptions, of course; the table suggests the impact of the Hungarian revolution; imprisonment in Hungary in 1960 was much higher than elsewhere in Eastern Europe. In every case, the absolute numbers of political prisoners run well into the thousands.

The second pattern is exemplified by Nepal, the Philippines, Singapore, Chad, the Ivory Coast, Honduras, Paraguay, Ghana, and Malawi. These nations have fairly stable, low long-term rates, though they vary from year to year. Even when the figures are those of the opposition, the rates do not ordinarily exceed 40 per 100,000 population. However, the data and other reports suggest that some prisoners may linger in prison for fairly long periods.

The third pattern is exemplified by Zanzibar, Bangladesh, Sri Lanka in the 1970s, Bolivia, Chile after 1973, Uruguay in the 1970s, and less clearly, India briefly in the mid-1970s, Argentina, Brazil, and Nicaragua. At a given time, the rate of political prisoners per 100,000 in these nations increases sharply (at least to 40, perhaps to more than 100) but then declines quickly. While this overall pattern fits India, Argentina, and Brazil, the actual rates do not. The worst Indian rate was 9, the worst Brazilian rate was 13 prisoners per 100,000 in 1970; the worst Argentine rate was 18 prisoners per 100,000 in 1977. However, the absolute numbers of political prisoners are very high. Brazil currently may belong primarily in this third pattern, though it might be moving in the direction of the fourth. As the data for Argentina, Brazil, and Zanzibar show, repressive periods may reappear after periods of relaxation.

The fourth pattern is exemplified by Mexico, Nigeria, and by many other countries that are not included. These countries ordinarily have few political prisoners (a rate of less than 1 prisoner per 100,000), and absolute numbers that rarely exceed the dozens or, in large countries, the low hundreds. In times of political crisis there may be arrests, but persons held for political crimes for a few weeks do not bring the rate over 5 per 100,000. The amount of time they spend in prison is also quite low. Some countries have had no political prisoners for many years; these, of course, are ideal, though a minority. One political prisoner is one too many. These countries fit a fifth pattern, in which nations have had no political prisoners at all for some time, a record that complies with international legal norms.

Perhaps the differences among patterns can most clearly be shown by comparing the performance of Chile's military government after 1973 with that of some other governments included in the table. According to the estimates of Amnesty International and those of the International Commission of Jurists, the rate per 100,000 population of Chileans arrested for a few days at the beginning of military rule was comparable to that of arrests in Communist countries, though not as high as the rates in some of those countries. (The rate for most Communist countries, except Cuba, does not show the peak rate of arrests, but rather the rate that pertained for some time after the new government came to full power.) Amnesty International estimates that the rate in Chile had dropped to about 67 within 10 months after the military takeover, which is comparable to the record of Rumania approximately 15 years after its regime assumed power, and is better than the rates in Hungary and East Germany. Within two years, the rate of political prisoners held by the Chilean government was about equal to the rate in the Communist countries included in Table 6 a decade and a half after a new regime came to power, or the rate in Indonesia after the regime had been in power for a decade; and by 1977 the rate dropped to no more than eight. This argument is certainly not an apology for the Chilean government, whose policies have led to a pattern of gross violation of many human rights. Nor should a judgment rest on one issue alone. This comparison simply illustrates that the performance of the Chilean government regarding political prisoners, though contrary to international norms, is not so bad as that of some other governments. (The amount of torture in Chile in the 1970s, however, appeared to exceed that of Communist countries, except Bulgaria, but it may not have been so great as the amount in some of these countries in the early years of their governments' consolidation, e.g., the Soviet Union in the 1930s.) The rate of political prisoners per 100,000 helps to distinguish among countries within the same cultural-geographic regions, which otherwise are often classed together. There is a great difference in degrees of repression between Brazil and Chile both at the peak of repression and after a lapse of time. There is an even greater difference between the repression under these two regimes and that under the limited authoritarianism of Mexico or in Nigeria under General Gowon. Honduras and Nicaragua are authoritarian neighboring small countries, but the latter is many times more repressive.

Evaluation of performance in the area of political prisoners therefore requires a prior assessment of the type of regime. International attention may be addressed to a regime that reaches a high rate of holding or to one whose rate of holding fails to decline soon enough. Judgments in this area must be closely coordinated with evaluations of the treatment of prisoners, and cast in the broad operational framework of human rights evaluation. Pragmatic considerations suggest that international objections to the level of prisoner holding shortly after a revolution or counterrevolution are not likely to be effective; a rise in the rate of political imprisonment is simply to be expected, however much deplored. Efforts to reduce the rate of holding quickly after a major change of regimes and, of course, to guarantee minimal standards of decent treatment are likely to be more effective. Here, as in the case of torture, addressing efforts toward governments that are more sensitive to deprivations of human rights, though less gross than others in violation of those rights, may be more effective.

A decline in the rate of political imprisonment may be a cause for rejoicing; however, the reason for a decline may be that a population has become so cowed that imprisonment is no longer necessary. For this reason, an issue-area approach is insufficient in assessing human rights; it must be coupled with a broader country profile to make sense of the decline of particular indicators. Yet a country profile alone would not tell us enough about a country's performance on the political imprisonment indicator; for a full assessment one would also need to know how the country's performance over time compared with that of similar countries.

FOUR

Conclusion

This essay has argued that human rights conditions should be evaluated in a broad context that has the formal consent of many countries. A broad framework is desirable, comprehensive, and consistent with empirical analyses. It does not treat all values equally; on the contrary, the essay has discussed different ways in which people, including the author, may weigh different values. If certain values are to be given more weight than others, the list should be organized in a nonexclusionary hierarchical fashion so that the comprehensive approach is still retained. This ranking would establish a clear threshold for human rights action, but it need not mean an abandonment of concern for and action on a fuller set of values. Even when action is triggered by specific violations of human rights, those who act should be fully informed about a country's performance in terms of a larger framework.

The case studies sought to indicate how the framework can be used for assessment and judgment. The perils and limitations of making the framework operational have already been noted. The framework and the case studies permitted comparisons of social systems as they change, or fail to change, over time. But case studies are not enough. Almost all countries do well on some values and less well, or poorly, on others. When certain values are deemed more important than others, they should be singled out for special discussion through issue analyses, which have cross-national patterns of their own. Some issues show worldwide trends, others do not. Some show improvement, others deterioration. The overall picture gained through knowledge of these patterns allows an observer to pick out instances of particularly egregious violations for evaluation more effectively than if country case studies alone were used.

This essay has tried to show how assessments can be made about human rights conditions by using empirical data for countries and specific issues. It has stressed the "How," but not the "What then?" But "What then?" is a question that will continue to face us all.

NOTES

1. See, for example, Kenneth Boulding, *The Impact of the Social Sciences* (New Brunswick, N.J.: Rutgers University Press, 1966); Karl W. Deutsch, "Toward an Inventory of Basic Trends and Patterns in Comparative and International Politics," *The American Political Science Review*, vol. 54 (March 1960); E. Sheldon and R. Parke, "Social Indicators," *Science*, vol. 188 (May 1975); and Charles Taylor and Michael Hudson, *World Handbook of Political and Social Indicators* (New Haven: Yale University Press, 1972). See also a closely related set of suggestions: Richard C. Snyder, Charles F. Hermann, and Harold D. Lasswell, "A Global Monitoring System: Appraising the Effects of Government on Human Dignity," *International Studies Quarterly*, vol. 20, no. 2 (June 1976), and the next two issues of this journal.

2. The importance attached in this essay to a broad framework for the study of human rights should not be taken to mean—far from it—that this author places less importance on the civil and political rights stressed with broad impact and appeal since the late eighteenth century, the human rights with which the general term is almost totally identified in common usage in the United States. My own biography underlines the high importance I attach to such human rights as political expression, unfettered political competition, criticism of government, freedom of information, political association, and international migration.

3. For a discussion of this topic, with bibliographic references, see Samuel P. Huntington and Jorge I. Domínguez, "Political Development," in Fred Greenstein and Nelson Polsby, eds., *Handbook of Political Science*, vol. 3 (Reading, Mass.: Addison-Wesley, 1975), pp. 5–6. See also references below.

4. See, for example, Hadley Cantril, *The Pattern of Human Concerns* (New Brunswick, N.J.: Rutgers University Press, 1965).

5. Raymond D. Gastil, "The New Criteria of Freedom," *Freedom at Issue*, no. 17 (January-February 1973); "Comparative Survey of Freedom, II,"

in no. 20, (July-August 1973); "Comparative Survey of Freedom, III," in no. 23 (January-February 1974); "Comparative Survey of Freedom, IV," in no. 26 (July-August 1974); "Comparative Survey of Freedom, V," in no. 29 (January-February 1975); "Comparative Survey of Freedom, VI," in no. 34 (January-February 1976).

6. Arthur S. Banks and Roger B. Textor, *A Cross-Polity Survey* (Cambridge: The M.I.T. Press, 1963); Robert A. Dahl, *Polyarchy: Participation and Opposition* (New Haven: Yale University Press, 1971), especially pp. 231–249; and Dankwart Rustow, *A World of Nations* (Washington, D.C.: The Brookings Institution, 1967), pp. 290–291.

7. See, for example, Carlos A. Mallman, "Quality of Life and Development Alternatives," paper presented at the Meeting on "Alternatives for Development," sponsored by the State Secretary for Planning and Economy, State of São Paulo, Brazil, November 1975, especially pp. 2–3; and M. Hopkins and Hugo Scolnik, with assistance from M. McLean, "Basic Needs, Growth and Redistribution: A Quantitative Approach," paper presented at the World Employment Conference, June 1976, especially p. 3. Both papers were presented at the Seminar on Global Opportunities and Constraints for Regional Development: A Review of Interdisciplinary Simulation Toward a World Model as a Framework for Studies of Regional Development, sponsored by the International Political Science Association et al., Cambridge, Mass., February, 1976.

8. Harold Lasswell and Abraham Kaplan, *Power and Society* (New Haven: Yale University Press, 1965), pp. 55–56, 74.

9. See Karl W. Deutsch, *Politics and Government*, 2d ed. (Boston: Houghton Mifflin, 1974), pp. 13–15, for some aspects of this idea.

10. See, for example, Harold Lasswell, Daniel Lerner, and John Montgomery, eds., *Values in Development* (Cambridge, Mass.: The M.I.T. Press, 1976); Henry Dobyns et al., *Peasants, Power and Applied Social Change: Views on a Model* (Beverly Hills: Sage Publications, 1971); G. D. Brewer and R. D. Brunner, eds., *Political Development and Change* (New York: The Free Press, 1975).

11. Much of the material on Cuba, and indeed the shape of the argument, can be found in Domínguez, "Revolutionary Values and Development Performance: China, Cuba and the Soviet Union," in Lasswell, Lerner, and Montgomery, eds. *Values in Development*. However, that argument had a different comparative purpose, including a limitation of the Cuban data to approximately 1970. That material has been updated here and other kinds of data introduced.

12. Richard Jolly, "Education: The Pre-revolutionary Background," in Dudley Seers, ed., *Cuba: The Economic and Social Revolution* (Chapel Hill, N.C.: University of North Carolina Press, 1964); Richard Fagen, *The Transformation of Political Culture in Cuba* (Stanford: Stanford University Press, 1969), pp. 33–68; Michael Huteau and Jacques Lautrey, *L'éducation à Cuba*

(Paris: Maspero, 1973), p. 27; María de los Angeles Periú, "Experiencias de la educación obrera y campesina en Cuba," *Cuba socialista*, no. 42 (February 1965); and *Granma Weekly Review*, March 9, 1975, p. 2. Computations from Dirección Estadística de Cuba, *Anuario estadístico de Cuba, 1972* (Havana: Junta Central de Planificación, 1974), pp. 18, 238–247, hereafter *Anuario 1972*; Dirección Central de Estadística, *Boletín estadístico de Cuba, 1971* (Havana: Junta Central de Planificación, 1973), pp. 270–273, 276–277, 280, hereafter *Boletín 1971*; and *Economía y desarrollo*, no. 25 (September-October 1974), p. 210.

13. Computed from the sources above, and from *Granma Weekly Review*, March 31, 1974, p. 7; and June 26, 1975, p. 1.

14. Samuel Bowles, "Cuban Education and the Revolutionary Ideology," *Harvard Educational Review*, vol. 41, no. 4 (November 1971), p. 497.

15. Computed from Bruce Russett et al., *World Handbook of Political and Social Indicators* (New Haven: Yale University Press, 1964), p. 108; *Granma Weekly Review*, June 4, 1967, p. 11; and United Nations, *Statistical Yearbook 1974* (New York: United Nations, 1974), p. 855, hereafter *Statistical Yearbook 1974*.

16. Computed from *Anuario 1972*, pp. 18, 22. For a discussion of statistical reporting (and an opposite argument, though without the data) see Peter Orris, "The Role of the Consumer in the Cuban National Health System" (New Haven: Yale University, unpublished M.P.H. thesis, 1970), p. 39.

17. Computed from *Boletín 1971*, pp. 295–297, and *Anuario 1972*, pp. 18, 25, supplemented where necessary by Roberto Hernández, "La atención médica en Cuba,"*Journal of Inter-American Studies and World Affairs*, vol. 11, no. 4 (October 1969), p. 553; Vicente Navarro, "Health Services in Cuba," *The New England Journal of Medicine*, vol. 287, no. 10 (November 9, 1972), pp. 957–958; *Granma Weekly Review*, October 13, 1974, p. 8; and *Granma*, June 12, 1975, p. 4.

18. *Granma Weekly Review*, May 11, 1969, p. 9.

19. Dirección Central de Estadística, *Boletín estadístico de Cuba, 1968* (Havana: Junta Central de Planificación, 1970), pp. 44–45; Dirección Central de Estadística, *Censo de población y viviendas, 6 de septiembre de 1970: datos preliminares* (Havana: Junta Central de Planificación, 1971), pp. 12–15; Oficina Nacional de los Censos Demográfico y Electoral, *Censos de población, vivienda y electoral: informe general (enero 28 de 1953)* (Havana: P. Fernández y Cia., 1955), pp. 49–50, hereafter *1953 Census*; Navarro, "Health Services," p. 956; Hernández, "La atención médica," pp. 550–551.

20. Computed from República de Cuba, *Informe general del censo de 1943* (Havana: P. Fernández y Cia., 1945), pp. 930–931, 1112–1114, 1203–1205.

21. For a statement of government policy, see José Felipe Carneado, "La

discriminación racial en Cuba no volverá jamás," *Cuba socialista*, no. 5 (January 1962).

22. See, for example, Carlos Moore, "Cuba: The Untold Story," *Présence africaine*, no. 24, English edition (1964); Carneado, "La discriminación," p. 65; Elizabeth Sutherland, *The Youngest Revolution: A Personal Report on Cuba* (New York: Dial Press, 1969), pp. 138–168; Barry Reckford, *Does Fidel Eat More than Your Father?* (London: Andre Deutsch, Ltd., 1971), pp. 127–128; John Clytus, with Jane Rieker, *Black Man in Red Cuba* (Coral Gables: University of Miami Press, 1970).

23. Computed from Lowry Nelson, *Rural Cuba* (Minneapolis: University of Minnesota Press, 1950), p. 157; and from Comisión de Orientación Revolucionaria, *Mil fotos: Cuba* (Havana: COR, 1966)

24. Domínguez, "Racial and Ethnic Relations in the Cuban Armed Forces: A Non-Topic," *Armed Forces and Society*, vol. 2, no. 2 (Winter 1976), pp. 283–287.

25. Detailed data available in Domínguez, *Cuba: Order and Revolution* (Cambridge: Belknap Press of the Harvard University Press, 1978), pp. 521–526, including about two dozen surveys before and after the revolution.

26. *1953 Census*, pp. 167–168; *Granma Weekly Review*, October 5, 1975, p. 5.

27. Computed from Ana Ramos, "La mujer y la revolución en Cuba," *Casa de las Americas*, vol. 11, nos. 65-66 (March-June 1971), p. 68; and *Granma Weekly Review*, August 31, 1969, p. 4.

28. Computed from *Anuario 1972*, p. 24.

29. *Granma Weekly Review*, May 11, 1969, p. 9.

30. Louis Jones et al., "Actitudes vocacionales de estudiantes de 1960 y 1965," *Psicología y educación,* vol. 2, no. 5 (January-March, 1965), p. 50.

31. Computed from Gustavo Toroella, *Estudio de la juventud cubana* (Havana: Comisión Nacional Cubana de la UNESCO, 1963), p. 102.

32. Mongo P., "Brochazos: La minifalda," *Bohemia*, vol. 67, no. 11 (March 14, 1975), p. 95.

33. Jorge Hernández et al., "Estudio sobre el divorcio," *Humanidades*, Serie no. 1, Ciencias Sociales, no. 3 (January 1973), p. 50.

34. Jones et al., "Actitudes," p. 47.

35. Computed from *Anuario 1972*, p. 24.

36. For example, *Aclaraciones: Periódico Hoy*, vol. 3 (Havana: Editora Política, 1966), p. 457.

37. Jorge I. Domínguez, "Cuban Catholics and Castro," *Worldview*, vol. 15, no. 2 (February 1972), p. 26.

38. Mateo Jover Marimón, "The Church," in Carmelo Mesa-Lago, ed., *Revolutionary Change in Cuba* (Pittsburgh: University of Pittsburgh Press, 1971), pp. 400–401. See also: Universidad Central "Marta Abreu" de Las Villas, *La educación rural en Las Villas* (Havana: Impresores Ucar, García, S.A., 1959), pp. 30, 32, 215; and Oscar Echevarría Salvat, *La agricultura cubana, 1934–1966* (Miami: Ediciones Universal, 1971), pp. 14–17.

39. René de la Huerta Aguiar, "Espiritismo y otras supersticiones en la población cubana," *Revista del hospital psiquiátrico de La Habana*, vol. 2, no. 1 (January-March 1960), pp. 45–47.

40. Torroella, *Estudio*, pp. 112–113, 129, 130–131; "La lucha contra el oscurantismo es una lucha ideológica," *Con la guardia en alto*, vol. 8, no. 6 (June 1969), p. 11.

41. For church statements, Alice L. Hageman and Philip E. Wheaton, *Religion in Cuba Today* (New York: Association Press, 1971), pp. 47–92, 191–269, 279–308.

42. For government statements, Fidel Castro, "A combatir al enemigo en todos los frentes," *Cuba socialista*, no. 20 (April 1963), pp. 5, 7–11; Blas Roca, "La lucha ideológica contra las sectas religiosas," *Cuba socialista*, no. 22 (June 1963).

43. Computed from Dirección Central de Estadística, *Boletín estadístico de Cuba, 1970* (Havana: Junta Central de Planificación, 1971), p. 30, hereafter *Boletín 1970*; *Anuario 1972*, pp. 18, 30; United Nations, *Monthly Bulletin of Statistics*, vol. 22 (June 1968), p. 182.

44. Food and Agriculture Organization (FAO), *Monthly Bulletin of Agricultural Economics and Statistics*, vol. 21 (January 1972), pp. 21, 23; United Nations, *Statistical Yearbook, 1974* (New York: 1975), p. 96.

45. Computed from *Boletín 1971*, pp. 78, 96–104, 123, 142–143, 166–178; *Anuario 1972*, pp. 69, 72–73, 107–109, 132, 141–144, 154.

46. See note 45, for *Anuario 1972*.

47. United Nations, *Statistical Yearbook, 1974*, p. 96.

48. *Granma Weekly Review*, November 25, 1973, p. 9, and January 13, 1974, p. 2.

49. International Labor Office, *Yearbook of Labor Statistics, 1959* (Geneva: ILO, 1959), p. 186; Kalman and Frieda Silvert, "Fate, Chance and Faith: Cuba," *American Universities Field Staff* (North American Series), vol. II, no. 2 (September 1974), p. 5.

50. *Granma Weekly Review*, November 25, 1973, p. 8; *Granma*, February 6, 1975, p. 2; and computed from Oscar Mazorra and Mario Montero,

"Estudio demográfico de 'Valle del Perú,' " *Economía y desarrollo,* no. 6 (April-June 1971), p. 136.

51. Computed from *Boletín 1970,* p. 36.

52. For example, *Granma Weekly Review,* August 5, 1973, pp. 2, 5; September 2, 1973, pp. 8–9; November 25, 1973, pp. 7, 10–11.

53. Ibid., May 11, 1969, pp. 7–8.

54. *Granma,* September 8, 1970, p. 5; and "La microemulación oriental del deber y el honor," *Bohemia,* vol. 65, no. 26 (June 29, 1973), pp. 91–92.

55. Ian McColl Kennedy, "Cuba's *Ley Contra la Vagancia*—The Law on Loafing," *UCLA Law Review,* vol. 20, no. 6 (August 1973).

56. Computed from G. Zafesov, "Cuba: Signs of Momentous Changes," *International Affairs* (Moscow), no. 9 (September 1974), p. 116; "Thirty Years of Socialist Progress," *World Marxist Review,* vol. 18, no. 1 (January 1975), p. 77; and Ted Morgan, "Cuba," *New York Times Magazine* (December 1, 1974), p. 108.

57. *Granma,* February 26, 1973, p. 4.

58. Computed from *Anuario 1972,* p. 18; Lee Lockwood, *Castro's Cuba, Cuba's Fidel* (New York: Vintage Books, 1969), p. 230; Frank Mankiewicz and Kirby Jones, *With Fidel* (Chicago: Playboy Press, 1975), p. 100.

59. For example, Jorge I. Domínguez, "Sectoral Clashes in Cuban Politics and Development," *Latin American Research Review,* vol. 6, no. 3 (Fall 1971).

60. *Granma,* February 8, 1974, p. 3; September 28, 1974, p. 7; *Granma Weekly Review,* February 28, 1971, p. 2; December 8, 1974, p. 6; *Bohemia,* vol. 67, no. 18 (May 2, 1975), p. 59.

61. Computed from *Granma,* November 19, 1970, p. 1; December 3, 1970, p. 1; *Granma Weekly Review,* August 1, 1971, p. 2, and May 7, 1972, p. 2; and Miguel Martín, "Informe al Congreso," *Cuba socialista,* no. 62 (October 1966), p. 108.

62. *Granma Weekly Review,* June 2, 1974, p. 4; June 9, 1974, p. 6; July 21, 1974, p. 1; August 4, 1974, p. 3; September 8, 1974, p. 3; Pedro Margolles, "Building Up a System of Representative Bodies," *World Marxist Review,* vol. 18, no. 2 (February 1975), p. 64; and *Constitución de los Organos de Poder Popular* (Havana: Departamento de Orientación Revolucionaria del Comité Central del Partido Communista de Cuba, 1974).

63. Computed from Dirección General de Estadística, *VIII censo general de población, 1960: resumen general* (Mexico: Dirección General de Estadística, 1962), p. 1, hereafter *1960 Census;* Dirección General de Estadística, *IX censo general de población, 1970: resumen general* (Mexico: Dirección General de Estadística, 1972), pp. 3, 271, 273, hereafter *1970 Census;* literacy is defined as the ability to read and write.

64. Computed from *1960 Census*, p. 1; and from Dirección General de Estadística, *Anuario estadístico de los Estados Unidos Mexicanos, 1941* (Mexico: Dirección General de Estadística, 1943), pp. 264, 271–272, hereafter *Anuario 1941*; Dirección General de Estadística, *Compendio estadístico de los Estados Unidos Mexicanos, 1960* (Mexico: Dirección General de Estadística, 1962), pp. 43, 47, hereafter *Compendio 1960*; Dirección General de Estadística, *Anuario estadístico de los Estados Unidos Mexicanos, 1970–1971* (Mexico: Dirección General de Estadística, 1973), pp. 228, 256, hereafter *Anuario 1970–1971*. We used 1959 enrollment data, and 1960 population data; the 1970 secondary and postprimary enrollment data (and only those) refer to enrollment at the end of the school year. The effect is to understate the real growth of Mexican postprimary education.

65. Computed from *1970 Census*, p. 299.

66. *1960 Census*, p. 1; *1970 Census*, p. 273.

67. Computed from *Anuario 1941*, pp. 264, 271–272; *Anuario 1970–1971*, pp. 229, 235, 240, 246; *1960 Census*, p. 1; *1970 Census*, p. 3. An "urban" community is defined by the Mexican government as one with a population of 2,500 persons or over.

68. Julio Durán Ochoa, "La explosión demográfica," *México: cincuenta años de revolución: la vida social* (Mexico: Fondo de Cultura Económica, 1961), pp. 8–9; hereafter *México: cincuenta*; and computed from Dirección General de Estadística, *Anuario estadístico de los Estados Unidos Mexicanos, 1962–1963* (Mexico: Dirección General de Estadística, 1965), p. 97; *Anuario 1970–1971*, p. 105; and United Nations, *Demographic Yearbook, 1974* (New York: United Nations, 1975), p. 347.

69. Moisés González Navarro, *Población y sociedad en México (1900–1970)* (Mexico: Universidad Nacional Autónoma de México, 1974), vol. I, pp. 297–299, and foldout after p. 320.

70. Ibid., p. 238.

71. Computed from *1970 Census*, p. 1081.

72. Computed from *1970 Census*, p. 135; *1960 Census*, p. 280; Dirección General de Estadística, *VII censo general de población, 1950: resumen general* (Mexico: Dirección General de Estadística, 1953), p. 87, hereafter *1950 Census*; Dirección General de Estadística, *VI censo de población, 1940: resumen general* (Mexico: Dirección General de Estadística, 1943), p. 71, hereafter *1940 Census*; and an unpublished manuscript by this author.

73. Computed from *Anuario 1941*, pp. 334–335; *Anuario 1970–1971*, p. 323; Dirección General de Estadística, *Anuario estadístico de los Estados Unidos Mexicanos 1968–1969* (Mexico: Dirección General de Estadística, 1971), p. 279; *1960 Census*, p. 1; *1970 Census*, p. 3.

74. González Navarro, *Población*, foldout after p. 320.

75. Computed from *1970 Census*, p. 259; *1960 Census*, p. 651; *1950 Census*, p. 52; *1940 Census*, p. 31; Dirección General de Estadística, *V Censo de población, 1930: resumen general* (Mexico: Dirección General de Estadística, 1934), p. 123; and Dirección de Estadística, *III censo de población, 1910* (Mexico: Dirección de Estadística, 1918), p. 451. The 1910 census assumed that children under five spoke the language of their parents.

76. *1940 Census*, p. 71.

77. *1970 Census*, p. 135.

78. On the general point, Huntington and Domínguez, "Political Development," Part VI.

79. For example, Lucio Mendieta y Núñez, *Efectos sociales de la reforma agraria en tres communidades ejidales de la República Mexicana* (Mexico: Universidad Nacional Autónoma de México, 1960), pp. 327–332.

80. Computed from *Anuario 1941*, p. 60; Ana María Flores, "La mujer en la sociedad," in *México: cincuenta*, p. 339; *1960 Census*, p. 1; *1970 Census*, p. 569.

81. Ward M. Morton, *Woman Suffrage in Mexico* (Gainesville: University of Florida Press, 1962), *passim*, especially pp. 110–111.

82. William J. Blough, "Political Attitudes of Mexican Women," *Journal of Inter-American Studies and World Affairs*, vol. 14, no. 2 (May, 1972), p. 214.

83. María del Carmen Elu de Leñero, *¿Hacia dónde va la mujer mexicana?* (Mexico: Instituto Mexicano de Estudios Sociales, 1969), pp. 46, 48, 126.

84. Ibid., pp. 82, 86, 88, 96.

85. González Navarro, *Población*, pp. 102–103.

86. Computed from *Anuario 1941*, pp. 334–335; *Anuario 1970–1971*, p. 323; *1960 Census*, p. 1; *1970 Census*, p. 3.

87. James W. Wilkie, "Statistical Indicators of the Impact of National Revolution on the Catholic Church in Mexico, 1910–1967," *Journal of Church and State*, vol. 12, no. 1 (Winter 1970), p. 97.

88. Ibid., pp. 91, 93, 95; and *1970 Census*, pp. 101, 147.

89. Elu de Leñero, *Hacia dónde*, pp. 69, 98.

90. Blough, "Political Attitudes," pp. 218, 222.

91. Clark W. Reynolds, *The Mexican Economy: Twentieth-Century Structure and Growth* (New Haven: Yale University Press, 1970), p. 22; and United Nations, *Statistical Yearbook, 1974*, p. 601.

92. Reynolds, *The Mexican Economy*, pp. 84–86.

93. Richard Weisskoff, "Income Distribution and Economic Growth in Puerto Rico, Argentina and Mexico," *Review of Income and Wealth*, Series 16,

no. 4 (December 1970), pp. 311–312; in a comparative Latin American study, Mexico had the fourth most concentrated income distribution pattern of eight Latin American countries in the mid-1960s studied by the Economic Commission for Latin America, in *Economic Survey of Latin America, 1969* (New York: United Nations, 1970), p. 365; in a different study of seven Latin American countries at about the same time, Mexico was exactly in the middle in terms of national income concentration, as shown by Adolfo Figueroa and Richard Weisskoff, "Visión de las piramides sociales: distribución del ingreso en América Latina," *Ensayos ECIEL*, no. 1 (November 1974), p. 123.

94. Economic Commission for Latin America, *Economic Survey of Latin America, 1972* (New York: United Nations, 1974), pp. 210, 232; hereafter ECLA *1972*.

95. Nacional Financiera, S.A., *Statistics on the Mexican Economy* (Mexico: Nacional Financiera, S.A., 1966), p. 49.

96. ECLA *1972*, p. 201.

97. J. W. Vaupel and J. P. Curhan, *The Making of the Multinational Enterprise* (Boston: Harvard Business School, 1969), p. 384; see also Susan Eckstein and Peter Evans, "The Revolution as Cataclysm and Coup: A Comparison of Mexico and Brazil," paper presented at the 68th Annual Meeting of the American Sociological Association (August 1973). See also: Economic Commission for Latin America, *Economic Survey of Latin America, 1970* (New York: United Nations, 1972), p. 270, hereafter ECLA *1970*; Howard F. Cline, *The United States and Mexico*, revised edition (New York: Atheneum, 1965), p. 350.

98. ECLA *1970*, p. 53, and foldout after p. 54.

99. U.S. Arms Control and Disarmament Agency, *World Military Expenditures and Arms Trade, 1963–1973* (Washington: U.S. Government Printing Office, 1975), pp. 3, 23, 26, 46.

100. Calvin P. Blair, "Nacional Financiera: Entrepreneurship in a Mixed Economy," in Raymond Vernon, ed., *Public Policy and Private Enterprise in Mexico* (Cambridge: Harvard University Press, 1964).

101. Miguel Wionczek, "Electric Power: The Uneasy Partnership," in ibid.

102. William E. Cole, *Steel and Economic Growth in Mexico* (Austin: University of Texas Press, 1967), pp. 23–40.

103. Raymond Vernon, *The Dilemma of Mexico's Development* (Cambridge: Harvard University Press, 1965), pp. 154–175; and Susan Kaufman Purcell, "Decision Making in an Authoritarian Regime: Theoretical Implications from a Mexican Case Study," *World Politics*, vol. 26, no. 1 (October 1973).

104. See Kevin J. Middlebrook, "Structure as Stability: The Political

Economy of Mexican Labor," unpublished manuscript, Department of Government, Harvard University, June 1975. Middlebrook's computations in Tables 21, 22 and 25 are based on data from Secretaría del Trabajo y Previsión Social de México, *Memoria de Labores*.

105.   Pablo González Casanova, *Democracy in Mexico* (London: Oxford University Press, 1970), pp. 198–200.

106.   Donald J. Mabry, "Mexico's Party Deputy System," *Journal of Inter-American Studies and World Affairs*, vol. 16, no. 2 (May 1974), p. 226.

107.   Computed from González Casanova, *Democracy*, p. 201; and from Mabry, "Mexico's Party Deputy System," p. 222.

108.   González Casanova, *Democracy*, pp. 21–24.

109.   James W. Wilkie, *The Mexican Revolution: Federal Expenditure and Social Change since 1910* (Berkeley: University of California Press, 1970), p. 3.

110.   Susan Kaufman Purcell and John Purcell, "Community Power and Benefits from the Nation: The Case of Mexico," paper presented at the Annual Meeting of the Latin American Studies Association, Madison, Wisconsin, 1973. However, the conclusion drawn in the text is at odds with the conclusion drawn by these authors.

111.   Computed from *Anuario 1970–1971*, pp. 331, 336, 340, 344.

112.   González Casanova, *Democracy*, p. 221.

113.   Franz von Sauer, *The Alienated "Loyal" Opposition: Mexico's Partido Acción Nacional* (Albuquerque: University of New Mexico Press, 1974), pp. 120, 133.

114.   Evelyn P. Stevens, "Legality and Extralegality in Mexico," *Journal of Inter-American Studies and World Affairs*, vol. 12, no. 1 (January 1970).

115.   For evidence of at least limited pluralism and government responsiveness even in crisis conditions, see Richard R. Fagen and Wayne A. Cornelius, Jr., *Political Power in Latin America* (Englewood Cliffs, N.J.: Prentice-Hall, 1970), pp. 299–301, 328–336.

116.   I have specifically used the following *New York Times* sources: August 1, 1968, p. 4; August 28, 1968, p. 9; September 22, 1968, p. 20; September 25, 1968, p. 1; October 10, 1968, p. 10; October 27, 1968, p. 11; October 30, 1968, p. 3; December 5, 1968, p. 52; December 25, 1968, p. 14; January 19, 1970, p. 18; July 9, 1970, p. 12; July 19, 1970, p. 18; November 29, 1970, p. 8; April 3, 1971, p. 5; June 12, 1971, p. 3; and June 20, 1971, IV, p. 3. The 1968 population has been extrapolated from *1970 Census*, p. 3, and *1960 Census*, p. 1.

117.   The best single source of data in five-year averages from 1920–1924 to 1960–1964 is Statistical Office of the United Nations, *Demographic Yearbook, 1966* (New York: United Nations, 1967), pp. 280–295, which has been

supplemented by Statistical Office of the United Nations, *Demographic Year-book, 1973* (New York: United Nations, 1974), pp. 256–262, and *Demographic Yearbook, 1974*, pp. 342–353.

118. *Demographic Yearbook, 1966*, pp. 286–287; *Demographic Yearbook, 1973*, p. 257; *Demographic Yearbook, 1974*, p. 345.

119. *Demographic Yearbook, 1966*, p. 284; *Demographic Yearbook, 1973*, p. 256.

120. Mohamed Awad, *Report on Slavery*, no. 67, XIV. 2 (New York: United Nations, 1966), pp. 25–29, 167–168, 170, 172, 175–179.

121. Ibid., pp. 24–29, 75–77, 122, 155–156, 171, 173, 184–185; *New York Times*, August 29, 1976, p. 37; on Brazilian Indians, see also "The Extermination of Indians in Brazil," *Bulletin of the International Commission of Jurists*, no. 35 (September 1968), pp. 20–21.

122. Awad, *Report*, pp. 23, 75–77, 170, 183.

123. Ibid., pp. 75–77, 170; *Boston Globe*, October 25, 1975, p. 2.

124. Awad, *Report*, pp. 25–29, 172.

125. Ibid., pp. 122, 173.

126. Ernst B. Haas, *Beyond the Nation-State: Functionalism and International Organization* (Stanford: Stanford University Press, 1964), pp. 221–225.

127. Amnesty International (hereafter AI), *Report on Torture* (London: Gerald Duckworth, 1973), p. 31, hereafter *Torture*.

128. Ibid., pp. 23–29.

129. Coded from Ibid., pp. 99–100, 114, 121–127, 134–135, 142–143, 145, 148–152, 162–168, 175, 182, 185–190, 192–201, 207–210, 214; from AI, *Report on Chile* (London: AI, 1974), pp. 57–63; and from *Amnesty International Newsletter* (hereafter *AI Newsletter*), the following issues: vol. 5, no. 4 (April 1975), special section in *Campaign for the Abolition of Torture Monthly Bulletin* (hereafter *Campaign*), p. 1; vol. 5, no. 5 (May 1975), p. 2; vol. 5, no. 6 (June 1975), *Campaign*, p. 1; vol. 5, no. 7 (July 1975), pp. 2–3; vol. 5, no. 8 (August 1975), *Campaign*, p. 2; vol. 5, no. 9 (September 1975), *Campaign*, pp. 1–2; vol. 5, no. 12 (December 1975), pp. 1–3, and *Campaign*, pp. 1–2; vol. 6, no. 1 (January 1976), *Campaign*, p. 2.

Because Cuba was a lengthy case study in an earlier section, its complex performance on this question should be highlighted. Amnesty International has summarized a judgment which I share. There was probably torture as an administrative practice in the early 1960s. In the 1970s, however, there is little or no evidence of physical torture. There is still evidence of very substantial psychological pressure on political prisoners. It also appears that the improvement of the Cuban economic growth performance in the 1970s has also helped to improve material conditions in the prisons. The government, beginning in the mid-1960s, has court-martialed some torturers and convicted them. *Torture*, p. 191; Jorge I. Domínguez, "The Civic Soldier in Cuba," in Catherine Kelleher (ed.), *Political-Military Systems: Comparative Perspectives* (Beverly Hills, Calif.: Sage Publications, 1974), p. 219.

130. *AI Newsletter*, vol. 5, no. 8 (August 1975), *Campaign*, p. 2; vol. 5, no. 9 (September 1975), *Campaign*, pp. 1–2.

131. *Torture*, p. 200.

132. Ibid., p. 113.

133. Ibid., pp. 138–139.

134. Ibid., pp. 172–175; *AI Newsletter*, vol. 6, no. 1 (January 1976), *Campaign*, p. 2.

135. *Torture*, see the case studies on Greece and the United Kingdom, at some length, plus pp. 162–168.

136. All population data taken from Statistical Office of the United Nations, *Demographic Yearbook, 1970* (New York: UN, 1971), pp. 126–135; from *Demographic Yearbook, 1973*, pp. 101–107; and from *Demographic Yearbook, 1974*, pp. 127–133. In each case the most up-to-date data were used. Population data for 1975–1976 were extrapolated from the previous population growth patterns. Population levels for Indonesia in the mid-1960s were recalculated to take into account the 1971 census; the effect of this procedure was to lower population estimates for the mid-1960s and to raise the estimate of the political imprisonment rate. The 1961 Cuban population is from *Anuario 1972*, p. 18. For Albania, AI, *Torture*, p. 172; for Bulgaria, *AI Newsletter*, vol. 6, no. 1, p. 2; AI, *Prison Conditions in East Germany: Conditions for Political Prisoners* (London: AI, 1966), pp. 12–14; *AI Newsletter*, vol. 3, no. 4 (April 1973), pp. 2–3; "Recent Legal Developments in Hungary," *Bulletin of the International Commission of Jurists*, no. 11 (December 1960), pp. 47–50, hereafter *Bulletin ICJ*; *Prison Conditions in Rumania: Conditions for Political Prisoners 1955–1964* (London: AI, 1965), pp. 1–4, 26; "Amnesties in Eastern Europe: Rumania, Poland, Bulgaria, East Germany," *Bulletin ICJ*, no. 21 (December, 1964), pp. 15–25; for the USSR, *AI Newsletter*, vol. 5, no. 12 (December 1975), pp. 1–2; for Bangladesh, *AI Newsletter*, vol. 3, no. 1 (January 1973), p. 2, and vol. 4, no. 4 (April 1974), pp. 2–3; for India, *AI Newsletter*, vol. 5, no. 9 (September 1975), p. 2; for Indonesia, *AI Newsletter*, vol. 1, no. 4 (April 1971), p. 2; vol. 1, no. 10 (October 1971), p. 2; vol. 2, no. 1 (January 1972), p. 3; vol. 3, no. 1 (January 1973), p. 3; and *New York Times*, November 30, 1975, p. 3; for Nepal, *AI Newsletter*, vol. 6, no. 2 (February 1976), p. 1; for Singapore, *AI Newsletter*, vol. 6, no. 2 (February 1976), p. 4; for Sri Lanka, *Torture*, pp. 151–152; for Chad, *AI Newsletter*, vol. 5, no. 6 (June 1975), p. 2; and vol. 6, no. 2 (February 1976), p. 2; "Recent Developments in Ghana," *Bulletin ICJ*, no. 24 (December 1965), pp. 21–25; *AI Newsletter*, vol. 2, no. 12 (December 1972), p. 2; for Ivory

Coast, *AI Newsletter*, vol. 4, no. 7 (July 1974), p. 4; and vol. 5, no. 4 (April 1975); "Malawi Since Independence," *Bulletin ICJ*, no. 27 (September 1966), pp. 20–25; *AI Newsletter*, vol. 4, no. 6 (June 1974), p. 3; for Nigeria, *AI Newsletter*, vol. 5, no. 9 (September 1975), p. 2; AI, *Prison Conditions in Rhodesia* (London: AI, 1966), p. viii, for African population in 1963, and p. 4 for estimates of political prisoners; "Zanzibar since the Revolution," *Bulletin ICJ*, no. 30 (June 1967), pp. 38–41; AI Newsletter, vol. 4, no. 4 (April 1974), p. 3; for Argentina, *AI Newsletter*, vol. 3, no. 6 (June 1973), p. 2; for Bolivia, "The Rule of Law in South America," *The Review: International Commission of Jurists*, no. 11 (December 1973), p. 15, hereafter *Review ICJ*; for Brazil, Brady Tyson, "Brazil: Nine Years of Military Tutelage," *Worldview*, vol. 16, no. 7 (July 1973), p. 30 (Tyson is a critic of the Brazilian government); *AI Newsletter*, vol. 5, no. 12 (December 1975), *Campaign*, p. 1; AI, *Chile*, pp. 6, 15–17; "The Legal System in Chile," *Review ICJ*, no. 13 (December 1974), pp. 46–47, 54; *Boston Globe*, October 25, 1975, p. 2, and December 14, 1975, p. 57; for Cuba and Mexico, see earlier sections; for Cuba, see also Hugh Thomas, *Cuba: The Pursuit of Freedom* (New York: Harper and Row, 1971), p. 1365; for Paraguay, AI, *Prison Conditions in Paraguay: Conditions for Political Prisoners* (London: AI, 1966), pp. 27–29, 33–34; "Paraguay," *Review ICJ*, no. 7 (December 1971), p. 13; *AI Newsletter*, vol. 5, no. 3 (March 1975), p. 2; vol. 6, no. 3 (March 1976), *Campaign*, p. 2; for Uruguay, *AI Newsletter*, vol. 6, no. 3 (March 1976), *Campaign*, p. 1. For 1976–1977 data, *New York Times*, January 2, 1977, pp. 1, 14, 18; and March 13, 1977, IV, p. 4.

Monitoring Human Rights Violations in the 1980s

Nigel S. Rodley

Introduction

This paper attempts to deal with the problem of monitoring information concerning compliance with or violations of human rights. By "monitoring" I mean nothing more complicated than the assembling, presentation, and dissemination of pertinent data in a form that enables human rights performance to be assessed according to agreed-upon international standards. Compliance with such standards could be measured according to the indicators examined by Jorge Domínguez in his preceding essay or by some other method of assessing state behavior toward its citizenry.

The national census is probably the classic monitoring technique. Its principal objective is to develop as accurately as possible information relating to population trends. From such information demographers and others can assess, for example, future demands on resources, while politicians can perhaps plan commensurate reallocation of resources. It hardly needs stating that in the field of human rights, particularly civil and political rights, the relevant information is incomparably more difficult to come by than that concerning the number of individuals residing in a particular area. (Indeed, it may be recalled that even national censuses can give rise to controversy as to what information they should contain. Should they, for example, include individuals' racial or religious backgrounds?) The difficulties of collecting information in human rights investigations will be considered below.

The question already arises: Why monitor? My own answer certainly is: To help diminish the incidence of human rights violations. It is based on the unverifiable assumption that the public display of state misbehavior can inhibit such misbehavior. An indication of the reasonableness of this assumption may be found in the resistance of governments to subjecting their human rights performance to the official scrutiny of international governmental bodies.

Another basic question arises: Who will monitor? It is clear that the brunt of the burden today is being assumed by a number of nongovernmental organizations (NGOs). The NGOs will almost certainly continue their key role into the 1980s, since the record to date of the international governmental community indicates that it will not be able to assume such a role by itself.

INTERGOVERNMENTAL ORGANIZATIONS AND CONCERN FOR HUMAN RIGHTS

International concern over violations of human rights within the frontiers of sovereign states is not new, though it has gained in intensity in the aftermath of World War II. Even in the nineteenth century, the high point of the doctrine of sovereignty in its most positivistic form, there were instances of military intervention justified, if not satisfactorily explained, on the basis of humanitarian concern for the fate of certain minorities who were at the mercy of the sovereign government.[1] The major development in the protection of individual rights during the nineteenth century was the international outlawry of chattel slavery; the Anti-Slavery Society, founded in 1823 in England, played a historic role as one of the first nongovernmental organizations concerned with human rights.

In the twentieth century, the League of Nations made some provision in its Covenant for the protection of minorities. In addition, the mandates system of the Covenant imposed on the mandatory power a standard of respect for the human rights of the peoples under its tutelage. It is to be noted that this concern with group or national rights on the part of an international organization was a natural development, precisely because World War I had shown so devastatingly how international conflicts could arise from competing claims to sovereignty over, access to, or exploitation of territories and resources belonging to minorities or even to indigenous majorities. Formal and systematic concern with defining and protecting the human rights of the individual, however, had to await the end of World War II.

With the creation of the Charter of the United Nations, for which the moral context was reaction to the monstrosity of nazism, the international community undertook a far broader obligation to promote respect for and observance of individual human rights and fundamental freedoms, and each state pledged itself to work separately and in cooperation with the UN to implement that obligation. For about the first 20 years of the UN's existence its membership considered that it was discharging its duties by formulating an international bill of rights (the Universal Declaration of Human Rights was proclaimed by the General Assembly on December 10, 1948; the International Covenant on Economic, Social and Cultural Rights, the International Covenant on Civil and Political Rights, and the Optional Protocol to the latter Covenant were all adopted by the assembly on December 16, 1966) and other international norm-creating instruments. The function of implementation would be according to the machinery created by these treaties.

Investigation and publication of alleged violations of human rights were, in the absence of a separate treaty obligation, deemed to be beyond the purview of the world body, since they could be interpreted according to Article 2(7) of the UN Charter as constituting intervention in matters falling essentially within the domestic jurisdiction of member states. This cautious approach was affirmed as early as 1947, when the UN Economic and Social Council (ECOSOC) approved the stand of its Commission on Human Rights that the commission had no power to take action on allegations concerning individual human rights. This position was reaffirmed in resolution 728 F(XXVIII) of July 30, 1959, although the same resolution set up a procedure whereby communications alleging specific human rights violations could be transmitted to the government concerned, with a confidential summary being made available to all commission members. Any replies from governments complained against might also be circulated to the members of the commission. This confidential process is still operative, and while the public hears nothing about it—indeed, in principle even the author of the complaint receives only an acknowledgment enclosing the texts of the relevant resolutions (728 F [1959], 1235[1967], 1503 [1970], and an implementing subcommission resolution)—it may safely be assumed that countries will frequently wish to reply to charges of injustices and may even rectify situations so that their answer puts them in a more favorable light.

It should be noted that many UN bodies, including the Commission on Human Rights, have investigated situations that were not covered by particular documents but that were deemed so serious as to justify being treated as exceptions to the domestic jurisdiction rule: violations in South Africa, Namibia, and Rhodesia; in Angola and Mozambique when they were Portuguese colonies; and the situation in the Israeli-occupied territories of the Middle East. (Apartheid and colonialism have for a long time been considered as matters of international concern raising questions of international peace and security. Foreign occupation is, by definition, no internal affair.) Eventually, by resolution 1235(XLII) of June 6, 1967, and resolution 1503(XLVIII) of May 27, 1970, ECOSOC authorized the commission to investigate situations that appear to reveal a consistent pattern of gross and reliably attested violations of human rights and fundamental freedoms. Such possible situations are to be determined by the Subcommission on Prevention of Discrimination and Protection of Minorities on the basis of confidentially examined information from various sources, including communications from individuals and nongovernmental organizations.

In 1975 the commission, at the previous suggestion of the subcommission, endorsed by the General Assembly, set up an ad hoc working group to inquire into the human rights situation in Chile. The ad hoc group—like the bodies carrying out inquiries in southern Africa and the Middle East—was not established pursuant to the procedure stipulated by ECOSOC resolution 1503(XLVIII). Nevertheless the Chile investigation was welcome both as a significant precedent and as a valuable contribution to the protection of human rights in that country. The willingness of states normally hostile to the idea of UN human rights investigations—except in southern Africa and the Middle East, where the element of international concern prevailed over the claim of domestic jurisdiction—to go along, albeit reluctantly, with an inquiry in Chile deserves more detailed analysis elsewhere. Suffice it to say here that the inquiry was made possible by a rare conjunction of widely shared feelings of repugnance for the junta that had replaced the constitutional government of President Salvador Allende Gossens in one of the last, oldest, and most stable Latin American democracies.

Such sporadic action is a far cry from sustained and thorough investigations of human rights violations throughout the world. In fact, the procedure laid down by resolution 1503(XLVIII) has not even yielded, at the time of writing, one thorough study or investigation. Furthermore, the campaign to establish a UN High Commissioner for Human Rights, which started early in the life of the UN, has been fruitlessly debated by the General Assembly for the past 15 years. Indeed it is currently on the agenda of the Thirty-third General Assembly.

It is generally felt among those seeking to promote further UN protection of individuals denied their rights that the best to be hoped for is the security from erosion of such gains as have already been achieved. It would, therefore, be rash to envisage the UN engaging in a systematic and impartial program of monitoring even the most serious incidents of human rights violations in the world, at least within the next generation.

The treaty-based mechanisms hold out little better prospect. The two international covenants referred to above only provide for the submission by states parties of reports on their compliance with the provisions of the treaties. While questions based on the reports may be addressed by the appropriate bodies to the submitting states, there is no provision for investigation of allegations of violations made by victims or others. At the time of writing, only 48 states have ratified the International Covenant on Economic, Social, and Cultural Rights, while only 46 have ratified that on Civil and Political Rights. It is true that states parties to the Optional Protocol to the latter Covenant (a mere 16, at present) grant the right of individual petition to the Human Rights Committee set up under the parent covenant. But it would be unwise to expect wide ratification of the Protocol in the near future and, in any event, the jurisdiction of the committee is limited to the study of individual complaints submitted by or on behalf of individual victims. There is no provision for the investigation of situations where there may be a pattern of violations. Arguably, the procedure relating to interstate complaints under Article 41 of the Convenant could help fill this gap, but so far only 6 states have made the necessary declarations under this article (10 such declarations are required even to render the procedure operative) and prospects for wide adherence are dismal. Nor does the history of the European Convention on Human Rights suggest that governments will freely make allegations of violations committed by other governments.

It is also highly unlikely that a worldwide monitoring network linking regional intergovernmental institutions will be established during this period. Neither the existing European or inter-American machinery—the Council of Europe's Human Rights Commission and Human Rights Court and the Inter-American Commission on Human Rights of the Organization of American States—is set up primarily for monitoring, and these bodies are not likely to change their basic orientation. In any event, even if the UN were to change its spots overnight, or if a new intergovernmental network were to be created, there is no reason to assume that the information available to NGOs would be less useful to these organizations than it has been to the UN in the past. NGOs provided enormous amounts of material, for example, to the groups investigating Chile and the southern African countries.

Thus a premise of this paper is that the principal role of monitoring human rights violations will remain with nongovernmental organizations. The most important of the NGOs, their methods of operation, and suggestions for strengthening their work will be discussed later. Finally, the paper will present a blueprint for a worldwide NGO—admittedly utopian in its ideal form but not inconceivable as a working approximation—that could extend the range and effectiveness of the currently existing groups.

PROBLEMS OF MONITORING

No matter who takes on the responsibility, monitoring human rights observance raises a number of problems. First, there is the question of the political, economic, and social context in which the monitoring takes place. Second, the subject matter of what is to be monitored must be considered. This involves a process of selection closely linked with the extent to which standards of human rights correspond to shared international values. Third, there are what might be called technical problems. They include such questions as who is the intended audience of the monitoring function, what techniques are suitable for reaching this audience, how should raw data be evaluated, and the central question of how access to data is secured in the first place.

The International Setting: The World of the 1980s

I am not a futurologist and there would be little value in making specific predictions regarding the state of the world in the 1980s. Ideally, it would be composed of libertarian democracies, be they socialist or capitalist, each of which would have strong civil liberties unions if they were needed, all of which could sustain and be nourished by an international civil liberties union. More likely, but still unlikely, the whole world could be engulfed by totalitarian regimes of the left or right, leaving no room for any international monitoring body. Presumably the world will, in fact, achieve neither of these extremes and the reality will differ only in degree, rather than in essence, from the present. Nevertheless, these differences will affect the climate for monitoring human rights conditions.

Work for human rights is most effectively conducted in a setting of peace. The first question that must be asked is what the prospects for peace are in the 1980s, and it is difficult to be sanguine about them. The bipolar structure of the world of the 1950s has already moved toward a certain multipolarity, and until recently it could have been safely argued that such multipolarity preserved intact the basic equilibrium that the previous bipolar world had established. However, this may no longer be the case.

Whatever one's reaction to the retreat of the West in Southeast Asia, southern Africa, and possibly elsewhere, it would certainly be possible for both a traditional, hardnosed Western strategist and a scientific Marxist in the Kremlin to see the beginnings of the collapse of Western power and preeminence in much of the world. If subsequent world developments were to confirm such a view to any measurable extent, it would be difficult to predict the reactions of either side. Western feelings of being seriously threatened, for example, or Soviet perceptions of such feelings could lead to the kind of tension that is not easily restrained from terminating in war. Likewise, if the Sino-Soviet dispute—which has traditionally been underestimated by Western commentators, if not Western governments—were to escalate into armed warfare, peace throughout the rest of the world might be in jeopardy. In a global war, concern for human rights would not be relevant; indeed, any such war could well put an end to social systems as we know them and the pertinence of human rights to their structures. However, like the two paradigms of worldwide libertarianism and worldwide totalitarianism mentioned above, the prospect of a global holocaust must be discarded in making any serious assessment of the possibilities of monitoring human rights observance.

A more likely prospect is that there will be a continuance of local conflicts, albeit with the involvement in various degrees of outside powers. This will necessarily affect human rights in the warring countries and in neighboring countries, and sometimes even farther afield. What should be the standard for human rights observance in a situation of armed conflict? All international treaties concerned with the protection of human rights—other than the rights during armed conflict that are codified in the Geneva Conventions—make provision for derogation from their right-granting provisions in situations of public emergency threatening the life of a nation. It may not be possible for any monitoring agency simply to consider itself bound by such exemption clauses. An agency may well seek to examine the legitimacy of a government's unilateral declaration of public emergency, as well as the extent to which derogating measures are strictly required by the exigencies of the situation even if the seriousness of the

126

emergency is verified. It may not be realistic to expect countries in conflict to be directly influenced by such investigations. Of greater importance is the attitude of the outside parties supporting the conflicting groups. Are these parties willing to pressure the belligerents to act more humanely? Unfortunately, for reasons of strategy that override considerations of human values, outside parties may side during conflicts with factions whose commitment to human rights—even in peacetime—is negligible if not nonexistent. In such cases, the reports of monitors will have an insignificant audience of relevance.

More positively, it is possible to envisage a significant reorientation of human rights concerns as the fortunes of various power groupings fluctuate. Today, for example, the gross and blatant violation of the human rights and dignity of majority black populations in southern Africa is the single most important human rights issue below the Sahara. The concept of human rights means virtually one thing to most people in that area: freedom, dignity, and self-determination. It is certainly not difficult to imagine that by the mid-1980s at the latest this situation will have changed radically, perhaps even in South Africa. It may well be that when this happens many black African countries—whose colonial history leads them to link the suffering of their brothers and the hypocrisy of the West, whose rhetoric promotes and purports to protect human rights even as its actions contribute to their wholesale violation in South Africa—will consider the importance of human rights in a more expansive and generous manner than they are now able to do. The less human rights can be perceived as an inseparable part of specific nationalist objectives, the greater will be the chances for more widely shared understanding of their universal importance. The barbarity of the Amin regime in Uganda has already been well documented and is not seriously challenged, even by African governments. In fact, these governments have combined to block any public international action by the UN or the Organization for African Unity (OAU) on the problem. It is to be hoped that monitoring in the 1980s will no longer have to face this "Hear no evil, see no evil, speak no evil" attitude, at present so strongly reinforced by the southern African situation.

127

Another aspect of respect for human rights is its relation, in a particular country, to economic and social well-being within that country. Very little work has been done to devise techniques of understanding this relationship, and cause and effect are not readily identifiable. Within the developing world, for example, the relative wealth of Iran does not seem to be able to provide the basis of a government that can rule without terror, but the poverty of Tanzania permits a relatively humane government to endure, even though its standard of respect for human rights may not be as high—at least as far as civil and political rights are concerned—as in some other countries. Costa Rica, not a wealthy country, is an island of relative liberty in a Central American sea of repression. Nevertheless, it does not seem unreasonable to assume that unless developing countries actually begin to improve their economic and social conditons, the turbulence they are prone to and the repression such turbulence often provokes is likely to continue and to preclude the kind of long-term social stability that regard for human rights requires. The legal protection of human rights is only as strong as the institutions charged with the task, and social stress, turmoil, or leaders' fear of losing power will cause them to be either abrogated or simply disregarded. If you cannot execute your enemy by application of the law, you may be tempted to do so by the creation of death squads.

I do not have the wisdom to predict how socioeconomic conditions will evolve in the developing countries. My personal suspicion is that little effective change will take place without left-wing revolutions; that such revolutions will be waged by forces that have little time for the concept of human rights, with the support of powers that demonstrate little respect for human rights in their own spheres; that the forces of economic and social repression they seek to overthrow will be supported by those who claim to be concerned with human rights and indeed who largely protect them for their own populations; and that successful revolutionary movements, for a long time to come, will not be required by their populations to demonstrate compliance with standards and norms inspired by the societies that contributed to their own previous repression. If this is so, the outlook for human rights is gloomy, and the outlook for any possible monitoring agency is commensurately gloomy.

Value Choices

Although the challenge of devising an index for quantifying a state's observance of human rights is taken up by Jorge Domínguez in this volume, this paper cannot ignore the implications of the scope of human endeavor subsumed by the concept of human rights. Even a cursory reading of the Universal Declaration of Human Rights—ranging, as it does, from enunciating the rights of freedom of speech and assembly, including the right to join trade unions, to acknowledging a right to a family life, food, clothing, housing, and education—demonstrates that the final realization of all the rights in question will herald the first day of utopia. It goes without saying that no single monitoring agency could hope to deal with the matters covered by the declaration. But it is at the point of selection that controversy has to arise. The international consensus reflected by the declaration is obtained, if at all, for the document as a whole. The separate parts do not command the same uniform allegiance. Indeed, much of the lip service paid to the high principles of the declaration may be explicable by the fact that by addressing itself to a universe of problems, the declaration may be interpreted to apply to none. Selection is necessary if realistic monitoring is to be done by one institution or even a group of institutions.

Such selection must take into account certain areas of value conflict if it is to be successful. The most obvious of these is the philosophical dialectic of the rights of the individual as a unit versus the rights of the person in society. The Western premise, generally considered to find its clearest articulation in Lockean philosophy, is that the person comes first and society second; the role of the latter is to be a mere accessory to the primacy of the liberty of the person. The premise of Marxist or would-be Marxist societies is that society comes first; it is only through the processes of society that the person acquires individuality; and thus only the welfare of society can ensure the welfare of the individual. In many ways, the dichotomy thus posed is artificial. The main function of the concept of human rights is to arbitrate not so much between the individual and society as between the individual and his or her government. Of course, it is usual for governments to identify their interests with those of society, but the history of human evolution is one of dissenting individuals capturing the aspirations of society in opposition to those of the persons in governmental control of the society. Nevertheless, for a human rights monitoring system to command respect, it will have to interpret human rights principles, whose broad formulation leads to controversy as to their application, in a way that is sensitive to the demands by societies, particularly weak ones, that individuals, particularly powerful ones, not be allowed to stifle their attempts to improve the lot of the majority.

Another area of value conflict, often reflecting the philosophical one but different from it, is the political one that gives primacy either to civil and political rights or to economic, social, and cultural rights. To state the problem simply: It is all very well to talk about freedom of speech and assembly and the right of participation in the political process, but of what use are these to an undernourished man, with no roof over his head, who fears that his children have only a 50 percent chance of surviving to the age of five? This is indeed a disarming question to a secure, middle-class Westerner, often all too aware of the injustice and even fragility of his own privileged condition. But if once again we remember that when talking of human rights we are talking of the relationship between individual and actual government, we may well ask: How can the lot of this starving, homeless man, half of whose children die, ever be improved unless he is able to give voice to his plight, organize to ensure his rights, and change the policy that permits his actual condition to continue? In this formulation the exercise of civil and political rights becomes the engine of achieving economic, social, and cultural rights. I have yet to see, in any case, a clear, convincing presentation of why, in a given situation, particular measures to improve the enjoyment of economic, social, and cultural rights necessarily entail infringements of specific civil and political rights.

It would probably be impossible to pin down the exact relationship between these two sets of rights. Political and civil rights could, at least in theory, be realized immediately by fiat, whereas it takes a long time for socioeconomic conditions to change—as recognized by the International Covenant on Economic, Social, and Cultural Rights. Implementation of the latter rights would have to be examined over a broad time period. Such an examination would also have to eschew the adoption of explicit or implicit assumptions that certain forms of social organization are more or less likely to promote the material welfare of the people. Ultimately human rights transcend specific social and political ideologies, the practitioners of which have, in any event, to be kept honest.

There remains an irreducible minimum of consensus from which an international standard of human rights behavior might be devised and developed. This is to be found, in the first place, in those rights from which no derogation is permitted, even in time of public emergency threatening the life of the nation, according to article 4 of the International Covenant on Civil and Political Rights. Thus, no amount of civil strife justifies a government in derogating from any of the rights in the covenant in any way involving discrimination solely on the ground of race, color, sex, language, religion, or social origin. Similarly, the inherent right to life, including the right not to be arbitrarily deprived of life, is nonderogable. So is the right not to be subjected to torture or to cruel, inhuman, or degrading treatment or punishment. The prohibition against being held in slavery or servitude also remains absolute. Imprisonment on the ground of inability to fulfill a contractual obligation is completely prohibited. Nonretroactivity of criminal offenses and penalties, perhaps the most fundamental principle of legality, is upheld in all circumstances, as is freedom of thought, conscience, and religion.

Of these rights, only that relating to nonimprisonment for nonfulfillment of a contractual obligation, which has become something of an anachronism, is not of fundamental importance in safeguarding the dignity and integrity of the human person. And it is this concept of the dignity and integrity of the human person that ultimately may be said ethically to reconcile the philosophical divergences discussed above. It may well be that there will be different views across cultures and political systems of the specific content of the rights enumerated above, but there will remain a universally accepted minimum. Ultimately it has to be recognized that often a government shrouds its violations of human rights in a tissue of philosophical pretexts that are to be taken only as seriously as is necessary to expose them.

Both the declaration and the Covenant on Civil and Political Rights deal separately with freedom of thought, conscience, and religion on the one hand and freedom of opinion and expression on the other. There is no clear philosophical distinction between the two. Freedom of thought and conscience, if not coextensive with freedom of opinion, shares a large mutual field of application with it. Nor is it the experience of the author that governments admit to imprisoning people just because of their views. Thus, while there will be inevitable disputes as to whether a particular factual situation constitutes a violation of freedom of thought/ conscience or freedom of opinion/expression, there will tend to be agreement that there is indeed a violation. Similar reasoning might apply to the right to freedom of association.

It is more difficult to establish a basis for including the right to freedom of movement, other than to observe the nature of most of the regimes that seek to limit or deny it. A society that properly guarantees the other rights already discussed does not seem to have to resort to the more draconian limitations on the right to stay, leave, or return. A comparable observation could be made concerning the procedural right to a fair trial. It, too, is a barometer of a society's respect for basic rights. Where the basic rights are respected, the rights above are more likely to exist.

In the field of economic and social rights, good indicators of a government's performance would be the intensity of its efforts to combat infant mortality, hunger, illiteracy, and homelessness. A monitoring agency that scrutinized these indicators as well as compliance with the other rights suggested in this section would be able to claim respect for the information it was compiling and presenting.

At this point it should be noted that intergovernmental bodies, particularly the international financial institutions, are keeping a pretty close watch on economic and social conditions throughout the world. With the possible exception of hunger—the struggle of nongovernmental aid-furnishing bodies to draw attention to the recent drought in the Sahel and the famine it was producing may be recalled—nongovernmental organizations would be able to add little information that has not already been systematically compiled and authoritatively presented at the international level. It follows that the technical problems of monitoring discussed below would not apply. Ultimately, therefore, if a new nongovernmental human rights monitoring institution were to be established, it would draw on socioeconomic information gathered elsewhere in making a broad assessment of governments' human rights performance. Perhaps a set of indicators such as those explored by Professor Domínguez could secure sufficient international acceptance to serve as a program for the monitoring body.

Technical Aspects

It is assumed that the object of international concern for human rights is to inhibit or terminate their violation by governments. Thus the function of monitoring/recording will be to put the information gleaned to the use best suited to the attainment of that objective. This instantly raises the question of the intended audience, the consumer of the product of the monitoring enterprise. Such an audience could include worldwide power elites, particularly of countries with which the described country has significant historical, cultural, political, strategic, or economic relations; worldwide intellectual elites; a mass international audience; or even a popular nongovernmental audience in the country described.

Of these audiences, the first three are easiest to reach. Governments, like individuals, have a passion to know what is said about them; and whatever their public posture—disdain, concern, or otherwise—they invest a lot of resources in establishing

133

the machinery and personnel (sometimes called diplomats) to find out. The intelligentsias of most countries, interrelated as they now usually are with government elites, are with some degree of variation also reachable. A mass international audience can be reached in some parts of the world on some occasions. Much will depend on the country criticized and its relations with other countries. Much will also depend on the tastes and prejudices of the audience in these other countries. Probably no country's internal situation can generate as much interest in the West, for example, as the Soviet Union's. This is not wholly attributable to that country's superpower status. It is also due to its claim to ideological leadership of a particular form of social organization and its implicit offering of itself as a model for emulation by others. By far the hardest audience to reach, except in a few countries, is that of the indigenous masses, though the number of such countries increases if we include those whose populations receive a certain amount of information, conveyed through the filter of governmental rejection, denial, denunciation, and other distortions. (The ability of the governed to read between the lines—and even of a controlled press to write in easily decipherable invisible ink—should not be underrated.)

All this presupposes the use of publicity as the medium of communicating the monitored information. Yet the value of such activity ought not to be assumed. Even if the information gets through in some form, there are significant professional, intellectual, and mass constituencies in many countries that will unite against perceived attacks on their group or national pride and self-respect. In addition, there is the common governmental phenomenon of retrenching in the face of public onslaught, whereas private persuasion may evoke a moderate response. Also, the likelihood of the "hard" reaction is increased if the information is perceived as being calculated to threaten the structure of a government's foreign relations. It is easier to denounce the use of human rights information if it can be characterized as politically motivated.

The above problems are compounded by the difficulties involved in selecting monitoring techniques. (I am not referring here to the difficulty of establishing sources and compiling information; that will be discussed later in this section.) The possibilities are legion. The following, none of which are mutually exclusive, are among the more obvious: the establishment of a public documentation center; the preparation of reports, regular or otherwise, on specific countries or worldwide situations; publishing any or all of the above or submitting them confidentially to the governments concerned with or without a view to future publication; publishing of press releases; submission to intergovernmental bodies; holding of hearings (tribunals, etc.); concentration on patterns of repression of individual cases, etc.

Before information is released, it has to be evaluated. How does the monitoring body undertake the difficult task of measuring compliance with its norms as opposed to noncompliance? A lot depends on what questions are asked. The UN Commission on Human Rights, for example, has been criticized for mandating an investigation into the human rights situation in territories occupied by Israel after the 1967 war in ways that precluded the body from examining anything other than fault.[2] The investigation was thus unable to acknowledge that Israel's occupation, albeit perhaps the longest noncolonial military occupation in history, has been relatively humane. Nevertheless, even favorable comparisons are odious—particularly in the field of human rights. It is patently silly to compare the situations in the United Kingdom and Uruguay; yet if one lowers one's sights and aims merely at reflecting progress or regression within a single country, the standard of judgment and the intensity of the description may well be distorted. In any one year, there may be a "plus" for Uruguay, if fewer people die under torture there than in the preceding year, and a "minus" for the United Kingdom because someone is put in jail for trying to persuade a soldier that he should not participate in what the prisoner considers an unjust war in Northern Ireland. It must also be borne in mind that however sophisticated the fact-finding network of the monitoring body, there will continue to be regimes where unpleasant facts are freely available and others where such facts, particularly the most repugnant, are either well hidden or at least not susceptible to convincing documentation. Comparisons thus become even more distortional.

135

This brings us to one of the most intractable problems of monitoring: securing access to the information required to assess compliance with the human rights in question. The best kind of information is, evidently, firsthand. The monitor can receive information direct from the victim of an alleged violation of human rights, with supporting documentation, and can test this information against that provided by the government alleged to be responsible for the violation, again with supporting documentation. Relevant public records, including the press, can be examined. A significant proportion of the world's population lives in societies where this paradigm functions. Even this optimal fact-finding is not free of difficulties. For example, much of what goes on in British prisons is subject to the rigors of the Official Secrets Act. Cases purportedly dealing with espionage are, in some countries, conducted behind closed doors. Vaguely worded laws can be applied to penalize what should be permissible behavior. Most troublesome of all from a monitoring point of view, the forces of law may, while respecting the external forms of law, act in concert deliberately to convict innocent persons of criminal offenses.

But these problems are relatively insignificant compared to those in societies commonly known as "closed." For the purposes of this discussion, a closed society is the opposite of the optimal model just described. There is no effective communication between the potential victim—or, for that matter, any other member of the citizenry—and the world beyond the frontiers of the society. Government information is strictly limited to that required to convey the desired external image. Any questions concerning social matters are ignored, rejected, or answered in an uncorroborable way. The press, needless to say, is confined to reporting the facts, lies, and opinions it pleases the authorities to see published. Frequently such countries generate a refugee population, even when they seek to close their frontiers and prevent emigration. These refugees may be a limited source of information, if they are not too terrorized by the perceived or actual threat to their kin remaining behind, by the activities of secret security agencies operating abroad, or by a combination of both. In any event, the nature of such information

136

will probably not be detailed and comprehensive enough to sustain an accurate depiction of specific human rights violations. Even when such information is available to a refugee population, it is not difficult for a government to discredit it on the basis of the presumed antiregime motivation of the source. There is no formula for dealing with this problem; one can only call attention to it where it exists and allow others to draw conclusions.

Fortunately, few societies manage to tie such an effective *cordon sanitaire* around themselves, at least for more than a limited period of time. Most societies fall at various points along a scale whose limits are the optimal and closed models. Thus it is not unknown for a government that resorts to the use of paramilitary and parapolice torture and death squads to permit the press to report on the discovery of bodies of missing persons, and their condition on discovery. Perhaps such news is presumed to have a deterrent function. In addition, there are few societies, however brutal their governments, that do not admit foreign journalists, business people, students, tourists, and other outsiders. Indeed, probably most societies permit those of their own citizens who can afford it to travel abroad. Many even encourage such travel; for example, they may send their students for training overseas. Diplomats and other itinerant official personnel, either representing or residing in the country in question, are clearly in a position to acquire information that may be made available to a monitoring agency or group, albeit on a confidential basis.

Many societies, not just the least repressive, in fact permit, or do not stand in the way of, foreign individuals or groups visiting their countries with a view to investigating the human rights situation. There is no doubt that such visits are important in establishing the credibility of information that is subsequently published. As to the detail and accuracy of the information gathered, much will depend on the level of fear existing in the society. The more nearly the society approaches the closed model, the less information will be available to a visiting person or team. Except when such visits succeed in eliciting information from the authorities (it should not be forgotten that governments may sometimes have an interest in settling for publication of the truth, however bad, rather than living with the dissemination of even worse exaggerations of the real situation), their function may amount to little more than the provision of window dressing for information possessed before the visit was undertaken.

A type of source that could be tapped by a body seeking to monitor human rights situations might be termed the external official source. Information developed by diplomatic personnel in a systematic way could, if made publicly available, provide reliable evidence of practices in various countries. Recent developments in the United States and United Kingdom suggest that this possibility is no longer in the realm of fantasy. Similarly, in those cases where intergovernmental organizations undertake investigative activities on human rights questions and make their findings public, this would be a useful store of information.

THE MONITORS TODAY: AN EMBRYO NETWORK

Apart from the limited work of intergovernmental organizations, which has already been alluded to, the rest of the task of monitoring human rights violations is carried out by NGOs. The range of objects and variety of structures subsumed under the notion of the NGO defies description. Every NGO, be it an association of innkeepers or a society of metallurgists, may well be involved in some way in the protection of human rights, or at least the human rights of its constituents. Even those NGOs whose concern for human rights is such as to induce them to paricipate in NGO human rights committees in New York or Geneva represent a wide field of interests. They include religious bodies (World Council of Churches, Quakers, World Muslim Congress, World Jewish Congress, Bahai International, Pax Romana), trade union bodies (International Confederation of Free Trade Unions, World Confederation of Labour, World Federation of Trade Unions), political bodies (Christian Democratic World Union, Socialist International, Afro-Asia Peoples' Solidarity Organization), peace groups (International Peace Bureau, World Federation of United Nations Associations, World Peace Council), youth groups (International Youth and Student Movement for the United Nations, World Assembly of Youth, World Federation of Democratic

Youth, World YMCA, World YWCA), women's groups (International Alliance of Women, International Council of Women, Women's International League for Peace and Freedom, Women's International Democratic Federation), and many others.

The work of many of these bodies for human rights is important, although there are only a few international organizations whose work is wholly or primarily in the field of human rights. The major ones are Amnesty International, the International Commission of Jurists, and the International Committee of the Red Cross. There are others that deserve mention, although they cannot be said to be as substantially engaged in the monitoring process as these three bodies. The International Federation of Human Rights has a long history of work in the field, but its prominence is mainly restricted to the francophone countries of western Europe, from which its membership is primarily drawn. The International League for Human Rights, an offshoot of the Federation that was founded in New York in 1941, tends to exert influence primarily in the United States. Its central directorate is smaller than necessary to discharge its tasks, although a number of individuals of very distinguished abilities do important work for the organization. The International Association of Democratic Lawyers, whose concerns include political ones extending beyond the human rights field, despite serious attempts has not yet successfully established the independence of policy required to distinguish fundamentally its own interests from those of its Soviet affiliate. The Arab Lawyers Union has done invaluable work in seeking to build an awareness of human rights in the region of its origin. The Anti-Slavery Society, a British organization that pioneered NGO human rights work in the nineteenth century, has a mandate that now covers the whole field of human rights. The small size of its staff restricts the amount of work it can do, which is invariably solid and newsworthy. The Minority Rights Group is presently applying for consultative status with the UN, and publishes important studies on specific minorities or oppressed groups.

Amnesty International (AI) was founded in 1961 in response to a felt need to do something about the "forgotten prisoners,"

139

by which was meant those detained all over the world simply because their political, religious, or other conscientiously held views caused their governments to silence them by separating them from society. Starting as a six-month campaign, AI developed into a movement of over 2,000 groups in some 35 countries covering all continents, although it is primarily European-based.

Today the overwhelming majority of AI's work—and documentation—relates to prisoners, mainly political prisoners. While such work makes relevant most of the civil and political rights enunciated in the Universal Declaration, the degree of relevance varies. Similarly, major areas of repression not resulting in imprisonment fall largely outside the scope of AI's activities. It is an action-oriented organization designed to campaign for individuals. Since AI acts on information it receives relevant to its mandate, particularly by giving publicity to that information, numerous sources, including but not limited to victims, are willing to expend the effort in providing information. (The expectation of tangible or immediate benefit for the victims may be, but is not necessarily, a consideration.) It may, nevertheless, decide not to publish information or to reduce the intensity of published information on a particular country if it feels that this would be in the interests of the prisoners.

A grass-roots participatory organization funded by its groups and members, AI works basically through the "adoption group," which consists usually of 10 or more private individuals. The group is assigned two or three "prisoners of conscience," as they are called, from countries of different ideological persuasion. This balance is intended as a guarantee of the political neutrality of AI's work. The main task of the adoption group is to work for the release of its "adopted prisoners," none of whom is a national of the group's country. This will be done by writing letters to the detaining government, by organizing demonstrations and letter- and card-writing campaigns, by seeking press publicity, and by using other techniques that may be appropriate in the circumstances. When necessary, and possible, groups will seek to provide relief to the prisoners' families. They are assigned their prisoners by an International Secretariat of over 100 full-time professionals at the organization's headquarters in London. The Secretariat, in addition to generating the information required for this group activity, is responsible for coordinating activities in particular countries and for the day-to-day functioning of the organization. This is done under the supervision of an International Executive Committee of nine persons, eight of whom are elected by an annual International Council in which all National Sections are represented, the ninth being elected by the staff of the Secretariat. The International Council is the supreme policy-making body of the organization.

In addition to group work, the organization sends observers to trials, publishes reports on particular countries or problems, engages in contacts and discussions with governments, and lobbies internationally for the strengthening and better enforcement of international human rights principles, particularly those governing torture or ill-treatment of prisoners, whether "of conscience" or not. AI opposes the use of capital punishment in all cases. It also works for a fair trial within a reasonable time for all political prisoners. Every year it publishes a report of its work in the previous year. It has consultative status or similar relations with the United Nations, UNESCO, the Council of Europe, the Organization of American States (OAS), and the OAU.

The International Commission of Jurists (ICJ), founded in West Berlin in 1952, consists of not more than 40 distinguished lawyers from all over the world who meet triennially. The International Secretariat is in Geneva, which maintains contact with some 50 National Sections. An Executive Committee, consisting of up to five members of the Commission, directs a small Secretariat and meets at least three times a year. As indicated by its origins, the ICJ started out as something of the political opposite of the International Association of Democratic Lawyers. However, its overall record is quite in keeping with the nonpolitical denomination prescribed by its statute. The objective of the ICJ is "the support and advancement of those principles of justice which constitute the basis of the Rule of Law," and it operates on the premise that the establishment and enforcement of a legal system that denies the fundamental rights of the individual violates the Rule of Law. The various reports of the ICJ on specific countries and problems and its biannual *Review*, which deals with national and international human rights developments, have acquired a reputation for competence and reliability. The ICJ sponsors private lectures, organizes public meetings and congresses, issues press releases, sends observers to trials and on missions of investigation in various countries, and lobbies for the international promotion and protection of human rights. It has consultative status with the United Nations, UNESCO, and the Council of Europe.

There are several points to note with respect to the ICJ. The strength of its work on countries where it has national sections is related to the strength of those sections, since, unlike AI, the sections are primarily responsible for promoting respect for the Rule of Law in their own countries. Its emphasis is on the promotion and protection of adjectival (i.e., due process) rather than substantive civil and political rights, though it is far from inattentive to the latter. It has an important access to worldwide legal elites and is particularly well qualified to intervene against persecution of lawyers, many of whom tend by virtue of their calling to be on the firing line of political tensions and repression. Indeed, it has recently established a separate Center for the Independence of Lawyers that promises to intensify the ICJ's work in this field. It relies on research and investigative missions for much of its direct information; its monitoring role is visible in a combination of its press statements, with or without reports, and articles in the *Review*. For a long time the ICJ was at the mercy of a few large donors, and it had to curtail its program radically when Ford Foundation funds were terminated in the late sixties. Happily, its financial position has recently been improving, although it is still materially constrained in the number of investigations it can carry out.

The International Committee of the Red Cross (ICRC), founded in 1863 in Geneva, where its headquarters is, is a constituent element of the International Red Cross, the other parts being the League of Red Cross Societies and the National Red Cross Societies. The Committee consists of not more than 25 members of Swiss nationality. The general conduct of its affairs is under the supervision of an Executive Board, whose members may not exceed seven and do not necessarily belong to the ICRC. Besides the specific tasks assigned to it by its statute, the ICRC accepts the mandates entrusted to it by the periodic International Conferences of the Red Cross, which are attended both by the above-mentioned elements and by governments of signatories to the Geneva Conventions for the Protection of Victims of War. This indicates what is confirmed by the role specifically assigned to it by the Geneva Conventions, namely, that the ICRC has an "official" international status and authority distinct from that of the other NGOs. The ICRC is the "guardian" of the Geneva Conventions and receives the close cooperation of the Swiss government in its periodic attempts to secure their revision. Its principal activities are the securing of humane treatment and the provision of humanitarian assistance in international and noninternational armed conflict. After World War I, and especially after World War II, the ICRC extended its concern to political prisoners in cases of "internal tensions."[3] It seeks access to prisons, and by presenting confidential reports, attempts to ensure the humane treatment of political prisoners. Equally confidentially, it sends observers to trials at which prisoners who would be objects of its concern might be convicted. It does not seek to challenge the legitimacy of detention any more than it questions the justness or legality of a particular war. Its aim is the mitigation of the excesses of both phenomena.

It should be noted that the ICRC is a monitoring body only in the sense that in its quest for the application of the norms of humanitarian law in armed conflict it amasses information pertinent to that quest; such information is particularly available to the extent that the ICRC gets access to prisoners through its inspections and relief activities. Its operations are strictly confidential and it publishes its reports only if the governments of the countries concerned issue selective or inaccurate versions. The ICRC is composed of an elite group of nationals of one neutral country. Its work depends on the cooperation of governments, which would terminate if it were to abandon its policy of confidentiality or its exclusive national base. Its role is not to judge whether or not the acts of governments are in compliance with human rights as such. However, humanitarian law, like international standards for human rights, explicitly prohibits torture or cruel, inhuman, or degrading treatment or punishment. There is no question that the ICRC has been able to alleviate the suffering of prisoners at the hands of governments.

It is clear from the above that these three organizations are structured in such a way that they could not be successfully merged into one organization. If the mandates of AI and the ICJ could conceivably be harmonized without doing too much damage to the world views of their respective constituencies, clearly that of the ICRC is not similarly adjustable. The latter organization's official international status removes it from the purely private level of the other two. Indeed, nothing would be less acceptable to AI and the ICJ than to accept a mandate that is politically determined by representatives of governments. The ICJ's policy is determined by the approximately 40 lawyers comprising it, while that of AI is set by its 35 national sections representing some 168,000 members.

Nevertheless, cooperation is possible. This is particularly the case with regard to international initiatives such as the improvement of humanitarian law applicable in armed conflict or the strengthening of intergovernmental standards against the use of torture. Such cooperation normally takes place at meetings of the special NGO committees on human rights referred to earlier. These provide a forum for isolating areas of common interest and mobilizing such joint activities as the adoption of joint resolutions for statements to be submitted to international conferences.

Direct cooperation between the three principal NGOs would be difficult to research outside the organizations themselves, since such cooperation might, for a number of reasons, not be felt suitable for public scrutiny. Certainly, between AI and the ICJ there is already substantial contact by way of exchanges of information. Often such information will give rise to initiatives by one or both organizations depending on a mutual appreciation of respective mandates and likely political effectiveness. In the past, for instance, shared information has resulted in decisions to send observers to certain trials. Indeed, joint missions are not unknown. As a result of one such mission—a 1974 visit to Uruguay by the Secretary-General of the ICJ and a regional expert from AI's International Secretariat—both organizations produced a number of reports and engaged in a variety of other actions exposing the steady transformation of "the Switzerland of Latin America" into a squalid reign of terror by the military.

Similarly, direct cooperation is not required to establish what may be perceived as a complementary relationship between the work of these two NGOs and the ICRC. Compatibility no more requires marriage than it requires public demonstration of its existence. The ICRC can only work efficiently if it has access to information from independent sources—it has, after all, to decide what countries to visit, what prisons to inspect in these countries, and which prisoners it might profitably seek to interview. To the extent that such visits help mitigate excesses on the part of detaining authorities, they can be said to complement the work of other NGOs. Conversely, the public activities of bodies such as AI and the ICJ may induce target governments to deal with the confidentially operating, more congenial Red Cross.[4]

It should go without saying that in my view the work of these bodies, hopefully supplemented by the increasing involvement of the churches in human rights questions, represents a valid and valuable attempt to tackle the worst of people's inhumanity to one another outside of warfare. I also believe that the inability of these bodies to come to grips with the deprivation of economic and social rights, sometimes called human needs, does not detract from the validity and value of their work. Interestingly, while the ICRC has on occasion been attacked for alleged political bias, as in the Vietnam quagmire,[5] it is not usually reproached for not concerning itself with economic and social matters. This charge is leveled, however, at the publicity-oriented organizations. But, as mentioned earlier, little else needs to be done to demonstrate governments' failure to ensure their citizens' social and economic well-being. The key information is already available from a variety of national and international institutions. It is in the field of civil and political rights that the NGOs fill what would otherwise be an information gap, as well as a gap in remedial action at the international level.

The question that remains to be answered is how their work could be strengthened or supplemented to ensure that human rights violations are monitored and controlled as effectively as possible in a medium-term future that, for the purposes of working toward these objectives, is not likely to be fundamentally different from the present. This question is probably best approached by seeking to identify the perceived weaknesses of AI and the ICJ:

1. The civil rights emphasis (as opposed to economic and social rights) opens them to the charge of Western orientation. But it is in this field that there is a gap, a need to be filled, and there is little likelihood of their accepting a broader mandate for image purposes.
2. Their constituencies are predominantly Western in terms of both internal structure and the audience for their published matter.
3. Their mandates (e.g., the prisoner orientation of AI and the Rule of Law orientation of the ICJ) do not cover the whole field of even civil and political rights.

In reply to the third criticism: AI and the ICJ already deal with the most egregious varieties of violation of civil rights, if not political rights, and it might well be that without recourse to violations of these rights governments would be denied the means of other forms of repression.

In reply to the other criticisms: Only the constituency of the NGOs can be at all adjusted, and even this is not so easy, since it is inevitable that only those relatively secure in the exercise of their rights are able to work publicly and freely on behalf of those who are not. Nevertheless, direct involvement in the Third World in ways that do not involve judging its malfeasances is both desirable and possible. The non-Western world is not monolithic, and the NGOs' already existing efforts to strengthen indigenous support there should be encouraged. Another, very closely related goal should be to diffuse knowledge of human rights matters to an audience that has little awareness of such things. Such an effort would involve a response to those who, within a number of bodies, including UNESCO, are seeking to stifle the flow of information in the Third World by confining it to that originating in official sources. Such an effort would have to be very sensitive to the charge that the present Western-dominated international agencies give a politically and culturally biased view of the non-Western world. There is a real challenge to the existing NGOs to seek methods of vastly expanding efforts in education on human rights concerns. Ultimately, human rights are guaranteed only by the awareness that such education could help stimulate. This involves imaginative, multidisciplinary, multiprofessional, and multicultural programs and experiments to reach beyond traditional audiences. Out of such a program it would not be inconceivable for a new human rights monitoring institution to be born.

AN IDEAL WORLDWIDE MONITORING INSTITUTION

What follows is an attempt to sketch out what a worldwide human rights monitoring institution might look like if it could be created from scratch. It is in no sense the expression of dissatisfaction with the very effective work of the existing NGOs; nor, indeed, would such a new institution be in competition with them. While there might be significant areas of overlap—as there are between AI and the ICJ—the substantive emphasis and the style of activity would be different. Its voice would be neither that of the lawyer nor that of the relatively free individual working for his or her unfree cousin. The mission of such an institution would be merely to report, in a manner approximating as closely as possible academic detachment. Its structure is designed to avoid the criticisms fair and unfair that have been leveled at the existing NGOs. Its range of concern would be broad enough and its authority respected enough that other NGOs would be able to invoke its output in pursuance of their own work. Being an ideal model, it may well be incapable of realization. It nevertheless illustrates targets that existing NGOs may still work toward.

The following are the principal desiderata of a new body:

1. It should be completely independent of governments.
2. It should be completely independent of all power elites, particularly economic ones.
3. It should be free of all ideological or politically partisan prejudice. It should not be committed to, or otherwise permeated by, any single sociocultural norm.
4. It should be staffed by and responsible to people who, individually or collectively, can ensure compliance with the above.
5. It should be financially secure.
6. It should be legally secure.
7. Its investigations should seek to approximate scientific accuracy.
8. The information it disseminates should be detailed and accurate.
9. It must have access to and seek to work effectively with such international media of communication as are willing to give it attention.
10. It should be based in a country that is stable enough to protect the human rights of its own citizens and to accept without retaliation such criticism as the institution may be called upon to level against it.

The Institutional Blueprint

1. *The founders*. The original sponsors might be some 75 former victims of oppression—e.g., political prisoners—or a similar number of former heads of state, or preferably both sets together. All members of either group would be from different countries.

2. *Functions*. The institution would produce an annual conspectus of the human rights situation in all countries, indi-

cating in its report the relative availability and quality of its information. In addition, after the first three years of its operation, it would embark on a program of investigations whereby it would seek to visit every country at least once every five years. The executive would be able to authorize investigations out of schedule in particularly unstable situations and publish the results. Investigations would only take place with the knowledge of the authorities. Under no circumstances would the institution engage in communication with governments other than to facilitate the mutual exchange of information. Any attempts to redress specific human rights violations would be outside the institution's scope; otherwise its effectiveness as a monitor would be compromised.

One way of disseminating information about violations would be through a documentation center. The information stored here would be available to all inquirers, except if it could be harmful to individuals or groups that supplied it or to the victims of human rights violations. The center would store information from all sources—not just the investigations that the institution undertook with the knowledge of governments.

The institution would be empowered to consider establishing its own radio broadcasting service.

3. *Consultative status with intergovernmental organizations.* In order to facilitate access to other organizations with similar concerns, the institution would seek consultative status with all intergovernmental organizations whose programs involve concern with human rights—particularly the UN, UNESCO, the Council of Europe, the Inter-American Commission of Human Rights of the OAS, and the International Labor Organization (ILO).

4. *Legal status.* The institution's only special legal status would be that of a tax-exempt body within the host state. No special legal regime would be sought, since concessions so obtained constitute a continuing—and terminable—donation from the government.

5. *Control bodies*. An executive that met not more than twice a year would consist of about ten persons elected by the founders or the assembly from among their number. The assembly would consist of the founders, plus one alternate to be nominated by each founder.

6. *Staff*. The Executive would appoint an international staff of the greatest efficiency, competence, and integrity. While high regard would be had for the affirmative value of equitable geographic distribution, the only geographical "quota" would be the rule that no country would be "represented" to the extent of more than 15 percent of the total staff.

7. *Funding*. The founders would launch a worldwide appeal for, say, $100 million, from all sources. No source, anonymous or otherwise, direct or indirect, would be permitted to contribute more than one percent of the target sum. Operations would not commence before half the target sum had been reached. The annual budget would be no more than 75 percent of the annual income generated by the capital on hand when operations began. Thereafter the budget would consist of all such annual income minus the percentage necessary to safeguard the capital sum against currency devaluation in the country of the institution's headquarters.

Every five years the executive could launch a limited fundraising campaign if the institution required additional resources to expand or satisfactorily maintain its operations.

The establishment of a worldwide monitoring body in 1984 would give that date a symbolism radically more hopeful than that created by the all-too-wise prophecies of George Orwell.

NOTES

1. See Ian Brownlie, *International Law and the Use of Force by States* (New York: Oxford University Press, 1963); Thomas M. Franck and Nigel S. Rodley, "After Bangladesh: The Law of Humanitarian Intervention by Military Force," *American Journal of International Law*, vol. 67, no. 275 (April 1973), pp. 279–283.

2. Nigel S. Rodley, "The United Nations and Human Rights in the Middle East," *Social Research*, vol. 38, no. 217 (Summer 1971).

3. See, generally, J. Moreillon, *Le Comité International de la Croix-Rouge et la Protection de la Protection des Détenus Politiques* (Lausanne: Editions L'Age d'Homme, 1973).

4. Ibid.

5. What happened was that the South Vietnamese government restricted access to places of detention and abused ICRC confidentiality by selective publication of its reports. The ICRC was blamed for allowing this to happen.

Human Rights Issues in Latin America

Bryce Wood

Introduction

The performance of all governments in demonstrating respect for the human rights of their citizens has, in the past 15 years, become an important element in their foreign relations. Poor performance may adversely affect governments' prestige, their status in international organizations, and their access to sources of external financial and military assistance.

The government of Chile, for instance, has evidently been embarrassed by the publicity of private agencies and the Inter-American and United Nations Commissions on Human Rights. A decade ago, the Council of Europe suspended Greece from participation in its activities because the European Human Rights Commission found the ruling Greek regime to have seriously violated the human rights of its people. The UN Security Council mandated the imposition of sanctions against Rhodesia, deeming the racially discriminatory policies of that government a threat to the peace. More recently, the United Kingdom government admitted before the European Human Rights Court that its handling of certain prisoners in Ulster amounted to practices of inhuman treatment and torture in violation of the European Convention. And in the United States, the Congress has enjoined the administration to refuse economic assistance to countries where, in the administration's judgment, "patterns of gross violations of internationally recognized human rights" are found to exist. The Congress itself prohibited any military assistance whatever to Chile and Uruguay on the basis of its own judgment of their violation of human rights. The Carter administration has committed itself at least to declarations in favor of respect for human rights as a worldwide policy.

In light of these developments, human rights seems likely to remain a significant aspect of international relations in the years to come. This study proposes to assess both the prospects for the observance of basic human rights in Latin America and the potential influence of contending domestic forces. It will also analyze the policies of public and private organizations, national and international, that may have some power to affect governments' performances and attempt to suggest likely developments in the 1980s.

BASIC HUMAN RIGHTS

For purposes of this paper, "basic human rights" will refer only to those classical rights painfully established over centuries to restrain the brutality of tyrants. These rights are intended to protect individuals from governmental acts that are directly and immediately harmful, such as murder, torture, imprisonment without trial, refusal of habeas corpus, cruel and unusual punishments, enforcement of penalties under ex post facto legislation or decrees. These rights are simple and specific in that their deprivation directly affects individual persons. They frequently present clear alternatives—is habeas corpus granted or not? Further, a government can grant them whether or not it has financial resources, which would be needed, in contrast, to comply with assertions of a right to health services. Basic human rights usually pose clear moral questions, at least in the traditional, liberal, Western view, on relations between officialdom and citizenry—cruelty, rather than neglect, for example. They provide the "freedom from fear" on which the gaining of other rights depends.

This discussion will not take up the questions posed by two other sets of rights: first, those associated with democratic polities, which include the rights to freedom of the press, to vote, to participate in decisions about taxes, and others; and second, those economic, cultural, and social needs that have recently begun to be considered rights. These include, among many others, as listed in the American Declaration of the Rights and Duties of Man (1948): education, preservation of health and well-being, and "the benefits of culture."

In addition to the characteristics mentioned above, there are several reasons for limiting the present discussion to "basic" rights. These rights are being flagrantly violated by many Latin American governments. Consequently, the other classes of rights are observed, if at all, only with respect to limited sectors of the populace. Moreover, international concern has been primarily focused on governmental performance in connection with basic rights. According to the Inter-American Commission on Human Rights (IACHR), the most that could be said of that performance during 1975 was that it was "not worse than in previous years." However, violence continued to be used by groups and by governments, and "in this framework of violence, life, liberty and personal security, that is, the basic rights set forth in Article I of the American Declaration of the Rights and Duties of Man, are in constant jeopardy and are frequently violated."[1] Again, if any protests or other actions are to be taken by other states, it is easier to secure convincing evidence of torture, for example, than it is of corruption in elections, or deprivation of the ballot. There are far more refugees from regimes that practice torture than from those that merely rig elections.

The triple combination of (1) widespread violations of human rights in Latin America, especially in certain countries where reasonably decent standards of governmental conduct had formerly prevailed; (2) the establishment of international commissions on human rights in Europe, the Americas, and the United Nations; and (3) the adoption by both the United States Congress and the Carter administration of policies aimed at encouraging foreign governments to treat their citizens more humanely has given rise to a novel set of issues both in inter-American relations and in the domestic politics of Latin American states. It is likely that they will perturb inter-American relationships over a substantial period of time.

ONE

The Latin American Scene

THE NEW MILITARY REGIMES IN LATIN AMERICA

Eight of the 12 South American countries are presently governed by military regimes. In varying degrees these governments share two characteristics rarely seen before in the region: first, a shift away from both personal dictatorships and democracy and toward the institutionalization of rule by the military and, second, the appearance of a "new professionalism," marked by military control of internal security and fostered by success in counterinsurgency measures, direct military involvement in political decisions, and the training of military officers to be political and economic specialists able to consult economists and other experts without being ignorantly dependent upon them. In Chile, Brazil, and elsewhere the military, despite a rhetoric of a return to democratic institutions, appear to be moving away from traditional roles as "moderators" or "caretakers" to those of directing and consolidating new types of authoritarian, corporative political systems.

The circumstances and outlooks in each country are different and can be treated adequately only in a larger context, but some broad generalizations may be ventured. The regimes seem to have several major concerns; rapid economic development of their societies; maintenance of internal security and order, meaning the destruction of organized opposition to regime plans and policies; and defense of the new powers and position of the military as an institution. These aims are variously interwoven. If Fidel Castro "learned" from the experience of the Guatemalan presidents in the early 1950s that the destruction of the traditional military command was essential for his plans for communism in Cuba, military men elsewhere in Latin America "learned" from him that their very existence depended on their preventing the rise of communism at home.

The Brazilian military establishment, for example, became seriously alarmed in 1963–1964 by the growth of trade unionism among enlisted men in the army, by President João Goulart's politically motivated promotions of military officers, by the President's encouragement of unrest among the cadre of sergeants, and by his plans for expropriation of large, privately owned estates. In alliance with some middle-class leaders, the main body of the army, air force, and navy quickly and with little fighting forced Goulart into exile in April 1964. The new military regime, headed by General Humberto Castello Branco, soon broke diplomatic relations with Cuba and initiated a new policy of economic development that offered a warm welcome to investments by foreign business enterprises. The regime has peaceably solved the problem of succession to the presidency and has governed continuously for the past 14 years, a period that has seen a remarkable increase in Brazil's gross national product.

The Brazilian military coup of 1964 marks the emergence of Brazil as the predominant power in South America. Its population, size, and resources had earlier provided the potential for outstripping its neighbors, but the new combination of political stability, technological and administrative competence, and economic policies emphasizing investment from abroad and development of exports of manufactured products created annual growth rates in gross domestic product averaging 10 percent from 1968 through 1974. This "Brazilian miracle" prompted discussions elsewhere in South America of a "Brazilian model" that included both Brazil's politico-military system and its economic policies.

The Brazilian politico-military system consists of several components. The first component shows the army's confidence in its strength, going back to combat experience in Italy in World

War II. There was sufficient unity among the army, air force, and navy to restore military discipline after April 1964, to suppress rural and urban guerrilla movements, and to embark upon a policy of rapid economic development involving a vast increase in state control and ownership of industrial enterprises, which was intended to assure Brazil's emergence as a world power. Yet the military, while countenancing a democratic facade of parties, congress, and elections, has in practice rendered the opposition nearly helpless to exert significant influence on policy or to make effective protests against increasing inequalities in the distribution of income induced by the policy of holding real wages nearly constant. In summary, the regimes' arguments run: "To support Brazilian greatness, a concentration of power is required, and opposition is therefore disloyalty. Subversion remains a palpable threat to the stability and therefore the growth and progress of the Brazilian state. Competitive politics is a breeding ground for antiregime elements and cannot be tolerated."[2] The measure of ferocity of nontoleration of such disloyalty will be considered later.

While the Brazilian authoritarian model was studied elsewhere in Latin America, it would hardly be correct to say that it was copied, for the circumstances in the several countries were too diverse for replication. Yet, all the several South American authoritarian regimes that have been established since 1963 are characterized by enhanced competence of the military forces themselves, and their infusion with a new sense of mission.

Competence has many facets. The embarrassingly feeble performance of Peru's armed forces in the Leticia conflict with Colombia in 1932–1933 prompted President Oscar Benavides to reorganize and reequip all services. Perhaps most important, the Higher War College was converted in 1950 from a somnolent institution into an effective planning agency, the Center for Higher Military Studies (CAEM), that instructed officers in economic and political as well as military subjects. Even before 1960, the Center was studying national development, with special reference to internal security; by the mid-sixties the Center, like the Superior War College (ESG), "had forged a doctrine that implicitly "legitimated" long-term military supervision of the development process."[3] Since its coup in 1968, the military has been applying the doctrine.

In these two most highly professionalized of Latin American military institutions, competence means sophisticated equipment, unity among the services, centralized police powers over the whole country, and the monopoly of the means of making warfare. No longer do army and navy become possible opponents by supporting rival civilian pretenders; no longer do dissident colonels make "pronouncements" in provincial capitals; and army domination over the police forces is fully established. Competence also means deep concern for and intensive study of the objectives and accomplishments of national economic and social policies. Finally, competence has grown from the elaboration and understanding of the basic doctrine that economic growth depends on internal order and discipline and that the military, as the only stable, cohesive, national force capable of directing and stimulating growth, has the mission to take the lead.

A comparison of these new roles with the three principal roles of armed forces in the past may suggest the significance of these new military regimes, not only at present, but for the next several years. In most countries of Central America and the Caribbean, where international conflict has been almost unknown since 1898, armies, more properly defined as police forces, were the creatures of dictators, and their principal function was to crush internal opponents. In certain countries of South America—notably Argentina between 1870 and 1930, Brazil for a half century after the termination of the monarchy, and Chile, Uruguay, and Colombia for longer periods—the military was nearly neutral in domestic politics; civilian presidents came to power and relinquished it through competitive party struggles via elections. For nearly half a century after the War of the Pacific in 1879–1883 between Chile, Bolivia, and Peru, there were no armed conflicts among the South American countries, and the principal occupation of officers in these states was the preparation of plans for defense. Finally, in Bolivia, Ecuador, and Honduras, for instance, armies frequently entered into the game of presidential politics on their own initiative, or on the invitation of one or another civilian candidate for the presidency.

The case of Mexico is distinct. For about 30 years after 1880, the police force of President Porfirio Díaz, famous as the *rurales*, served the dictator's purposes in maintaining order. From the Mexican revolution until 1946, successive presidents were ex-generals. Since then, all Mexican presidents have been civilians, and the institutionalization of civilian control in an essentially one-party system has kept the army small, efficient, and nearly politically neutral.

Although there are significant local differences in the timing and manner of securing power, the eight existing military regimes do share, with varying emphases, the essential characteristics of the "new professionalism" of the armed services. Some features of these local differences are worth examining before considering human rights. While the doctrine of military rule implies control by the military over the policies affecting economic and social development, it does not mandate any given development policy. Thus, while the Brazilian and Peruvian military are principally responsible for creating the doctrine, their own policies have differed significantly on the important matter of land reform. The Brazilians, in destroying rural guerrilla movements, maintained the existing system of land tenure, while the Peruvians, having also crushed rural guerrillas, decreed the expropriation of large estates and their division among small holders and workers in order to avoid further uprisings in the countryside. The Peruvians also expropriated foreign oil companies and nationalized the important fish meal industry. They have, of course, had problems implementing the land reform and have again let private industries operate the fish meal industry, but this turn to the right indicates that successive regimes adhering to the broad lines of the doctrine may yet have diverse policies.

Of the other countries, Argentina, having experienced several army presidencies since the ousting of Juan Perón in 1955, is now under the rule of a military regime whose principal immediate task is stifling terrorism. The regime appears to be winning the struggle. Yet it is uncertain whether, once internal security is established, the military will return power to civil authorities or will endeavor to make an effort similar to Juan Carlos Onganía's in the late 1960s to set up a durable authoritarian regime.

The example of Uruguay is not encouraging: The crushing in 1972 of the Tupamaros, a terrorist group, has resulted not in a return to representative democracy, but in the establishment of a military-dominated government installed by a coup in 1973.

The Paraguayan military regime is an older type—a personal dictatorship founded more than twenty years ago by President Alfredo Stroessner. The regime, whose power base is an efficient police force, has been brought into the ambit of modern developmental policies through its intimate cooperation with Brazil in the building of the great Itaipu dam on the upper Paraná River. Bolivia has not been as stable as Paraguay, but like Paraguay it has in recent years been strongly influenced by Brazil, which appears likely to have assisted the planners of the coup that placed General Hugo Banzer in control in La Paz in 1971 and has continued to support his government.

The Chilean military regime, which came to power in 1973, has given firm evidence that it intends to rule for a long time: on March 12, 1977, it decreed the illegality of all political parties in Chile. Its economic policies, somewhat similar to those of Brazil, include measures of austerity to restrain inflation, a return to the pre-1970 pattern of landholding, and efforts to attract foreign investment through measures that have brought about its withdrawal from the Andean Pact. In Ecuador, as in Peru, the military junta has been able to survive one change in the presidency. Aided by revenues from substantial exports of petroleum via its trans-Andean pipeline, the military shows no signs of relinquishing control, and it has not had serious opposition either from guerrillas or from the remnants of political parties, primarily dependent on the personal power of a single leader, such as those associated with the several-times ex-President José María Velasco Ibarra.

SECURITY, DEVELOPMENT, AND REPRESSION

The military regimes in the major countries seem to be firmly established and capable of defending themselves against any new attempts by insurgents. Although in Ecuador and Peru severe measures have been infrequent since 1966, the six regimes in the so-called Southern Cone—Argentina, Bolivia, Brazil, Chile, Paraguay, and Uruguay—have been responsibly charged by refugees, Catholic and Protestant churches, international agencies, private groups, and in some cases, by the Congress and government of the United States, with serious, even atrocious, violations of basic human rights. These violations have included murders of prisoners, torture, and refusal of habeas corpus. Among other countries, Cuba has been denounced by the IACHR in several reports for cruelty in treatment of political prisoners. In Central America, the Commission has reported serious abuses on the part of Guatemala, Nicaragua, and El Salvador.

The Latin American scene is thus a varied one, but conditions in general are not encouraging. Amnesty International reports that "throughout 1975–1976 there has been a slight but unmistakeable deterioration in the overall human rights situation in the Americas, particularly in the *cono sur* (Southern Cone) countries of Latin America."[4] The regimes of this region, with the exception of Argentina's, have succeeded in suppressing guerrillas, and their police and intelligence forces appear to be cooperating effectively in counterinsurgency techniques. It seems likely, therefore, that violent, brutal treatment of persons regarded as dangerous to the structure or policies of existing regimes will continue to endanger human rights in these countries.[5]

Yet, if these regimes are apparently so stable, why do they find it necessary to carry out extreme and enduring violations of human rights? There are several reasons. First, military-dominated governments equate national security with the stability of the governing regime; they identify the safety of the country with the continuation of military rule. The fundamental danger to both is "Communist totalitarianism," which, in the case of Chile, is claimed to have been manifested when "Marxist aggression attempted systematically to destroy the machinery of peace and order and economic and administrative structures, to debase public morals and to eliminate by assassination those who endeavored to resist."[6]

Second, in countries where charges of "Communist totalitarianism" have even less validity than in the Chilean case, a broader category of "subversion" is used to justify repression. As a leading analyst of Brazilian military politics has put it, for the War College, "National security . . . was seen to a great extent as a function of rationally maximizing the output of the economy and minimizing all sources of cleavage and disunity within the country." Thus, by the early 1960s, as the Brazilian crisis deepened, the War College's emphasis on the need for a total development strategy to combat internal subversion found an increasingly receptive audience in the military.[7]

This view is supported by the recent declaration of the National Conference of Bishops of Brazil. According to the declaration, national security doctrines originating in Latin American military schools after World War II stressed the firm link between national security and economic growth, indicated that threats to security existed both inside and outside the country, and assigned to the military the role of maintaining the security vital to economic growth. The document went on to say that "regimes of force, claiming to fight Communism and carry out economic development, declare an antisubversive war against all those who do not agree with an authoritarian vision of society."[8] It seems evident that, where security becomes the prerequisite for economic growth, domestic criticism of development strategies—wage or housing policies, for example—may be regarded as dangerous to the security of the state, and hence a justifiable target of severe measures.

The third reason stable regimes find it necessary to violate human rights is that Brazil's and Uruguay's successful, if painful, experiences in combating terrorists do not incline governments to deal humanely with any new opposition groups. The Argentine government, adapting to worldwide protests against the brutalities attributed directly to the Pinochet regime in Chile, has apparently followed Brazil's example: Authorities have connived at the formation of "private" terrorist groups that complement the work of the regular army in dealing with antigovernment terrorism.

Fourth, in the view of former ambassador Ben Stephansky, "Brazil considers the violation of human rights a necessary condition for economic development."[9] This is a charge that is difficult to document explicitly. At various times severe restrictions on freedom of speech and association have been customary in the military regimes. In Brazil, Chile, and Peru, labor unions have been suppressed or have been subjected to leaders appointed by the governments. Occasional cases of murder and torture in prison are well known, notably that of Olavo Hansen, a leader of textile workers in São Paulo, who was killed while in police custody. Regarding Hansen's death, the IACHR asserted that the Brazilian government had permitted "exceedingly grave violations of the right to life."[10] In connection with this and other cases, the government has not permitted members of the IACHR to visit Brazil and it has largely ignored the Commission's requests for information, so that no clarification of positions has been displayed, as has occurred with respect to national security, which was suggested earlier.

Fifth, it may well be the case for now and some time to come that political estrangement in Latin America between the military and their civilian collaborators, on the one hand, and remaining elements in the political spectrum, on the other, is so deep and bitter that violations of human rights are to be expected as a matter of established policy. The Latin American governments now defending themselves against charges that they have violated human rights have not failed to assert a position on moral grounds. They claim, first, that they are acting within the terms of their own constitutions and laws, and second, that they are defending the rights of their citizens to enjoy peace and order. As stated by a spokesman for one of these governments, the case is that in an extreme "emergency" governments are obliged to protect their citizens, and if they do not, they will indeed be violating human rights, because they will not be fulfilling the fundamental purpose of a nation, which is that of making it possible for "decent people" to live in liberty and tranquillity. These latter mandates are claimed to be of "a higher order" in the moral hierarchy than the rights which have been violated.

But when the rights to life or freedom from torture are subordinated to governmentally defined "higher" human rights, and murder and torture become regarded as routine techniques for

167

keeping the populace obedient and deferential, then a realm of ethical and political conceptions is delineated where there is no place for the rights of man in the classical liberal tradition, or as set forth in the American Declaration of 1948. It may be here that the Latin American authoritarian regimes of left and right share a common characteristic. In exalting the rights of society above the rights of the individual, they are both intolerant of the opposition.

A final significant factor that is difficult to evaluate in relating the new professionalism to human rights is the training by United States specialists of many Latin American military and police officers in techniques of counterinsurgency and civic action, including guidance on intelligence, use and maintenance of arms and machinery, and methods of guerrilla warfare.[11] For example, the Bolivian army units that destroyed the small force led by Ché Guevara were aided by United States advisers.

Whether this United States training had any effect on the development of the new professionalism is largely conjectural. It is not intended to suggest here that United States instructors or advisers on the organization and operations of police forces in Latin America were associated in any way with torture as an intelligence technique. It does seem likely, though, that United States instruction encouraged the labeling of "insurgents" as Communists, if only because courses on military and police intelligence began to be offered in the early 1960s when the confrontation with the Soviet Union in the Western Hemisphere became acute.

It is evident that in many Latin American countries the existence of military regimes that want to remain in power, maintain internal security, and achieve rapid economic development has created new sets of governmental policies that endanger and can sharply curtail basic human rights of their citizens. Further, current deprivations of human rights are not simply a continuation of policies of previous regimes that did not possess the military/bureaucratic competence of those now in power. In several cases, notably Chile and Uruguay, constitutional governments had closely followed the liberal tradition with respect to human rights and tolerance of the political opposition for decades. These new policies are noteworthy for having no recent precedents in some of the most important South American countries.[12] The new military regimes have confronted—and largely vanquished— a surprisingly ineffective local opposition. Guerrilla movements in the 1960s were decisively beaten either before the new regimes gained power (in Bolivia, Peru, Uruguay) or shortly afterwards (in Brazil).[13] In no country was there a struggle approaching a civil war. The situation in Argentina is exceptional, but it should be noted that the terrorist groups now opposing the government were organized and active prior to the coup by the military headed by President Jorge Rafael Videla.

Domestic civilian groups have been unable to present any serious or sustained resistance to the military. Political parties have either been proscribed, as in Chile, or, when officially sanctioned, as in Brazil, have become part of sham parliamentary institutions. "Opposition" party members of Congress in Brasília, for example, are unable to use the floor of the house as a platform for freedom of speech, as they have no parliamentary immunity. Labor unions have either been outlawed or thoroughly co-opted as subordinate institutions of the regime.

There have, however, been domestic protests against violations of human rights, notably by lawyers in Brazil and Chile and by the Catholic churches in Brazil and Nicaragua, but these seem to have had little effect so far on government practices. In Chile the Catholic Church, the World Council of Churches, and other religious groups organized the Committee for Peace in 1973 to assist refugees, but the Committee was disbanded at the request of the government in early 1976 and replaced by the Vicarate of Solidarity as a wholly Catholic agency. In Brazil, the National Conference of Bishops of the Roman Catholic church in 1976 issued a document charging that the government of President Ernesto Geisel, like other "regimes of force" in Latin America, had begun to "take on the same characteristics and practices of Communist regimes: the abuse of power by the state, arbitrary imprisonment, torture and the suppression of liberty of thought."[14] The two most prominent of five Chilean lawyers who jointly and publicly protested their government's nonobservance of human rights during the meeting of the Organization of American States

(OAS) General Assembly in Santiago were summarily exiled despite a resolution voted by the Assembly that appealed to the Chilean government to afford "appropriate guarantees" to persons providing evidence concerning matters of human rights. There has been no significant, continent-wide protest by the national Catholic churches, nor have such organizations as the Inter-American Press Association or the Inter-American Bar Association found it possible to mount any protest campaign to which influential segments of opinion might rally. A meeting in South America comparable to that held in Madrid in 1976 by Communist party leaders of France, Italy, and Spain is unthinkable, and even Socialist or Christian Democratic party leaders would find it impossible to meet anywhere south of Colombia.

Sympathy for refugees and grants of temporary residence were offered to thousands of persons fleeing from Chile in 1973 and 1974 by certain countries, notably Argentina, Mexico, and Peru. One private, specialized agency, the Latin American Social Science Council (CLACSO), organized a register of qualified refugees and exiles and found fellowships, teaching posts, and other positions for some of them in other Latin American countries and in the United States and Europe. These were, of course, more like welfare activities than political protests.

The near absence of any kind of transnational cooperation in Latin America among those opposing violations of human rights stands in sharp and even macabre contrast to the close collaboration of police forces among several countries. For example, Brazilian police officers appeared in Santiago within a few days of the coup of September 1973, allegedly to secure information about—or to arrest—certain Brazilians associated with the Allende regime. The abduction and murder in 1976 of two Uruguayan parliamentarians, Zelmar Michelini and Hector Gutierrez Ruiz, were, it is charged, committed "by officials of the Argentine Government acting under orders from the equally murderous Uruguayan Government."[15] In addition, officers of the Brazilian secret police are reliably reported to be "coaching" the Paraguayan police.[16] Cooperation of this type may be expected to continue and to strengthen the internal security capabilities of the regimes. It is even possible to contemplate the future possibility of police and military cooperation in support of a military regime that appears to be in danger of losing its grip.

Thus, violations of human rights are regarded by military regimes, at least for the time being, as an essential element in their stability. For the present military governments, which have attached moral justification to political expediency and institutional survival, there is no domestic issue of human rights because domestic opposition has been shattered. Opponents are kept demoralized and terrorized by murder and torture, when necessary. A remark attributed to ex-President Juan M. Bordaberry of Uruguay may well apply beyond his own country. Addressing a special meeting of Uruguayan ambassadors, he is reported to have said that torture is "indispensable" because "it is a methodology."[17]

The principal way in which human rights do exist as a domestic issue in these countries is through the protests by national Catholic churches. These protests, however, seem to carry little weight in government circles, and in Brazil at least, even church officials are not immune from government retribution. In 1976, a priest who went to a jail to inquire about a woman who had been arrested was shot and killed by a military policeman; and in Ecuador, 37 Catholic clergymen from several countries who were attending a conference on human rights and other matters were arrested, held overnight, and deported.[18] Since, as one diplomat has stated, "the Church is simply the last bastion of articulate criticism in Chile," it is evident that there is no other group capable of creating issues. The influence of the church over time, however, should not be written off, and it is possible that its work may at least be able to mitigate the worst excesses of mailed-fist "methodologies."

Finally, it may simply be noted that there are, except possibly in Nicaragua and Argentina, no pockets of armed resistance to the present military regimes. There is no Yenan in South America, and no prospect that exiles might be able to mount land-based military expeditions from either Colombia or Venezuela.

TWO

The International Scene

In an earlier time, Latin American governments violating human rights could confidently have viewed the consequent issues as purely domestic. Since World War II, however, the international climate has significantly been altered by both revulsion against wartime atrocities and the currents of opinion that led to the Genocide Convention and the Universal and American declarations on human rights.

In the Americas, prior to 1948 and for some years afterwards, governments—much less the OAS or the UN—rarely attempted to defend citizens of other Hemisphere states from repressive acts of their own rulers. Indeed, at the present time there are still serious differences of opinion among international lawyers and statesmen regarding the legal obligation of a government to defer to any external agency or international standard in matters concerning its treatment of its own nationals. The practical situation in the Americas was altered, however, when human rights formally became a subject of international concern with the signatures of the American Declaration on the Rights and Duties of Man (1948) and the American Convention on Human Rights (1969), and the creation of the Inter-American Commission on Human Rights in 1959.

The American Declaration is simply an affirmation of broad categories of individual rights, a statement of the nature of rights and duties that does not impose any obligations on governments. The American Convention, however, is an agreement that came into effect in mid-1978 among eleven ratifying states; it requires them to respect the enumerated human rights and, should disputes arise, to accept decisions of the Inter-American Court of Human Rights, which will have its seat in Costa Rica. The United States has recently signed the Convention, but the securing of senatorial consent to the ratification may be a difficult process. Other nonratifiers include the major countries of Argentina, Brazil, Chile, and Mexico; Colombia, Venezuela, and, since 1977, the United States, have led a campaign for the Convention's entry into force. A major issue for the immediate future is the relationship between the IACHR and nonratifying states, since the Commission's new conventional status will apparently give it legal recognition only among parties to the Convention.

The Convention originated in the late 1950s when for brief periods in certain countries, including Peru and Venezuela, democratic statesmen were deeply concerned about rights and democratic liberties. They secured in 1959 the adoption of the Declaration of Santiago by the Fifth Meeting of Consultation of Ministers of Foreign Affairs of the American Republics. The Meeting also passed resolutions favoring the drafting of a convention on human rights, and most importantly, for the creation of the IACHR to promote the observance of human rights. The Commission was to be organized immediately, on the assumption that it would function until the proposed convention should come into effect. The Commission held its first meeting in 1960 on the authority of a statute adopted by the Permanent Council of the OAS. The statute was amended in 1965 to enhance the powers of the IACHR, partly because the Commission had effectively carried out its functions of promoting and defending human rights in the preceding five years, but mainly because of its on-the-spot work in the Dominican Republic in 1965, when it was able to secure humane treatment of prisoners and to assist in caring for refugees.

As a result, Latin American regimes of the 1970s find that an inter-American institution created by their predecessors in 1960 has turned out to be a more troublesome creator of human rights issues than any domestic institution or group, with the possible exception of the Catholic church. The men of 1960 may have built better than they might have thought possible, and it is ironical but no accident that the IACHR they bequeathed has now come under menacing attack from unwilling beneficiaries who, both domestically and internationally, would reject their liberal patrimony.

THE INTER-AMERICAN COMMISSION
ON HUMAN RIGHTS

The IACHR is a group of seven persons, selected by the Permanent Council of the OAS to serve four-year terms in their individual capacities and not as representatives or delegates of governments. The purpose of the Commission is to promote and defend the observance of human rights in the Americas and to be an advisory and consultative body to the OAS and member states. The range of its powers and activities is set forth in its Statute; perhaps because it operated in obscurity for most of its life, the Commission has been able to adopt interpretations of the Statute that give it a freedom of action probably not intended by its founding fathers. The glare of publicity accompanying the coup of 1973 in Chile has led to a reexamination by the Permanent Council of the Commission's freedom of action, especially as concerns the preparation and issuance of reports.

In brief, the IACHR accomplishes its principal purpose by receiving complaints of violations of human rights from individuals and other sources; by communicating with governments and asking for information about complaints; by investigating situations through visits to countries, but only with the consent of the affected government; by compiling annual and special reports on the observance of human rights; and by making such special studies as its scanty resources permit, which have taken the form mainly of articles and memoranda by Commission members.

The reports of the Commission are not mere bland, perfunctory, generalized expressions of concern. They name individuals, detail methods of torture, quote from tape-recorded interviews with political prisoners, and finally, they make certain types of judgments about the performance of governments. In the case of Brazil, as already noted, the IACHR has stated that the government had been responsible for "exceedingly grave violations of the right to life"; and more recently, in the case of Chile, the Commission boldly asserted in 1976, in language quite untypical of OAS bodies, that "the practice of arbitrary jailings and persecution and tortures continues up to the present," although "decrees are being issued for the purpose of tranquilizing or confusing world opinion."[19]

However, the IACHR has no coercive power, nor can it, in the absence of a Convention in force, hale governments before a nonexistent court. It relies on publicity, and the persuasive influence of its authority as being formally one of the "principal organs" of the OAS. One phase of its work is well illustrated by its position on the critical issue of measures permissible to maintain regime stability. The nature of the issue is defined in two articles of the text of the convention. Article 27 states that "in time of war, public danger, or other emergency that threatens the independence or security of a State Party, it may take measures derogating from its obligations under the present Convention to the extent and for the period of time strictly required by the exigencies of the situation." However, Article 28 provides that such derogation "does not authorize any suspension" of rights of individuals under certain other articles of the Convention, such as those to life, humane treatment, and freedom from ex post facto laws.

The IACHR has concurred that governments that "reach power through a revolutionary movement are forced in such convulsive periods to suspend certain guarantees," but it also has insisted that conditions of "war, public danger, or other emergency" do not authorize "deprivation of life, torture, or retroactive application of the more severe laws. . . ."

In the still primitive inter-American political system, the member states are thus free to make the critical decisions about the danger and duration of an "emergency." In cases of insurgency, guerrilla warfare, and terrorism, severe repressive measures are customary, and there is little inclination even in the IACHR to censure governments. It is in the far more controversial area of "subversion" that the confrontation arises between the IACHR and member states. As the delegate of the United States declared in the General Assembly's First Committee at Santiago in June 1976: "No one here is talking about emergency measures when they are called for to combat terrorism. What the IACHR is talking about, it seems to us, are prohibitions on the activities of political parties, lack of respect for individual rights of persons who under no circumstances can be considered as enemies of the state in any accepted sense of the word; and lack of proper judicial safeguards."[20]

The IACHR determines the existence of and publicizes violations of human rights, but it does not presume to judge whether governments' decisions are justified. As the chairman of the IACHR, Andrés Aguilar, explained at the Santiago session, the mission of the IACHR "is not to condemn nor put states in the dock to demonstrate their derelictions, but to promote respect for human rights," and for this purpose its only resource is the moral value that may accompany its opinions, and its recommendations that are made to the political organs of the OAS.

Moral rectitude is of little use for an institution like the IACHR without effective publicity. For 15 years its reports were given no consideration by other organs of the OAS. Even the General Assembly, at its first five sessions, beginning in 1970, merely noted the existence of the reports, thanked the Commission for its work, and passed on to other matters. At the Assembly's session in June 1976 in Santiago, Chile, however, the Commission's second report on Chile could not be ignored, as was the first. The chairman of the Commission was for the first time permitted to present the report. The resolutions that emerged from the ensuing debate expressed the hope that Chile would continue to make efforts to ensure respect for human rights, thus implying criticism of its efforts so far. Chile countered by referring to the Permanent Council two draft resolutions obviously aimed at emasculating the IACHR. The Commission staunchly defended its Statute and Regulations in February 1977, and again urged members of the OAS to sign and ratify the Convention, to collaborate in the work of the Commission, and to give it adequate resources to carry out its functions.

Stimulated by the unprecedented attention given by the General Assembly to the IACHR, Secretary General Alejandro Orfila of the OAS has made several notable statements placing concern for human rights as one of three principal items on the agenda of the OAS for the near future. He has asserted that the OAS should do everything possible to upgrade inter-American standards and expand practices in defense of human rights anywhere in the Hemisphere, stating: "No persons, group or movement, no matter what their motives, no matter what their objectives, no matter what their role in society, can justify themselves if their actions rely upon violence and destruction of human life."[21] Such statements and the opening of debate at Santiago presage a new, serious, official confrontation with human rights on the part of the OAS.

At issue now are the Commission's methods of securing information, notably by accepting direct communications from individuals; its manner of reporting, including singling out specific governments as having committed violations of human rights; and its independence in being able to issue its reports without prior approval by the governments at whose infractions they are aimed. The Chilean draft resolutions stress the consultative and advisory services of the IACHR and ostensibly seek to increase "cooperation" between the Commission and the member states, but cooperation as the Chileans intend it will clearly diminish the Commission's scope of independent action. Former U.S. Secretary of State Kissinger, in contrast, asserted at Santiago not only that the record of the Commission justified "strengthening further its independence, evenhandedness, and constructive potential," but that its mandate should be broadened "so that instead of waiting for complaints, it can report regularly on the status of human rights throughout the hemisphere." Further, he suggested that for these purposes the budget and staff of the Commission should be increased. In October 1976, the Permanent Council of the OAS, with reluctant approval by Brazil and Panama, accepted the sum of $102,000, expressly voted by the United States Congress, as a special contribution above the regular U.S. assessment of 66 percent of the OAS budget, for the specific purpose of expanding the IACHR's capabilities. The issue of the IACHR's future has thus been joined, and the United States government is on record as a firm upholder of the Commission's role.

At the seventh meeting of the General Assembly, held at Grenada in June 1977, issues of human rights and the status of the IACHR dominated the agenda. Two important resolutions were passed. The first, sponsored by the United States and other delegations, was supported by a vote of 14, the minimum absolute majority required, against 8 abstentions and 3 absences.[22] In this resolution, the General Assembly commended the Commission for its work, approved an increase in its resources, and urged that member states "cooperate fully with the Commission." The second resolution, offered by Colombia, was passed by a vote of 18 in favor, with abstentions by the Dominican Republic, Panama, the United States, and Venezuela. This resolution noted that earlier stages of economic development and capital formation had created "serious social tensions and a political climate that is not conducive to the necessary respect for and protection of human rights." It asked the IACHR to make a study of methods of investigating human rights violations based on principles recognizing the "juridical equality of states"—which apparently means that the IACHR was being requested to stop issuing reports that singled out specific states for criticism. The study would be reviewed by the Permanent Council of the OAS. Finally, the resolution called on the "developed countries" to abolish protectionist policies in international trade, reduce armament expenditures, and promote capital investment in the developing countries; these actions were to be undertaken so as to "create favorable conditions for the functioning of democratic systems and the full effectiveness of human rights."

It is evident that the two resolutions were employing two very different concepts of the scope of "human rights"; that a majority was indirectly critical of the work of the IACHR, and that many delegations were using an appeal to human rights as the basis for a broad attack on the economic policies of the United States.

With respect to the IACHR, the prospect for augmented finances to aid new staff will facilitate more rapid handling of a backlog of over 2,000 complaints. The basic powers of the Commission, however, especially with respect to investigations and reports, remain under attack by the Colombian resolution; the Commission's mandate to study its own procedures, and any action the Permanent Council may take on this study, will be of

179

fundamental significance for its future operations. The recognition given at Grenada to the importance of human rights issues in inter-American affairs has, however, established the IACHR in fact, as well as in name, as a principal organ of the OAS.

A final concern at the Grenada meeting was terrorism. An attempt, through a resolution sponsored by Argentina, to justify abuses of human rights by governments in suppressing terrorism was defeated. The General Assembly accepted the views expressed by Mexican and Venezuelan delegates that political freedom is the antidote to terrorism, and that terrorism by individuals does not justify the state's response in kind.

THE POLICY OF THE UNITED STATES

Unilateral Aid

If the IACHR is one important external means by which many Latin American governments are brought face-to-face with human rights issues, a second source is the policy of the United States, first forced upon a reluctant Secretary Kissinger by the Congress in 1976 and then independently espoused in 1977 by President Jimmy Carter and his new Secretary of State, Cyrus R. Vance. The new policy consists of several features that include (1) the publication of reports by the Department of State on the situation with regard to human rights in all countries receiving security assistance from the United States; (2) public expressions of disapproval of violations of human rights; (3) prohibition of security assistance to violating countries; (4) limitations on economic assistance to such countries; (5) opposition in the Inter-American Development Bank (IDB) to certain types of loans; and (6) establishment of an Office of Humanitarian Affairs in the Department of State. This policy is creating issues not only for Latin American countries but also for the United States, both in its bilateral relations with other countries of the Americas and in its role as a leading member of the OAS.

Until 1976, the Department of State acquiesced in the refusal of the General Assembly of the OAS to consider questions of human rights, specifically the reports of the IACHR. However, beginning in 1973, there were efforts in the U.S. Congress to limit or terminate United States economic aid and security assistance to countries notoriously violating human rights.

Hearings held shortly after the Chilean military coup of September 1973, by the Senate Judiciary Committee's Subcommittee to Investigate Problems Connected with Refugees and Escapees, made clear that the Department of State had previously paid little or no attention to the work of the IACHR. Department representatives took the position that one government could not formally determine whether another was observing a basic minimum of human rights. Further, it would not have been consonant with the maintenance of a "low profile" in the Americas—the policy of the time—for the United States to make judgments that would incite resentment.

In 1974 the Assistant Secretary for International Organization Affairs moderated this position by admitting that action by an international body such as the IACHR would provide "a natural point of departure" for the United States in bilateral negotiations with the states concerned, since the United States would not then have to take responsibility for initiating charges; but he added that giving attention to an adverse judgment by the IACHR would be much easier if the relations between the United States and the country in question were not very close, since special consideration in security matters would have to be given to those countries regarded as allies.

This response did not satisfy Congress, which in 1974 asked the Secretary of State for annual reports on the "observance of and respect for internationally recognized human rights" for the countries for which security assistance was proposed. Secretary Kissinger did not comply with this request; instead, he presented a general report on human rights throughout the world which neither named countries nor differentiated among their performances in observing human rights. In 1976, therefore, Congress made a new demand, drafted so as to preclude evasion, for country-by-country reports.

An important feature of the reports is that the Department of

State must give consideration to the findings of international organizations, including those of the IACHR, particularly regarding the willingness of a government charged with violations of human rights to permit "an unimpeded investigation" by monitoring organizations. Secretary Kissinger was presumably bowing to this steady congressional pressure when he formally stated to the OAS General Assembly in Santiago that "the condition of human rights as assessed by the Inter-American Commission on Human Rights has impaired our relationship with Chile and will continue to do so."

The Congress has in this fashion drastically reduced the freedom of action and flexibility of the Department of State in making decisions about supplying both armaments and economic aid to Latin American countries. Further, before the Department acted, the Congress demonstrated both the importance it assigns to human rights and its lack of confidence in the Department of State by prohibiting any security assistance whatever to Chile and Uruguay. Fulfilling congressional instructions, the Department began to collect data on the situation in individual countries in the autumn of 1976, resulting in *Human Rights Reports*, including reports on the 82 countries that receive security assistance, published on March 12, 1977, by the Subcommittee on Foreign Assistance of the Senate Committee on Foreign Relations. Violations of human rights were found to exist in most countries. In March 1977 the Administration proposed that security assistance should be terminated in the case of three particularly egregious offenders: Argentina, Ethiopia, and Uruguay.

With respect to economic aid, the Congress in 1974 approved a generalized amendment to foreign aid legislation that could, in certain circumstances, suspend economic aid to any country for not observing the rights of its citizens. The following provisions of the existing legislation indicate the scope of contemplated action:

Sec. 116. Human Rights.—(a) No assistance may be provided under this part to the government of any country which engages in a consistent pattern of gross violations of internationally recognized human rights, including torture or cruel, inhuman, or degrading treatment or punishment, prolonged detention without charges, or other flagrant denial of the right to life, liberty, and the security of person, unless such assistance will directly benefit the needy people in such country. . . . (c) In determining whether or not a government falls within the provisions of subsection (a), consideration shall be given to the extent of cooperation of such government in permitting an unimpeded investigation of alleged violations of internationally recognized human rights by appropriate international organizations, including the International Committee of the Red Cross, or groups or persons acting under the authority of the United Nations or of the Organization of American States.[23]

The Congress left it to the administration to define the phrases "consistent pattern of gross violations" and "directly benefit the needy people." Prohibiting security assistance could be justified under any circumstances, but the Congress did not wish to penalize poor people because their own government was behaving in an inhumane fashion.

However, again demonstrating lack of confidence that the Department of State would carry out its intent, the Congress itself decided to limit total economic aid to Chile in 1976–1977 to $27,000,000, in addition to prohibiting all security assistance. In October 1976, the Chilean government declared that it would not accept this limited amount. By doing so, it may have wished to deny any linkage between United States aid limitation and its own subsequent decision to release some 300 political prisoners.

Multilateral Aid

In 1975 a reluctant Department of State made the most of loopholes such as "consistent violations" and "needy people" to tortuously defend allocations of funds for housing guarantees in Chile; but in 1976, the Department cast an unprecedented negative vote on a proposed $21 million Inter-American Development Bank loan to aid small industry in Chile, specifically on the ground that the Chilean government was derelict in observing human rights. The acting IDB director for the United States, Ian Ross, referred to findings of the IACHR showing "a pattern of Chilean violations that precluded United States approval under the Harkin Amendment.'' That amendment—named for Representative Thomas R. Harkin of Iowa—applied the same restrictions to United States votes in the IDB (but not in the World Bank) as had been approved for prohibition of direct economic aid by the United States. Mr. Ross stated, further, that this loan could not be interpreted ''as directly assisting the needy.''[24]

Not only was this an unprecedented action; it was also a ''judgment call.'' The Department might have claimed, for example, that the findings of the IACHR were out of date, as it in effect had done when it agreed to refrain from any discussion of the IACHR's first report on Chile at the 1975 session of the General Assembly. Or it might have argued that some effects of this loan would ''spill over'' and ''trickle down'' to ''needy people.'' Instead it accepted the IACHR's description of the Chilean violations as accurate, and began to narrow the definition of what would ''benefit the needy people,'' so that the phrase is no longer likely to be used to cover all development aid to any regime, however inhumane.

This stance was the high water mark of the Ford administration's recognition of human rights as an important element of foreign policy, for in December 1976 the Department of the Treasury, adopting the view that only economic considerations should bear upon loans made by the World Bank, voted for two loans to Chile. Even the IDB loan that the State Department had opposed was in fact made: the United States' 44 percent share of the total IDB vote was insufficient to carry the issue against the combined votes of all the other members. New United States policy on human rights will evolve from existing legislation on economic and security assistance. The Congress adopted that legislation primarily because the administration ignored its informal requests to withhold aid from governments violating human rights, notably in the case of Chile. Under President Salvador Allende—opposed by the United States administration—aid to Chile had been reduced. When the military regime headed by General Augusto Pinochet seized power from the Allende government, a relieved United States administration sharply increased aid to the country and remained indifferent to Chilean violations of human rights. Arms aid ended in 1976 not by the administration's action, but by congressional prohibition; and economic aid, limited by the Congress, ended the same year with Chile's refusal to accept it.

The view has been widespread in Washington that the current legislation unreasonably requires the Department of State to decide when a regime has, for example, committed "gross violations" of human rights. The law, however, was specifically designed to force a reluctant administration to stop helping brutal regimes: Foot-dragging officials customarily cite the lack of objective standards of performance when they do not want, for other reasons, to make a decision. It may well be that, as the Congress develops greater confidence that the administration shares its basic purposes regarding promotion of human rights, the legislation may be made more permissive.

GENERAL CONSIDERATIONS

Unilateral Aid

These developments do not, however, mean that there will not be serious problems in the future stemming from the changing nature of the United States relationship with Latin American governments. The latter now protest against any vocabulary depicting a "special relationship" between the United States and other American states. Many Latin American countries indeed no longer are objects in the "sphere of influence" of the United States but have raised independent voices in world politics. Ecuador and Venezuela, for example, are members of the Organization of Petroleum Exporting Countries (OPEC), and Brazil exerts an increasingly powerful economic influence far beyond the Hemisphere.

Two major aims of the United States in the Americas are long-standing: (1) preventing the lodgment of the "European system," once monarchy, now Communism, in the Americas; and (2) promoting democratic institutions—once free elections, now (because imposed free elections, as in Nicaragua, did not prosper) human rights. New policies are now being tested at a time when inter-American solidarity has become seriously weakened; the inclination of the United States to play the role of global law enforcer has markedly declined; and continued violations of human rights in Latin America may regretfully be expected.

The ability of the United States to prevent those violations is in fact quite limited. Withholding aid, whether military or economic, is not likely to be an effective pressure to ameliorate human rights performance by Latin American governments. For the principal Latin American countries United States economic aid—declining for several years—has reached very small figures. Loans and grants to Brazil, for example, have declined from a total of $329 million in 1966 to $17.2 million in 1974. Comparable figures could be cited for Argentina, Colombia, Mexico, Peru, and Venezuela, to mention only major countries. Chile is the principal exception to this trend. In 1966 it received $111.3 million; when the Allende government was toppled in 1973, the figure had fallen to $3.8 million; but in 1974 and 1975 the amounts rose to $9.8 and $95.5 million. The Carter administration is not likely to be so favorably disposed. For some of the smaller countries, such as Haiti, El Salvador, and others, totals have continued at about the same level over the decade, but with much smaller absolute figures. Given the small magnitude of United States aid, given the fact that Latin American governments can turn to multilateral lending institutions or to private sources (or even to the Brazilian government, which has made loans to Chile recently) for assistance, and given that the military regimes in the Southern Cone and other governments regard their variously repressive policies as vitally important both to their internal security and to economic development, it is highly probable that they would regard a complete termination of loans and grants by AID as a wholly inadequate inducement to change their policies with respect to human rights. As Chile's rejection of $27 million from the United States "for needy people" in 1976 showed, human rights policies are now no more negotiable with the Chileans than was the repudiation of free elections with the Peruvian military a decade earlier.

The ineffectiveness of withholding economic aid to achieve more humane practices in the treatment of political opposition, however, does not mean there is no case for refusing aid to governments that condone brutality. The residual case is that the United States government should in no way assist or appear to give approval to such governments. This position admits the humanitarian claims of undernourished children, for example; but it also asserts that there is no other purpose for which aid might be given that is more important to the United States than its claim of a revival of its own respect for basic human rights in an attempt to help victims of persecution in Latin America. Further, even if cessation of aid is ineffective, the United States would no longer be the object of bitter recriminations for continuing to give assistance to such a government as Uruguay's. Former Uruguayan Senator Wilson Ferreira-Aldunate's testimony in the U.S. House of Representatives offers an eloquent example of this type of charge.

With respect to military assistance, the situation seems equally clear. For virtually all of the countries of the hemisphere, armaments are useful only for internal order, for which purpose the military forces are well supplied. They have been useful for protection in territorial or frontier conflicts only infrequently during the past hundred years. Existing border disputes appear unlikely to give rise to serious fighting. The total military aid to Latin America of $133.3 million in 1966 fell to $26.7 million in 1969, and then gradually rose to $157.2 million in 1975. Of the total funds that year, 34 percent went to Brazil, 15 percent to Argentina, 10 percent each to Chile and Peru, and 6 percent each to Uruguay and Venezuela. Several of the major countries have demonstrated that they do not need to rely on the United States as a source of arms. In 1976, for instance, Peru made a major purchase of military aircraft from the Soviet Union. Thus, there does not seem to be any strong reason for considering that the ending of military aid or denial of weapons sales would in itself be critically influential in changing a Latin American country's policy on human rights.[25]

This view is strongly supported by the reaction in Argentina, Brazil, El Salvador, and Guatemala to the previously mentioned publication in March 1977 of the *Human Rights Reports* compiled by the Department of State. All these governments have stated publicly that they will reject further security assistance from the United States because they regard the Department's characterizations of their human rights policies as unjustifiable interference in their domestic affairs. Chile and Uruguay may be added as the fifth and sixth nations in this group, although arms aid to them had been terminated earlier by the United States Congress.

In conclusion, a policy of halting or limiting either economic or military aid or both is likely to have little or no effect in itself on the amelioration of human rights of Latin American nationals. (The only apparent exception is the release by the Paraguayan government in January 1977 of four members of the Communist party who had each been in prison for more than twenty years.) Equally ineffective would probably be any measure of exclusion from trade preferences, such as Congress mandated regarding Ecuador and Venezuela in the winter of 1973–1974 because of their membership in OPEC, despite the fact that they did not joint the Arab members in their oil embargo of the United States. This much-resented U.S. action has led to Latin American proposals for interdiction of "economic aggression" in the proposed revision of the OAS Charter. Comparably, future trade agreements might depend on demonstrated respect for human rights. This was the purpose of the Jackson amendment to the legislation putting into effect the proposed trade agreement with the Soviet Union. Countries less powerful than the U.S.S.R. might be willing to modify quietly some attitudes, especially if the United States declared in advance that it intended to use economic influence as part of a broad policy of fostering human rights abroad. However, restrictions on trade are more difficult to apply than termination of aid, if only because their effects on immediate interests of United States businesses would probably give rise to domestic political pressures.

Multilateral Aid

Since 1969 the IDB has become a source of development funds for Latin American countries substantially more important than the Agency for International Development. In addition, the Latin American majority of votes in the IDB on "hard loans" is not limited in any way by considerations of the human rights policies of claimant governments.

If the United States government strongly desires to bring maximum economic pressure against the more flagrantly inhumane Latin American regimes, it may decide to reduce in whole or in part the substantial funds it has been subscribing for support of the IDB. It was defeated on the Chilean loan in 1976, where the issue was specifically human rights versus economic feasibility. If it limits its direct assistance in order to try to protect human rights, it must then confront the question of whether it should continue to allow the IDB to frustrate its intent by channeling funds the Congress has appropriated for multilateral disposition to the very countries it is trying unilaterally to deter, however ineffectually at present. Unless the United States can persuade other governments to refrain from voting loans via the IDB to egregious violators of human rights, the efficacy of economic leverage will be very slight.

The United States would seem to have two related options on policy toward the IDB. The first would be to try to obtain cooperation from other members through quiet diplomacy, perhaps with the help of Canada and newly admitted European countries, in denying loans to violators of human rights. The second would be to terminate its funding of IDB. When the United States representative explained his negative vote on the loan to Chile, the Venezuelan delegate stated that "the Bank is not a forum for considering political questions." Commenting, Deputy Assistant Secretary of State Joseph Grunwald is reported to have declared that the general application of the Venezuelan's principle "could destroy the bank."[26]

Since the destruction of the IDB would constitute a far more serious setback to development investments in Latin American countries than would the termination of grants and loans from AID, a successful campaign by the United States to limit IDB loans would probably constitute the strongest type of economic pressure that could be exerted. Whether it would be effective in changing the policies of delinquent states, however, is quite uncertain.

The complexity of the situation and the issues is exemplified by the favorable vote by the U.S. Treasury on the World Bank loans to Chile. Contesting the Treasury's "apolitical" view, which is shared by the president of the World Bank, one member of the Congress, while admitting that the Harkin amendment applied (among lending agencies) only to the IDB, asserted that "it is the clear intent of Congress that we not support such repressive regimes through any economic assistance channel."[27] If this view is maintained in Congress, it is possible that the Harkin amendment may be applied to World Bank loans as well as to those of the IDB, thus extending the range of controversy over human rights to clients of the World Bank outside Latin America.

In addition, investments by private firms and loans by private banks provide a special type of support for some of the Latin American military regimes, notably Chile and Brazil. If public unilateral and multilateral aid is to be restricted by the United States in the interests of human rights, a case may be made for studying the possibility of restraining corporations and banks from investing in those countries "certified," as in the *Human Rights Reports*, as being ineligible for security or economic assistance. But for obvious political reasons, limiting opportunities for investment would be far more difficult than cutting off expenditure of public monies.

THE UNITED STATES AND THE OAS

Acting on its own, the United States is bound to create resentment in Latin America by cutting off aid. Are there also possibilities for working within the OAS, in a less exposed position, to foster observance of human rights? The only possibility here is the IACHR. The American Convention on Human Rights is not going to come into effect soon, and no state in which there are deep divisions over abortion is going to allow an inter-American court to have the chance to hear a case in which the state might be charged with violating the right to life. The Permanent Council or General Assembly of the OAS is not going to apply any sanctions to a member state for deprivations of human rights.

The legal complexities are thick and deep here, and to them may be added the notorious reluctance of Latin Americans to contemplate interference, however collective, in one another's "domestic" affairs.

In any intergovernmental effort to induce nations to display greater respect for human rights, a reputable, nonpartisan source of information and analysis must be established. The IACHR is capable of performing this function, but only if its resources are greatly increased and its present powers are not reduced. Its work has expanded enormously in the last few years, as it has tried to deal with an increasing flood of communications from individuals and organizations protesting denials of their rights and liberties. However, the structures of the Commission, whose part-time members meet no more than eight weeks a year, has not been changed; its budget is still less than 1 percent of the total OAS budget; and its staff of five professional and four clerical employees, while competent, is far too small to perform its duties effectively. Acceptance of the special sum of $102,000 for the IACHR from the United States is useful in legitimizing an irregular form of support, but this sum is insufficient, and its continuance is not assured.

If the United States wishes to promote human rights over the next decade, it must work to improve the capacity of the Commission, both to make available more, and more intelligible, information and to help the United States to justify preferential policies in economic and other assistance by reliance on judgments of this authoritative, international body.

In this connection, it should be noted that the Commission is nearly entirely dependent for its information on complaints, and that well over half of its annual report for 1975 consists of technical accounts of negotiations over cases that are difficult to penetrate and baffling to follow in detail. The Commission has not found it possible, largely because of the press of immediate business and the lack of staff, to prepare reports assessing individual governments' records of observance of human rights over a period of years. Comparative judgments are completely lacking.

The Department of State does plan to discuss with the representatives of member states the idea that the IACHR might make routine visits to each of them, including the United States. The Commission could then issue regular, informed reports on all the countries. However, if these efforts should fail because of Latin American opposition, and if the Department of State intends to give to human rights an important place in foreign policy, it must be prepared to use other evidence as the basis for its decisions.

In this regard, the initial success and eventual demise of the Inter-American Peace Committee (IAPC) may be instructive, in a melancholy way. One of the main achievements of the Charter of Bogotá was to centralize the whole process of settlement of disputes in the OAS. A key element in the new system was the ability of the IAPC to proceed immediately, at the Permanent Council's request, to the scene of hostilities without previous consent of the parties to the dispute. This vital ability had not been expressly conferred on the Committee, but the Committee had acted, with the consent of the Council, on its own interpretation of the Treaty of Rio de Janeiro of 1947. After several successful settlements of disputes between 1946 and 1955, however, certain Latin American governments decided that the Committee's powers were too great. They determined that after 1956 it could make such visits only at the request of both combatants. If the restrictive purposes of the Chilean draft resolutions concerning the IACHR are adopted by the OAS, a comparable restraint will be placed on a second enterprising organ of the OAS, and the value to the United States of the IACHR, and of the OAS as a whole, will be seriously attenuated.

To sum up, the policy of the United States at present creates several issues for various Latin American governments:

- How to respond to assessments by the Department of State about each state's human rights performance;

- How to react to the termination or suspension of economic or security assistance or both by the United States;

- What type of policy, presumably collective, should be adopted in response to United States attempts to inject human rights considerations into decisions of the IDB, and, possibly, the World Bank;

- What sort of measures should be taken to respond to the expressed intent of the United States to expand the resources and functions of the IACHR.

Different countries will of course evaluate these issues in different ways. Nor can the policies of any one country be expected to be consistent. The same Mexican government that refused to attend the OAS General Assembly in Santiago in order to protest the excesses of the Pinochet regime voted in the same month for the IDB loan to Chile. The Venezuelan director of the IDB voted with Mexico on the Chilean loan several months after the Venezuelan Senate had passed a resolution condemning the tyrannical regime in Uruguay as being not only illegal in its origins but opposed to the great democratic traditions of the Uruguayan nation.

MORALITY AND FOREIGN POLICY

Governments of the Third World exhibit greater concern about the satisfaction of their peoples' human needs—food, housing, health care, education—than about protection of their citizens' basic human rights. The wealthier countries, out of sympathy, religious principles, and a desire to engender development that might permanently improve local capabilities to achieve a higher standard of living, have since World War II contributed food, capital, and technology. But while economic and technical aid intended to help governments provide for human needs is usually welcomed as buttressing official objectives of which the donor approves, any move to promote observance of basic human rights is generally perceived as an effort to interfere in domestic affairs and thus resented. The political opposition in a country may be emboldened by a relaxation of oppression; but it may be weakened by the success of programs of agricultural assistance with which the local government is associated.

193

It may be useful to distinguish between the morality of generosity and the morality of outrage. The first is expressed in developmental assistance and disaster relief, which may nevertheless be tinged with self-interest in the long run, for underlying it is the hope that revolutionary movements can be avoided by co-optation. The second—outrage at governmental cruelty to individuals—seeks, largely through deprivations, to persuade a pantherish regime to change its spots.

The morality of outrage has a strong tendency toward absolutism, and its adherents demand consistency in policy as a matter of principle. Illustrative of their attitude is the remark that "there is no such thing as a little permissible torture." The ultimate rationale of this view is that automatic, identical penalties should be applied to comparable violations of basic human rights.

This view, respectable in itself, is not one that can be fully adopted in foreign policy, simply because the promotion of human rights must compete variously at different times with other objectives, such as the defense of the nation or of its economic viability. The Carter administration has indicated that despite its concern about human rights violations in South Korea and the Philippines, the strategic importance of those countries to the United States justifies the continuance of economic and military assistance.

One of the inevitable accompaniments of applying moral principles to foreign policy is the albatross of inconsistency. It is possible to consistently denounce inhumanity in other countries as long as no names are mentioned. However, if some regions but not others are penalized, consistency becomes nearly impossible to maintain. The difficulty is not that consistency itself is virtuous, but that inconsistency shreds the moral fiber of the principles a state has proclaimed. In Latin America, however, the United States can be evenhanded in denouncing Brazil as well as Cuba, and, indeed, any Latin American country for its disrespect of human rights, since no other fundamental United States interests are at stake. Inconsistency would become an issue only if Argentina should claim that it should not be excluded from arms aid because its practices were no worse than those of Guatemala, for example. Allied to the issue of inconsistency is the charge that the United States is hypocritical in arrogating to itself the lofty tone of preaching against other nations' ways of life when it is still some way from being a shining example of the practice of its own moral principles. The defense, if there is one, is that although individual cases of outrages by police may from time to time occur, the United States does not practice or condone violations of basic human rights as a matter of governmental policy.

Latin Americans have varying views about the purposes of President Carter's pronouncements on human rights and his evident determination to employ economic and military aid as a means of pressure on Latin American regimes. One view is that the President is practicing clever politics for home consumption. Latin American diplomats are presumably familiar with a recent Harris poll that found that "a thumping majority" of the United States public believed that the United States was less respected abroad than it was a decade ago, due principally to Watergate, the Vietnam War, our interference in the internal affairs of other countries, and our lack of compassion for humanitarian aims.

A second view is that President Carter may well be sincerely distressed at the suffering of people living under repressive rule abroad, and that, even though United States aid may be temporarily stopped, some evidence even of innocuous changes in policy on human rights may be sufficient to satisfy him and to start aid flowing again.

A third view, however, is that Carter and the Congress, particularly now that they appear to see eye-to-eye, are really launching a political offensive aimed at unseating Latin American military regimes, and not simply intended to persuade them to use gentler techniques for suppressing political dissidents.

Finally, as one official in Washington has put it: "The Latins are naturally perplexed by the human rights furor, after they have done for years exactly what they thought the United States wanted them to do." What was the purpose of cooperation in training on tactics and strategy of counterinsurgency if not to contain Communist infiltration and local uprisings? The magnitude of covert activities by the CIA against the Cuban and Chilean regimes in recent years is sufficiently well documented so that it should not be strange that Latin American political leaders find it puzzling to be assailed in the United States Congress for dealing effectively with what they had been led to believe was the common enemy. It is even possible to detect a feeling of incomprehension among representatives of the Chilean government, who have a hard time understanding why they should be criticized for having brought an end, in whatever fashion, to the first Marxist government to be elected to office in the Americas. Implicit in this attitude is the opinion that the political left, at least as represented by terrorist groups, is as responsible as the military governments for violations of human rights and, further, that if it is not destroyed it might come to power and be no less inhumane than are present regimes.[28]

President Carter has said to the Soviet Union that while he will continue to speak out on human rights in that country, he has no intention of using any stronger measures of persuasion. He has not made a comparable public statement to Latin American regimes. A clarification of his plans, at least in broad outline, would settle some issues for Latin Americans and perhaps would create new ones, but it would at least commence a dialogue between Washington and those Latin American governments that have rejected future arms aid on the ground that criticism of their human rights performance is an inadmissible attempt to interfere in their domestic affairs. On this platform, if on no other, they have hoisted banners of sovereignty of the same color as those flown by the Soviet Union. They utterly reject President Carter's view that a government's disrespect for human rights is a proper matter for international concern.

Their defiance of United States policy raises the question whether measures such as denial of aid might be counterproductive. While effective retaliation seems unlikely, at least three possibilities call for our attention. The first is that heavy pressure from the United States might actually cause the plight of victims of repression to deteriorate as governments tried to show they could not be bullied. The second is that such pressure might recruit new and unexpected support for military regimes. It is reported, for example, that the legal opposition party in Brazil has publicly declared its support of the defense of national sovereignty expressed by President Ernesto Geisel's rejection of further arms aid and denunciation of the arms agreement with Washington. The third possibility is that severe condemnation by the United States might accentuate the centrifugal forces already operating in the Americas, causing the OAS to lose some of its members or even to be dismantled.

The resentment of Latin American countries might be mitigated and their responses might improve in practice if the policy of the United States were expressed in firm but quiet tones, without publicity. It is possible that the Congress might not insist on punitive legislation or on publicity for the Department of State's assessments if it were assured that private admonitions and unpublicized pressures were being used and—more important—were likely to be effective.

Finally, the potential influence of positive measures—such as reducing but not prohibiting aid to offending governments while augmenting it to those who modified their policies in directions approved in Washington—might be explored. A less heavy-handed and possibly more effective policy than termination of aid might be a flexible policy of discrimination in favor of countries respecting human rights.

THREE

Latin American Issues: The Outlook

At present, the most important issue facing the Latin American regimes that are least respectful of human rights is that of the extent to which the United States will employ its power to dissuade them from their present courses. They can safely assume that the United States will not intervene militarily and that they can get along without its arms aid, but some of the economic measures mentioned above might disrupt their countries' development programs. Such a slowdown however, would probably not in itself promote fundamental change. A possible (but very unlikely) exception may be Chile, where the continuance of rigid repression suggests that the government is seriously concerned about threats to stability; where inflation and unemployment continue high; and where evidence of foreign pressures might offer encouragement to opponents of the "hard line," both within and without the government.

In the coming decade the military-dominated corporative governments of the Southern Cone will probably be able to maintain themselves, and the less repressive military governments in Ecuador and Peru will probably be able to continue their own, somewhat different, courses, with the state assuming growing control over economic and social affairs. In Guatemala and Nicaragua the regimes hardly seem likely to lose quickly their well-established reputations for brutality. In contrast, Colombia, Costa Rica, Mexico, and Venezuela will continue to set the highest standards among Latin American governments in observance of human rights. Cuba, as a special case, can be expected to continue to keep substantial numbers of political prisoners for long terms in conditions regarded as censurable by the IACHR.

Since the authoritarian regimes have demonstrated formidable competence by the firmness of their political control and their own internal unity, and since they have been able to exile thousands of former political leaders and terrorize and muzzle the remainder, it is likely that they will be capable of surviving any ordinary economic and political vicissitudes. Only crises of unusual severity, such as an economic depression comparable to that of the 1930s or disastrous international conflicts, might cause them to lose their dominating positions.

Brazil's adoption of a leadership role enhances the likelihood that current regimes will remain in power. Once described by a British diplomat in the 1940s as "a kind of sheepdog of the United States," Brazil is emerging as its own herdsman, at least for the smaller countries on its southern periphery—Bolivia, Paraguay, and Uruguay. Brazil helps train their police, invests in their economies—heavily in Paraguay—influences their internal politics, and may confidently be expected to assist their highly compatible regimes to stay in office. It would be no less concerned about the installation of a "subversive" regime in Paraguay than was the United States about a "radical" change in the government of the Dominican Republic in 1965.

With respect to human rights, the military regimes will continue to employ their extreme repressive measures to maintain political stability and enhance rapid economic growth, in accordance with their established doctrines.[29] However, there will be fewer violations of human rights, even if not less severe ones. There will also be fewer murders of exiles, such as that of Orlando Letelier in Washington, and more political prisoners freed if only because of the passage of time. Occasional, well-planned violence may replace large-scale atrocities as a method of intimidation. "How can one, in the formulation of the Chinese proverb, 'kill just one and frighten ten thousand others'? One mode is to cow by a combination of ferocity and capriciousness."[30] This proverb seems to have had an echo in Brazil.

More sophisticated and less easily traceable techniques of repression may also be developed. In Chile, for example, ways have reportedly been found for quietly arresting persons, sending them to secret places of confinement, and denying any knowledge of sequestration. It is thought some have been sent to Argentina, exemplifying a high degree of cooperation among police forces.[31]

"Our countries are being occupied by our own armies," one civilian Latin American leader has said, and, short of economic disaster or defeat in war, it is those armies that will ultimately make decisions about human rights and about the timing and manner of return to systems of party politics, which some of them profess to envisage. They are powerful; they possess an elaborate justification for their retention of control; and, at least in Brazil, they have forged an alliance with technological and industrial elites which has given them a civilian base. However, they do not have an ideology that evokes widespread popular support; in Brazil, at least, the government is trying to compensate for this lacuna by intensifying nationalistic sentiment. Defiance of pressures exerted by the United States may further their efforts to excite patriotic zeal.

Still, the sparks of peoples' desires for liberty and equality can never be wholly extinguished, and new generations of students and political leaders will continue to make demands for more open societies. Over the years, the military regimes may find it possible to relinquish control to civilians, perhaps to a one-party system, if they are assured of their own security as an institution and of the perpetuation of certain of the basic principles to which they adhere. If so, the new administrations may not scent "subversion"[32] in every protest against economic conditions or in every attempt to gain a greater share in decision making and may not meet expressions of desire for greater equality with savage measures of suppression.

The examples of Colombia, Mexico, and Venezuela may be influential in this connection, as may be the constant, moderating presence of the church. The United States, especially if it can discover useful ways of working together with these three countries and other like-minded American governments (such as those of Jamaica and Costa Rica), may also be helpful. Finally, strengthening the capabilities of the IACHR is a prerequisite for any attempt to bring international sources of persuasion to bear on the protection of basic human rights in America.

NOTES

1. Inter-American Commission on Human Rights, *Annual Report, 1975* (Washington, D.C.: General Secretariat, Organization of American States, 1976)

2. Riordan Roett, ed., *Brazil in the Seventies* (Washington, D.C.: American Enterprise Institute for Public Policy Research, 1976), p. 6.

3. Alfred Stepan, ed., *Authoritarian Brazil: Origins, Policies and Future* (New Haven: Yale University Press, 1973), p. 59.

4. *The Amnesty International Report, 1 June 1975–31 May 1976* (London: Amnesty International Publications, 1976), p. 83.

5. Details on methods of repression may be found, e.g., in *Report on Allegations of Torture in Brazil* (London: Amnesty International Publications, 1976), and *Human Rights in Uruguay and Paraguay*, hearings before the Subcommittee on International Organizations of the Committee on International Relations, House of Representatives, June 17, July 27 and 28, and August 4, 1976 (Washington, D.C.: U.S.G.P.O., 1976).

6. OAS, General Assembly, 6th Session, Santiago, Chile, Minutes of the 1st Committee, June 15, 1976, OEA/Ser.P.AG/Com. I, pp. 3–4.

7. Alfred Stepan, *The Military in Politics: Changing Patterns in Brazil* (Princeton, N.J.: Princeton University Press, 1971), pp. 179, 180.

8. *New York Times*, November 19, 1976.

9. " 'New Dialogue' on Latin America: The Cost of Policy Neglect," in Ronald G. Hellman and H. Jon Rosenbaum, eds., *Latin America: The Search for a New International Role* (New York: Halsted Press, 1975), p. 166. Similarly, see Joseph Comblin, "The National Security Doctrine," in Jean Louis Weil, Joseph Comblin, and Judge Senese, *The Repressive State: The Brazilian 'National Security Doctrine' and Latin America* (Toronto: Brazilian Studies, 1976), pp. 36–65.

10. *Annual Report*, 1973, pp. 32–45, 45–74.

11. See Willard F. Barber and C. Neale Ronning, *Internal Security and Military Power: Counterinsurgency and Civic Action in Latin America* (Columbus: Ohio State University Press, 1966).

12. Stepan, *The Military in Politics*, p. 5; Thomas E. Skidmore, "Brazil's Changing Role in the International System: Implications for U.S. Policy," in Roett, *Brazil in the Seventies*, pp. 20, 21.

13. Richard Gott, *Rural Guerillas in Latin America* (Harmondsworth, England: Penguin Books, 1973), p. 542. On courses and sites of training, see *Human Rights in Nicaragua, Guatemala, and El Salvador: Implications for U.S. Policy*, hearings before the Subcommittee on International Organizations of the Committee on International Relations, House of Representatives, June 8 and 9, 1976 (Washington, D.C.: U.S.G.P.O., 1976), pp. 231 ff., and 222 ff.

14. Untitled document quoted in dispatch by Jonathan Kandell, *New York Times*, November 20, 1976.

15. Statement by Wilson Ferreira-Aldunate, in *Human Rights in Uruguay and Paraguay*, p. 6.

16. "Report of the Commission of Enquiry into Human Rights in Paraguay of the International League for Human Rights, July 6–15, 1976," by Ben Stephansky and Robert J. Alexander, in ibid., p. 177.

17. Testimony by Wilson Ferreira-Aldunate, in ibid., p. 21.

18. Jonathan Kandell, *New York Times*, January 2, 1977.

19. IACHR, "Second Report on the Situation of Human Rights in Chile," approved March 12, 1976, p. 119.

20. Statement by Robert E. White, in minutes of the First Committee, June 16, 1976.

21. Speech to the National Press Club, Washington, D.C., Sept. 15, 1976, mimeo (Washington, D.C.: General Secretariat, Organization of American States).

22. Voting for: Barbados, Costa Rica, Dominican Republic, Ecuador, Grenada, Haiti, Jamaica, Mexico, Panama, Peru, Surinam, Trinidad and Tobago, United States, Venezuela.
     Abstaining: Argentina, Brazil, Chile, Colombia, El Salvador, Guatemala, Paraguay, Uruguay.
     Absent: Bolivia, Honduras, Nicaragua.

23. Text in, e.g., *Chile: The Status of Human Rights and Its Relationship to U.S. Economic Assistance Programs*, hearings before the Subcommittee on International Organizations of the Committee on International Relations, House of Representatives, April 29 and May 5, 1976, p. 106 ff. This is, in part, the text of Sec. 116 of the Foreign Assistance Act of 1961, as amended by Sec. 310 of the International Development and Food Assistance Act of 1975.

24. Lewis H. Diuguid, *Washington Post*, July 9, 1976.

25. It may be noted, incidentally, that there is little likelihood that any Latin American state could effectively retaliate against a cessation of United States

aid. No Latin American state is an exclusive supplier of any raw material of importance to United States. Moreover, no Latin American state holds hostage important United States naval or air bases. The Panama Canal is not at Panama's mercy, nor is it likely that Cuba will make any attempt to forcibly expel the United States from Guantanamo Bay. Thus, a United States administration would not feel it necessary to accept compromises on human rights performance in Latin America for reasons of national security, as has been the case, by contrast, with regard to the Philippines, owing largely to the important naval facilities at Subic Bay.

26. *Washington Post*, July 9, 1976.

27. Quoted in the *New York Times,* December 12, 1976.

28. See the dispatch by Juan de Onis, *New York Times*, March 13, 1977.

29. For interesting discussions relevant to these doctrines, see Gunnar Myrdal, *The Challenge of Third World Poverty* (New York: Pantheon, 1970), p. 54, who argues that "greater equality in underdeveloped countries is almost a condition for more rapid growth"; Hollis Chenery et al., *Redistribution with Growth* (New York: Oxford University Press, 1974), where Tanzania, Sri Lanka, South Korea, and Taiwan are offered as examples of countries in which improvements in distribution of wealth have been accompanied by rapid growth, mainly through education, land reform, and other types of equity-oriented public investment; and Irma Adelman and Cynthia Taft Morris, *Economic Growth and Social Equity in Developing Countries* (Stanford, Calif.: Stanford University Press, 1973), who point out that in most countries inequality of distribution of the national income has increased as a result of international aid programs since 1945.

30. See the chilling, clinical dissection of this topic in Nathan Leites and Charles Wold, Jr., *Rebellion and Authority: An Analytic Essay on Insurgent Conflicts* (Santa Monica, Calif.: Rand Corporation, 1970), p. 99.

31. Tom Wicker, *New York Times*, March 20, 1977.

32. See the remark attributed to Gen. Hermán Bejares of the Chilean junta, who described a reported proposal for "democratic recuperation" in Chile, recently made by two leading Christian Democrats, as a move that would be "called subversion in any country," *New York Times*, March 13, 1977.

Responding to Severe Violations

Richard Falk

Introduction

Any serious violation of human rights represents some debasement of political process, as well as a deprivation for those whose rights are abridged. When violation of human rights becomes part of a systematic pattern of governance, it undermines the prospect of humane relations between government and citizenry. At present, in a large number of states the systematic and deliberate violation of human rights is an integral part of the governing process. Indicative of this disturbing feature of the modern world is the 1977 Amnesty International annual report, which concludes that serious human rights violations appear to be occurring in at least 116 countries.[1]

There are many reasons to be skeptical about how much can be done to improve this lamentable situation. Violations of human rights generally arise from the way a government treats individuals and groups within its territory. Territorial sovereignty is the basic characteristic of international relations, has become even more so in recent years as a result of decolonialization, and is likely to remain so through the 1980s. Almost every state is jealous of its sovereign rights and places the highest premium on the protection of its polity against various forms of encroachment. Generally, political leaders also recognize that their own claim to sovereign rights depends on respecting comparable rights of other states. Even the most powerful states are exceedingly touchy about any outside pressures that can be construed as "interventionary." The sanctity of state sovereignty is one of the most insistent demands of strong, as well as of weak states. At the same time, the reality of interventionary statecraft is associated with the impositions of the strong upon the weak. In the present period of international history virtually all governments, however weak and dependent they may be, want to appear as sovereign as possible, and thereby make a rallying cry of norms of nonintervention. The priority accorded the nonintervention concept as the basic juridical guideline of international behavior is also expressed by the extreme reluctance of most governments to endorse intervention in foreign societies, even if under international or regional auspices or in response to what is generally condemned as an extreme abuse of human rights. Governments seem wary that the sword used against others today could be turned against them tomorrow. Hence, there is reluctance about any undertaking that could be generalized beyond a particular situation and turned into a precedent. In this regard, anti-apartheid intervention gathers widespread support because the situation in South Africa seems sui generis, whereas anti-Amin intervention is impossible to organize because it would create a precedent perceived as dangerous.

Underneath support for the nonintervention norm is a generalized anxiety that creating exceptions for humanitarian purposes will open up additional possibilities for the strong to impose their will on the weak.[2] John Vincent, perhaps the most authoritative modern interpreter of interventionary practice, can discover only the French intervention in Syria in 1860 to save Christian Maronite tribes from abuse by Moslem Druses as an instance of pure humanitarianism.[3] The record of statecraft is the story of self-interested uses of power, and this makes it especially problematic to lend approval to any generalized right of intervention, regardless of alleged motives. Aside from states that are neighbors and may have a common interest in a given situation, the impulse to intervene is largely associated with the most powerful states active in a particular period of international history. But the motives and interests of these states make them least trustworthy as custodians of international morality.[4]

Also, within international society there is no consistently authoritative way to determine the existence of human rights

208

abuses. Regional organizations often function more like alliances than community organizations; aside from the European setting, regional actors are very deferential to sovereign rights except in cases of a regional pariah—e.g., Cuba versus the Organization of American States (OAS), Israel versus the Arab League, South Africa versus the Organization of African Unity (OAU). It is difficult, therefore, to maintain that judgment at the regional level of when humanitarian intervention is appropriate is likely to be more objective than the judgment made by the governments of the largest states.

The United Nations is a body more representative of principal international tendencies, and hence has never singled out Cuba, in the manner of the OAS, as an appropriate target of community pressure because of its adherence to Marxism-Leninism. Nevertheless, the UN can be an intensely partisan arena in which a fair consideration of the realities is unlikely to occur. For this reason the political organs of the UN are increasingly regarded as more likely to reflect arbitrary crosscurrents of international politics than to provide an arena for their transcendence.

The severity of an abuse of human rights is not enough to generate a serious effort to do something about it. For instance, although criticism may be directed in a variety of directions, no real consideration is ever given to organizing coercive responses to human rights violations occurring in large states. Also, in the case of smaller states that are closely aligned with a large one, a prudent forbearance dissipates serious attention at the global level to their human rights violations.

For these reasons, nongovernmental organizations (NGOs) in the human rights area have played an increasingly important role recently in identifying and documenting human rights violations. However, these organizations can operate only to the extent that they are tolerated by territorial sovereigns. Furthermore, they are dependent on private funding, the character of which may introduce elements of bias. The liberal democracies provide the main base of operations for NGOs in the human rights area: government policy in these countries can make it more or less likely that such organizations can operate independently and successfully. One of the solid gains of President Jimmy Carter's stress on human rights is to raise the stature of these NGOs and to encourage government officials to support their activities in countless ways through informal cooperation.

In addition, the legal situation pertaining to human rights, although it is evolving rapidly, remains ambiguous. The generalized norms of international law as set forth in the main legal instruments on human rights are either "declaratory" in stature (as is the case with the Universal Declaration), nonbinding because not widely enough ratified (as is the case with two international covenants covering the gamut of human rights), or simply discounted because they are perceived as "soft" law.[5]

Part of the difficulty, here, is a product of an overgeneralized debate on human rights. Especially in the United States there has been a cycle of high hopes and disillusionment. In idealistic statements by Woodrow Wilson, Franklin Roosevelt, John F. Kennedy, and most recently by Jimmy Carter in the early months of his Presidency, there have been periodic ardent endorsements of human rights as the foundation of world peace. At such times, the norms of human rights are proclaimed as universal, applicable to friend and foe alike. Conservatives tend to regard this posture as pompous and foolish. They regard them as self-righteous lectures to others about matters that are essentially the domestic concern of each state; and they believe that such a stance is bad foreign policy to the extent that it weakens bonds that hold geopolitical allies together in a world of conflict. The split in world politics between communist and anticommunist societies accentuates the domestic debate as to whether the promotion of human rights should be based on universal standards or should focus on the shortcomings of the other side.

At the bottom of this debate are different conceptions of human nature and international society. Those who believe in the universal promotion of human rights are generally optimistic about eliminating aggressive behavior through reform and believe that in time a harmonious human community can, will, and must emerge; they also tend to believe that democratically and humanely governed political systems are more stable, and that therefore it is practical to encourage allies, as well as adversaries, to uphold human rights. Those who are skeptical of universalism believe that conflict is endemic in the world and that it is best to look after one's own interests without entertaining the illusion that the world can be made into a more humane place; they tend to believe that human rights and democratic procedures are ill suited for poorer countries and non-Western cultures, and that it is a mistake to insist upon universal standards of application.

The dynamics of the state system seem to lend greater support to the more skeptical position on human rights. Governments rarely shape their foreign policy according to moral considerations. As has often been argued, perhaps most influentially by Machiavelli in *The Prince,* a statesman's main task is to advance the security and interests of his own polity. To expend resources or endanger friendships for the sake of reforming a foreign society or the world as a whole is, in this view, dangerous and sentimental. It is dangerous because it can be provocative, and it is sentimental because it ignores the wellspring of statecraft. All the norms and indignation in the world are powerless against a determined government with the repressive apparatus required to control its own population. And the upsurge of partisanship and propagandizing on human rights issues in the UN, often the work of spokespeople for some of the more reprehensible regimes, does nothing to discount this skeptical assessment.

Yet there is a healthy refusal on the part of many to accept this kind of cynical realism as definitive. Despite the larger context of constraint, some possibilities exist to cope with human rights violations. The modern consciousness of global interdependence makes it virtually impossible to seek humane goals for one's own society while ignoring the extreme sufferings of others. For the sake of our own self-esteem and dignity, a concern for human rights is one element in the recognition of the unity of the human race. This sense of unity is being formed, slowly and indistinctly, in part as a by-product of the space age, which has allowed us to see the planet as a whole. This sense of wholeness carries with it the implication that political boundaries are artificial, that if we care about hungry people in Appalachia and the South Bronx, we also will care about them in the Sahel or Calcutta.

Also, so-called realists often overstate their case by under-estimating idealistic elements in human experience. The existence of widely supported legal norms can have mobilizing effects in the domestic arenas that are the scene of violation. This seems to have been the case with Soviet dissenters who frequently ground their actions in an appeal to international human rights instruments that have been endorsed by their own government. Some violations of human rights may be curtailed by making foreign political leaders believe that without reform other serious interests of their state will suffer; these modifications may turn out to be more "cosmetic" than "structural," but, even if this is the case, particular individuals may be freed, torture may be eliminated or reduced, and the degree of repression may be diminished.

Finally, there are certain situations in which a global consensus can be achieved. In the present period, the campaign against official racism in South Africa is the best illustration. Whether sincere or not, all major governments have joined in denouncing the racist features of South Africa. The common cause against apartheid is premised on the importance of eliminating severe abuses of human rights. It is partly a moral reaction to the indecency of extreme and official racism. But it is also in part pragmatic, representing a concern that unless something is done on behalf of the victims, a race war is likely to ensue that would present unacceptable choices, especially for the white industrial governments of the West.

What "doing something" involves is a subject of intense debate. The moderate position is to induce the ruling elites to make a series of voluntary reforms; the more radical position is to insist that a new elite representing the victims achieves power, by armed struggle if necessary. The tactical controversy is due in part to a discrepancy in assumptions about change that occurs in societal relations. This issue will be considered later.

The main thesis of this essay is that the state system imposes drastic limits on what can be done at the international level to improve respect for human rights, but with an awareness of these limits in mind it is still possible to imagine some useful international responses to severe violations. It should be understood that severe violations usually express either pathological or structural realities, and are, therefore, particularly resistant to outside pressures that appeal to the rationality or good will of the violator.[6] This type of pressure does not enter in the cost-benefit calculus of the government violating rights except in the tactical sense that a target regime will deal with the pressures in such a way as to minimize their impact. Thus those who seek change must necessarily employ *coercive* strategies. Somehow, the regime violating human rights must be toppled or its leaders induced to make fundamental changes. This can be done either through domestic struggle, outside intervention, or a mixture of the two. Coercion can be applied internationally through psychological and diplomatic pressure, economic sanctions, embargoes on exports, boycotts on imports, and the resort to military force.

Before considering the narrow circumstances under which it is possible to respond effectively to severe violations of human rights by coercive means, it seems important to consider the types of severe violations of human rights that it would be desirable to do something about and the kinds of governments or leaders that engage in these violations.

ONE

Types of Severe Violations

We are assuming that a government and its officials are normally responsible for violations of human rights that occur within their borders. Usually this connection is an active one, that is, they either engage in the objectionable behavior as a matter of policy, rely on state resources and personnel, or deputize others to act on their behalf. Occasionally, the connection may be more passive, for example when certain individuals are not protected from destructive and unjust forms of private or semiprivate action. It is also conceivable that the situation giving rise to concern is beyond the control of the territorial sovereign, as when certain terrorist groups operate in weak states, when civil strife leads to the commission of atrocities, or when corruption brings about severe abuse of rights. The Lebanese Civil War of 1976–1977 illustrates several dimensions of the assault upon human values that can result from the breakdown of domestic order.

Defining a pattern of behavior as a severe human rights violation depends on several interrelated standards of appraisal. First, and foremost, are self-evident convictions about right and wrong. These require neither proof nor assent to be authoritative. For example, whether or not there is a prohibitive norm, the practice of torture or genocide seems "criminal" to the ordinary person. In effect, we affirm a natural law position. That is, certain patterns of behavior are forbidden and subject to corrective action whether or not a government sanctions prohibitive norms and independent of condemnation by the organized international community. Therefore, although the norms of international law are indicative of the standards of natural law, they are neither exhaustive nor are they all essential. That is, international treaties and customs incorporate most standards of behavior implicit in natural law, but their bindingness rests more on the fundamental foundation of international morality than on formal consent and codification. In recent years, despite its shortcomings as a politicized arena, the General Assembly of the UN has helped articulate this human rights core of international relations.

Second, we can identify offenses as severe by their incompatibility with widely endorsed standards of behavior. The endorsement can be formalized in binding international treaties or inferred from informal agreements. For instance, widespread assent to a nonbinding resolution of the UN General Assembly can be relied upon as evidence of what is regarded as forbidden behavior in the human rights field. There are two elements operative: the *consent* of particular governments and widespread *agreement* within the international community on the content of minimum human rights.

Third, we can assess offenses as severe by reference to the amount of harm and pain that they inflict. A situation can very persuasively be judged as severe when large numbers of people are harmed. It makes a difference in evaluating the Indo-Pakistan War or in assessing Idi Amin's rule in Uganda whether there were many victims or just a few. Although each victim's circumstance deserves concern and protection, there is a quantitative threshold that places domestic activities into the international arena for the protection of human rights. There is no way to supply numbers that establish these thresholds. Each situation needs to be assessed in context to determine whether the number of victims qualifies the offense as severe. Given, for instance, the small numbers of Aché Indians living in Paraguay, it seems plausible to regard them as victims of genocide even if the number of verified killings is small.[7]

Fourth, the continuing character of the violations is also important. If the objectionable behavior has ended, then the humanitarian impulse and the case for intervention is gravely weakened. A punitive mission would remain possible, but given the

216

difficulty of doing anything effective about ongoing abuses in the first place, it would seem foolish to concentrate on such a cause. Of course, if the harm done was of especially grave character or the government was expected to renew its violations, then it might make sense to take action.

According to these standards of appraisal, the following categories of human rights offenses seem severe:

Type A: Genocide

Type B: Official racism

Type C: Large-scale official terrorism

Type D: Totalitarian governance

Type E: Deliberate refusal to satisfy basic human needs

Type F: Ecocide

Type G: War crimes

The 1980s will probably witness governments that commit violations in each of these categories. Because of the prevailing influence of nonintervention logic and in the absence of effective supranational capabilities, most of these violations will be impossible to do anything about—beyond improving the capacity to take notice. Only exceptional violations will provoke significant response. Before considering the possibilities for response, it seems useful to describe each type of human rights offense.

TYPE A: GENOCIDE

The intentional killing, mutilation, or humiliation of a distinct ethnic group within a society is an extreme and self-evident abuse of human rights. Hitler's infamous "final solution" for Jews (and other disfavored groups) constitutes a paradigm for "severity" in the violation of human rights. After World War II, this assessment was given a formal legal character in the Nuremberg Judgment, the Nuremberg Principles endorsed by the UN General Assembly, and the Genocide Convention of 1950.

217

Despite the moral and legal status of genocide, it is often difficult to generate international concern unless victims have a powerful transnational constituency. For instance, considerable evidence of genocidal killing of tribal adversaries (Tutsis and Hutu) as a matter of official policy in both Rwanda (1964) and Burundi (1972) was treated with virtual indifference by governments and institutions in international society. Still greater neglect, extending to the media, was accorded the substantial allegations of genocidal behavior on the part of the Indian government in the course of its counterinsurgency war against the Naga and Mizo peoples in the period 1956–1964. In recent years, a series of large-scale genocidal campaigns has been waged against tribal populations in Africa and Latin America. Some individuals have tried to report on these instances of genocide, but it has been difficult to mobilize effective response because of the unwillingness of governments to become involved. In certain situations, adverse publicity discourages genocide to some extent. Often, genocidal policies are motivated by a mixture of economic and ethnic motives, and do not necessarily reflect a formal policy of the government to commit genocide per se; genocide, in such a situation, is an unintended by-product, but one for which there is responsibility, as it is the natural consequence of policies deliberately pursued. For instance, the destruction of American Indian peoples throughout the Western Hemisphere is most centrally associated with seizing land or devoting it to more profitable uses.[8] Such activity, since it is now marginal to the development of the dominant society, has some prospect of being inhibited by publicity and a private campaign of censure designed to discredit the regime in world public opinion. These issues, despite their seriousness for the people involved, rarely engage the formal attention of foreign governments or the organized international community. The former tend to be disinterested because of the absence of any specific national interest, whereas the latter is deterred by nonintervention considerations and by the absence of any outside state or group of states that is deeply engaged on behalf of the victims.

Uganda and Pakistan stand as partial exceptions. The pursuit of genocidal policies via widespread killings directed at minority tribes in Uganda has been coupled with inflammatory instances of terror directed at Christian leaders and Westerners.[9] Amin has also taunted Western sensibilities in a variety of respects, adding a posture of defiance to the abuse of rights and giving the objectionable domestic behavior an international character. These elements in addition to genocide have generated relatively serious international concern, although it is centered in Great Britain and the United States.

The brutal repression of Bengali nationalism in 1971 by the West Pakistani Army possessed a genocidal character. Unarmed civilians with any leadership potential were systematically killed and as many as 1 million deaths (some estimates run as high as 3 million) resulted. Another 10 million Bengalis fled across the border to India. Numerous horrifying crimes against humanity were reported and authenticated.[10] This chain of events did provoke military intervention by India. It was an effective operation, leading to the birth of the separate sovereign state of Bangladesh in what had been formerly East Pakistan, under the initial leadership of Sheik Mujibur Rahman, whose popular movement for regional autonomy had brought on the initial repression. India's motives for intervening were undoubtedly a complex mixture of geopolitical opportunism and humanitarian concern.

Some national situations exhibit genocidal features, for example, in Equatorial Guinea or Cambodia, but are better treated as instances of large-scale terror because the ethnic identity of the victims is not the essence of the crime. Also, official policies often erode the cultural identity of a people and thereby inflict "genocidal damage" without actually threatening individuals with physical death.[11] A typical example is the Canadian intention to build a pipeline along the Mackenzie Valley that would disrupt the traditional tribal lands of the Dene Indians.[12] These deprivations of human rights can cause irreversible damage for the group in question and should be considered "severe" if the internationally recognized territorial government does not establish its own procedures for protection. At the same time, given the problems associated with humanitarian intervention on behalf of such victims, it is inconceivable that anything more coercive than fact-finding and criticism would be undertaken by outside governments or intergovernmental groups. Nongovernmental organizations may go further and propose a variety of economic measures, especially a privately enforced boycott on exports, although normally NGOs' ability to mobilize coercive responses is very limited.

TYPE B: OFFICIAL RACISM

When a government endorses racial discrimination by official laws and practices, it flagrantly violates widely accepted norms of racial equality. The salience of such patterns of racism will depend on how extreme the discriminatory policies are, as well as on the degree of humiliation associated with belonging to the subordinated race(s). It will also depend significantly on the degree to which outsiders identify with the fate of the victims, and their ability to do something about it.

Apartheid in South Africa is currently the prime instance of official racism, which is perceived as a severe challenge to human rights.[13] In South Africa racism is buttressed by brutal repression directed against even moderate opponents of the present situation. From the massacre of unarmed demonstrators at Sharpville in 1960 to the apparent muder of Steven Biko in 1977 by prison officials, there exists a chain of unmistakable evidence that the South African government and its officials will stop at nothing to prevent any challenge of the racist structure of the state.

The apartheid context is distinctive because it combines a series of elements. Black political leaders in surrounding countries identify directly with the victims of apartheid. Also, the economic, social, and cultural stratification of South Africa is both a precursor and a legacy of the colonial period. The retention of a white-dominated bastion of power and wealth on the African continent has further antagonized black African governments and the Third World generally. The United States, with its own domestic struggle to move from slavery to racial equity, and the Soviet Union, with a clear anticolonial, anti-Western line on African issues, are united in opposing apartheid. A virtually universal consensus has formed in opposition to apartheid, but, as we shall discuss later, there is still much disagreement on what to do about it. The consensus has been reinforced by a steady stream of actions in the UN and other international forums, especially those organized by Third World countries. The Convention on the Elimination of Racial Discrimination, drafted in 1965, embodies this minimum consensus on opposition to apartheid in a widely endorsed legal form.

It is fair to wonder whether or not this consensus is opportunistic, making South Africa, in effect, a scapegoat. Is it fair to single out South Africa when racial discrimination has been rampant in other societies in the world? For instance, Asians in East Africa, especially in Uganda, have been deprived of their wealth and livelihood after generations of residency and in some cases have been forced to emigrate. Victims of genocide, as in Burundi or East Pakistan, have received very little attention from outsiders even though their fate has been worse than the victims of apartheid.

Such arguments are valid, and yet largely irrelevant from a descriptive and normative point of view. First, objective observers agree that apartheid involves a deprivation of basic rights and dignities that qualifies as a severe offense. But second, the racism associated with apartheid is not a minor and trivial case of racism. In sum, the classification of a human rights violation as severe appropriately draws on political factors, including perceptions, priorities, and the willingness to act. For these reasons apartheid deserves to be treated as a continuing, severe violation of human rights; and the fact that it mobilizes and unites the international community creates a greater opportunity to act. That is, while the emphasis on apartheid may be arbitrary in relation to other forms of racism, it helps establish a situation where it might be possible to do something.

TYPE C: LARGE-SCALE, OFFICIAL TERRORISM

When a government systematically engages in terror to maintain its political control or intimidate its opposition, it can be defined as large-scale official terrorism. It differs from genocide in that

221

it is a means of directly exerting authority rather than a campaign of persecution directed against ethnically distinct elements. Of course, as in Hitler's Germany or Amin's Uganda, there may be a generalized terrorist style of rule that complements official genocide.

Official terror can take many forms. Its essential character has to do with killing, maiming, and torturing members of the society without due process of law. It may be carried out by elements of the state apparatus—e.g., the National Security Information and Security Organization in Iran, known as the SAVAK, the Korean Central Intelligence Agency (KCIA) in South Korea— or by para-governmental "death squads"—e.g., in Argentina during the period of General Videla's rule. Official terror may also occur in the brutal repression of peaceful labor and student activity or other citizen demonstrations—e.g., Thailand in 1975.

The scale and persistence of official terror are significant. A regime that relies on continual terror places itself in a special subcategory of aggravated offender. For instance, Amin in Uganda, Masie Nguema Biyogo in Equatorial Guinea, or Somoza in Nicaragua rely on persistent terror as an ongoing feature of their regime. In certain crisis situations, a government may resort temporarily to large-scale terror, as Cambodia did in 1975 when it resettled its urban population in the countryside. The events in Cambodia remain obscure and controversial, although in recent months the scale and scope of terror seem to have diminished, if not altogether disappeared. In contrast, Stalin's regime became cumulatively more and more terroristic. Sometimes official terror is associated with a regime in which a single individual dominates the government for an indefinite period of time. However, the generals who have run Brazil since 1964 have relied on the periodic use of terror whenever such tactics seemed relevant to the maintenance of their political authority.

Private terror directed against the civilian population is also a severe violation if its perpetration can be reasonably attributed to a political entity, such as a government or liberation movement. If the conduct occurs in a situation of war, then it also belongs to type G: large-scale war crimes, which will be discussed later. Certainly several of the Palestinian liberation factions and their leaders are guilty of terrorism against civilians. Governments that support terroristic activities—by granting asylum and lending support to perpetrators—join in the violation as accessories. Qadhafi in Libya has played such a role in the mid-1970s, especially in relation to Palestinian terrorism.

Another type of accessory is a state that grants terrorist organizations a base of operations. This may occur in a strong state eager to cause trouble elsewhere; the auspices and encouragement given to anti-Castro operations of the Cuban exiles by the United States during the 1960s illustrate this pattern. It may also occur in a state too weak to assert full sovereign control over its territory, as has arguably been the case in Jordan and Lebanon in relation to the Palestine Liberation Organization (PLO) at various stages of the Arab-Israeli conflict. The point here is that governmental encouragement or inability to exercise control may produce a de facto situation of large-scale official terrorism that would qualify as a severe violation of human rights.

This category of severe offenses also includes governmental policies that support various domestic groups. The evidence suggests that elements within the Argentinian government have encouraged right-wing ultras to pursue "leftists" by terroristic means, including kidnapping and murder, with the assurance that such acts will be ignored by the police. If the pattern is widespread, and in Argentina hundreds of deaths and disappearances appear to have resulted from such means, the large-scale official terror can be said to occur even though it is not directly committed by government operatives.

TYPE D: TOTALITARIAN GOVERNANCE

The special feature of totalitarian rule is the comprehensiveness of governmental interference in the full range of civil, political, and cultural rights. Totalitarian rule does not have to extend to large-scale terrorism or genocide, as it did in Hitler's Germany and Stalin's Russia. It may involve merely an efficient bureaucratic apparatus that rigidly constrains freedoms of thought and action, the sort of polity so vividly portrayed in George Orwell's *1984*.

Totalitarian governance can mean centralization of authority that does not necessarily imply a dictator. With modernization comes the expansion of the state role. In the process most governments become more efficient and almost automatically acquire a totalitarian potential, that is, the means and rationale to stifle dissent and opposition. If pressures from below on consensual and moderate government continue to grow, as the outbursts of terrorism seem to suggest, then we can expect many currently democratic polities to become vulnerable to what Jean-François Revel has recently described as "the totalitarian temptation."[14]

Some Eastern European countries (e.g., Albania, Bulgaria, and East Germany) appear to be administered in a totalitarian fashion. Whether it is appropriate to characterize the Soviet Union as totalitarian in the Brezhnev era is a matter of controversy among experts. Surely it has totalitarian features, including the bureaucratic insistence on regulating virtually all features of society, on refusing to open channels for dissent, and on employing extra-legal forms of mistreatment against political prisoners. However, moderating trends are visible, including less harsh repressive tactics and greater toleration of grass roots autonomy in civic and regional affairs.

In a totalitarian state the pattern of rule is difficult to transform from within or without, especially if the regime can solve the succession problem. As post-Franco Spain and post-Fascist Portugal suggest, it is sometimes possible to end patterns of highly authoritarian rule rather bloodlessly, but the bureaucratic apparatus of repression never fully penetrated several major domains of activity within the Spanish and Portuguese societies. Also, it must be admitted that the threat of a recurrence of repressive rule has not been fully removed, especially in Portugal.

TYPE E: DELIBERATE REFUSAL TO SATISFY BASIC HUMAN NEEDS

Unlike types A through D, the deliberate refusal to satisfy minimum human needs is a category of human rights offense that is not yet generally accepted or fully understood as a violation.

To contend that individuals are entitled, as a matter of human rights, to have their basic human needs satisfied is tantamount to insisting that governments—and the international community—are legally and morally compelled to perform, at least to a minimum degree, as a "welfare state."

An obligation like this is nowhere spelled out. However, the constituent rights are endorsed in the Universal Declaration, and further specified in the International Covenant on Economic, Social, and Cultural Rights. In Article 23(1) of the Universal Declaration, for instance, "the right to work" is affirmed, and Article 25(1) details "the right to a standard of living adequate for the health and well-being of himself and of his family, including food, clothing, housing, medical care and necessary social services, and the right to security in the event of unemployment, sickness, disability, widowhood, old age or other lack of livelihood in circumstances beyond his control." Article 24 even affirms "the right to rest and leisure."[15] Whether or not they are embodied in a formally binding legal instrument, it seems correct as a matter of customary international law and of international morality to regard such prescriptions as emergent authoritative norms.[16]

The satisfaction of basic human needs is beginning to be seen as a realizable goal. It is possible to view the agitation around the new international economic order as a movement to assure that individual governments are provided with the capabilities to satisfy the basic needs of their citizens. The emphasis of the World Bank and other international aid and lending efforts in recent years has been upon policies designed to help the poorer countries and the poorest strata in these countries. Furthermore, on practical and moral grounds, leaders of rich countries have acknowledged the obligation to work toward the rapid elimination of world poverty. Recent research strongly suggests that most Third World countries possess the resources to eliminate poverty and satisfy basic human needs if their policy makers were so inclined.[17]

To speak of basic needs as human rights refers to the minimum requirements for sustaining physical life, that is, health, food, housing, clothing, work, literacy. Broader conceptions of basic needs are often affirmed, but I think it would be difficult to ascribe authoritative status to them as "rights."[18] These minimum requirements of physical and social well-being can be regarded as "rights" at this stage, and the deliberate failure of a government to satisfy these minima, especially when it is in a position to do so, is a severe violation. Such patterns of violation are widespread, and can be discerned in a preliminary way by the disparities between gross national product (GNP) and the innovative Overseas Development Council's Physical Quality of Life Index (PQLI). The PQLI is based on calculating relative achievement in life expectancy, infant mortality, and literacy.[19] Johan Galtung and others have described official policies that lead to mass misery and short life expectancy as "structural violence" to accentuate the severe character of the governmental practices.[20]

In effect, then, a government that maintains an economic situation in which a small proportion of the population gains most of the wealth while a large majority subsists at or below the poverty line is guilty of violating this category of human rights. Furthermore, as governments are increasingly expected to meet the basic needs of their citizens, there is a tendency to demand results in militant terms. To neutralize such demands and also mobilize the society for growth-oriented development can lead governments to employ repressive techniques.[21] On the other side, meeting basic human needs may also lead a government to rely on terrorism to achieve its goals. A revolutionary elite may feel it must engage in large-scale terror to achieve the transition to a needs-oriented society. In the early years of Mao's rule in China, for instance, many dispossessed landlords, merchants, and privileged elements from the prior social order were killed.[22]

The deprivation of basic human needs can be used to achieve explicit political ends, such as the denial of food in settling an ethnic conflict. Characteristically, the central government may deprive an ethnically distinct antagonistic component of its population of food so as to starve it into submission, as has been alleged in several African interethnic conflicts—the Ibos in Nigeria and the Somalis and Eritreans in Ethiopia. If this deprivation results in the decimation of the target group, it amounts to genocide. Given the prevalence of ethnic conflict, it is important in the context of human rights to become more attentive to those national situations where a government deliberately deprives an ethnic group of basic needs in order to impose its will.

Although it is possible to identify a basic human needs violation by reference to "waste" or a highly disproportionate income distribution, there is no consensus yet on the proper economic and social policies for a given society to adopt. Some commentators have argued that only socialism can meet mass needs in a nonindustrialized country that is experiencing rapid population growth.[23] Others have endorsed capitalist approaches based on order, growth, and a corporative state to assure the well-being of all societal sectors. It should also be appreciated that Hitler's Germany and Mussolini's Italy did well by needs criteria as compared to their more moderate predecessors—e.g., standard of living of workers improved in both countries.[24] At this time, the choice of *means* to achieve basic needs is a matter of national discretion, as long as the policies do not violate other standards of human rights.

TYPE F: ECOCIDE

The protection of the environment is understood increasingly to be vital for human well-being, if not survival. The Stockholm Conference of 1972 on the Human Environment formulated a Declaration of Principles that was endorsed with some modification by the UN General Assembly. The protective principles of this Declaration are an emergent area of international law, mainly perceived at this time as a series of declaratory duties imposed on governments. Human dependence on environmental quality is becoming so evident that it seems assured that it will begin to be treated as a dimension of human rights in the 1980s.

Suppose a government carries on atmospheric tests of nuclear devices despite the evidence that harm results to foreign societies, or continues to permit use of aerosol sprays despite indication of global ozone depletion, or licenses unseaworthy tankers, or orbits unspaceworthy satellites, or disposes of toxic

227

wastes in the oceans? These "offenses" are not traditionally dealt with in human rights instruments, but they involve official conduct that seriously endangers the life, health, and serenity of current and future generations. The notion of human rights is incomplete to the extent that it fails to encompass those forms of deliberate behavior that produce serious environmental damage.

This set of concerns is not an exotic or marginal category. In an increasingly interdependent global setting where elaborate technology is used and where even higher levels of industrialization are contemplated, environmental quality is a critical dimension of human dignity that may have a significant impact on development, and even survival, of mankind. At minimum, this reality should be acknowledged in the strongest possible normative terms.

TYPE G: WAR CRIMES

As with Type F, it is not yet usual to consider war crimes as a violation of human rights.[25] However, it is an artificial exclusion. Michael Walzer in his recent comprehensive book on war crimes grounds his concern with justice in wartime on a human rights argument.[26] The obligation of states to refrain from aggression and abhorrent practices in war arises from the concept of the sanctity of innocent life. Rules against causing unnecessary suffering and cruel tactics and weapons are based on a human rights rationale that regards even combatants as protected persons under certain conditions.

This last rationale can be most vividly observed, perhaps, in relation to legal, moral, and political efforts to safeguard prisoners of war. The reality of this concern was dramatically expressed on behalf of the several hundred American pilots held captive by North Vietnam during the Vietnam War. The treatment of these prisoners became a major issue of domestic politics and influenced the peace negotiations.[27]

A government that initiates war for aggressive purposes, that subjects a civilian population to inhumane treatment, and that wages war without regard for legal norms is guilty of severe violations of human rights. "Aggression" is difficult to define objectively, as are the facts surrounding war policies. The notion of "military necessity," as well as the behavior of other belligerents, may also complicate the task of assessing whether a severe pattern of violation has occurred.

In the background is the status of modern strategic doctrine, particularly as associated with nuclear deterrence. The deterrent posture is based on a threat to inflict indiscriminate devastation on enemy populations, with deaths numbering in the tens of millions in the event of general nuclear war. It also implies causing collateral damage through radioactive fallout on the peoples and environments of nonbelligerent third countries. In the 1980s the question may well be posed as to whether or not governments that base their national security on threats to use nuclear weapons violate fundamental human rights.

TWO

What Can Be Done about Severe Violations?

Because an intervenor may not be trustworthy, because the effects of intervention may be damaging to the people of the target society, and because interventionary precedents once set are likely to be extended to more dubious instances, it is plain that interventionary approaches to human rights violations, however severe, should be recommended with extreme caution. This caution is reinforced by the structure and history of international relations. In addition to these concerns about the *wisdom* of intervention are the problems connected with its *feasibility*. However severe the violation of human rights there is no reason on that basis alone to expect responsive action at the international level. The fundamental limits of action are set by the realization that it would normally require a significant mobilization of capabilities to intervene effectively from outside, that successful intervention would often require military means and include the establishment of new governments, and that geopolitical interests often insulate the violator from pressure. In effect, there are three sets of inhibitions:

- Insufficient motivation to devote the resources required for successful intervention
- Unwillingness to protect human rights through coercive intervention in internal affairs
- Mixed geopolitical interests that preclude the formation of an enforcement consensus

231

In addition, intervention is a problematic remedy. If it is nonmilitary, for example in the form of sanctions, then it generally seems ineffectual. If it takes military forms, then it amounts to a virtual declaration of war against the target state. Even unpopular regimes can mobilize against outside intervention, and hence the costs of intervention may be large and its effects may be indefinite. For this reason, interventionary response confined to the territory of the human rights violator seems implausible no matter how severe the outrage. If there is an active domestic resistance to the violator, or if the government is very small and within the sphere of influence of a large state, then a humanitarian intervention may occasionally occur. An example of the latter is the official American impulse to encourage, or at least acquiesce, in plans for the assassination of General Trujillo, the leader of the Dominican Republic from 1930 to 1961.[28]

RESPONSES TO GENOCIDE, RACISM, TERRORISM, AND TOTALITARIANISM

Several considerations always bear on the possibility of doing something about a severe pattern of human rights violation:

- *Prudence*. Does the response seriously endanger more valued policy goals including world peace, the integrity of alliance relations, and the protection of foreign economic interests?

- *Motivation*. Does some important government(s) favor taking coercive action designed to put pressure on the violative regime? If so, that usually presupposes either a strong domestic constituency that identifies directly with the victims or strong geopolitical grounds for eliminating the regime and its leaders.

- *Leverage*. Is the target polity relatively weak, small, and especially vulnerable to nonmilitary coercive measures (e.g., boycotts, embargoes directed at particular products, discontinuance of outside aid)?

- *Mandate*. Do the coercive measures have the support and authorization of the world community as a whole as well as the backing of most governments in the region? Have the facts of the case been verified by independent and objective sources, especially by respected NGOs in the human rights field? Has the target regime any significant transnational support?

- *Legitimacy.* Do the claims advanced have the backing of widely accepted norms of international law and morality? Has a reasonable effort been made over a sufficient period of time to induce compliance by persuasive means?

To cross the above hurdles is very difficult. Indeed, it is difficult to identify a real world situation in which these various conditions have been generally satisfied. Only in conjunction with other elements can one imagine that severe violations of humans will be removed by international action:

- *Independent provocation.* Has the violator also infringed vital interests of foreign states by seizing territory, withholding critical raw materials, confiscating foreign investments, repudiating debts, interfering with international navigation?
- *Alien victims.* Do the persons harmed owe allegiance or have juristic and emotional ties with powerful outside states (e.g., execution or torture of foreign nationals)?

In these special sets of circumstances the basis for coercive action may exist even if the conditions set forth above are not entirely satisfied. At best, the parallel rationale of human rights violations helps shape the cover story, although it does not account for the real interventionary motivation. The struggle against Nazism and Fascism during World War II was mainly geopolitical in character, and only incidentally did the Allied victory result in ending patterns of severe violations of human rights on the part of the defeated countries. Although it is true that as the extent of Nazi crimes became known in the course of the war, the human rights motivation seemed to grow more integral to the war effort as well as help to shape postwar arrangements. The nuclear dimension of post-1945 world politics greatly reinforces prudence in foreign policy and makes it even

233

more difficult to organize coercive action to overcome human rights deprivations.

Nevertheless, even in the current international setting, there are several situations of severe deprivation in which international interventionary responses are relevant. To illustrate the approach, consider in schematic form the impulses and the inhibitions toward intervention in the Ugandan (Amin) and South African (apartheid) cases.

The Ugandan Case

The challenge: genocidal elimination of specific tribal elements from positions of influence and a more generalized reign of terror associated with the regime of Idi Amin Dada.

The following is an assessment of whether conditions exist to support coercive measures, and if so, at what level of coerciveness:

- *Prudence.* There is no reason to suppose that coercive measures to topple the Amin regime would endanger world peace, although they might raise East-West and North-South tensions if the intervention were an American military initiative or otherwise predominantly conceived, staffed, and supported by NATO countries. There might, in other words, be geopolitical costs of short duration. Less coercive measures, such as a boycott on Uganda's coffee crop, although of smaller magnitude, might have a similar impact.

  If there is no reasonable vision of how intervention will improve the overall situation in Uganda, it may be imprudent to intervene. Suppose intervention were likely to unleash a civil war or result in Amin being replaced by a military leader who embarked on a new campaign of large-scale terror. Prudence involves having reasonable assurance that a positive precedent will emerge, both in relation to the form of intervention and its effect on the target society.

- *Motivation.* The United States and Western European governments seem shocked and outraged by Amin's actions, which in part is a response to the anti-white, anti-Christian, and anti-foreign animus of his regime. Some African governments have been critical, and Tanzania and Kenya have given varying degrees of support to anti-Amin plots. By and large, the Soviet and Arab blocs have maintained normal and friendly relations with Amin, including providing some economic and military assistance.

- *Leverage.* Uganda is a relatively small and weak country, but it has a considerable army with modern equipment for an African country of its size. It is shaky and allegedly vulnerable to boycotts, especially by purchasers of its coffee crop, a principal source of export earnings. Some have speculated that even a unilateral boycott by the United States, currently buying one-third of Uganda's export crop, might exert significant pressure.[29]

- *Mandate.* There is no reasonable prospect for an explicit authorization of coercive measures by either the OAU or the UN. Offsetting this, however, is abundant, uncontradicted verification by human rights NGOs and respected individuals of the large-scale descent into barbarism that has occurred during the period of Amin's rule and is likely to continue.

- *Legitimacy.* The documentation that provides the mandate also establishes a persistent pattern of transgressions in relation to the most basic and universal norms of international law and morality. There is also a long record of attempts to moderate Amin's policies through negotiation and persuasion.

- *Resistance.* It is difficult to assess the degree of organized resistance to Amin's regime. Several coup attempts have failed since his assumption of power, and there seems to be firm evidence of widespread latent opposition. But there is also considerable intimidation on the part of Amin's regime. It seems necessary to conclude that there is no significant resistance movement currently operating. Although opposition in the military sector could possibly succeed with a coup, without the support of popular resistance it can be argued that no significant intervention is possible. Paradoxically, if there were significant popular resistance, a coup would not be necessary. This situation suggests that there must be evidence of a viable alternative to the present regime before outside intervention can accomplish its goals.

- *Performance*. With respect to development goals, Uganda's progress under Amin has been poor—whether development is measured in conventional terms or by reference to satisfying the basic needs of the population as a whole. There are also reports of widespread corruption, stagnation, and a deteriorating international credit situation, although these elements would not distinguish Uganda from a large number of other Third World countries.

It seems evident that some of the conditions for international action are satisfied, but not all, and that no decisive inhibitions on coercive measures are present. Therefore, the Uganda challenge falls into a gray area where no significant action against Amin is likely to occur without some developments independent of the barbarism present now. That is, intervention would be more likely if Uganda gets involved in large-scale warfare with neighboring countries, especially if it can be plausibly cast in the "aggressor" role, or if Amin unleashes terror directed at the several hundred aliens still residing in Uganda, or if he lends support to terrorism in foreign societies.

Any one of these aggravating developments would probably increase the pressure within the United States and Europe to adopt coercive measures directed at Amin's regime. If the OAU response supported or acquiesced to military measures, effective action might be forthcoming. The stark reality, however, is that as long as Amin remains at peace with other African states, succeeds in terrorizing Ugandan opposition, and leaves the bulk of foreign residents as a whole more or less alone, he is reasonably secure against outside intervention. To be sure, some symbolic acts of disapproval, such as his exclusion from the Commonwealth meeting in 1977, are likely to occur, but these are probably of little consequence for the endurance or character of his rule.

The South African Case

The challenge: systematic, official racism administered in brutal fashion by a government of the minority white race, involving economic, social, cultural, and political discrimination carried out in a harsh and humiliating manner. The severity of the racism entails the commission of other violations: genocide, terrorism, and totalitarian rule.

Do conditions exist to support coercive measures, and if so, what kind of coerciveness?

- *Prudence.* There is no reason to suppose that coercive measures would provoke a wider war, although there is every reason to expect South Africa's modern military and paramilitary forces to put up a ferocious fight. Given the advanced weaponry at South Africa's disposal and the sequestration of the African population in easily contained urban townships, a direct interventionary effort to topple the white regime would produce a major war and a great loss of life. There is also the possibility of conflict spilling over into neighboring countries. If armed intervention proceeded with wide backing, this would be a major step in cooperative human rights enforcement, although its execution might produce sharp competition among participants over shaping the orientation of the black successor regime. As time passes, the conditions for coercive measures may ripen, but the reluctance to intervene will increase if it is believed that South Africa possesses even a small arsenal of nuclear weapons. South Africa is a major supplier of uranium, and it might withhold this critical nuclear fuel from states that join in mounting a coercive movement.[30] However, South Africa, despite a large stockpile of emergency reserves, is relatively vulnerable to an oil embargo. The uncertainty of the effects of intervention in this case are also inhibiting; it is often claimed that the main victims of outside intervention would be the supposed beneficiaries—namely, the black majority. Also, insufficient coercion might result in intensifying repression or unleashing a prolonged period of civil strife and chaos.

- *Motivation.* The African countries are united in their hatred of apartheid, although several regional governments carry on normal trade relations with South Africa because their geographical position and extreme poverty creates the practical necessity or because of opportunism. Third World countries, in general, dislike the South African system because it appears to be a white legacy of the colonial era, and an alien presence within the Third World. The Soviet bloc and China dislike apartheid and its accompanying political and economic system because it is so avidly anti-Communist and closely linked to the United States and the United Kingdom in economic and strategic terms. It is a sober truth that apartheid has no supporters in international society, although South Africa has managed to work out some cooperative relations with other pariah states and commercial relations with some societies.

- *Leverage.* South Africa is strong, prosperous, efficient, and generally stable. Aside from oil it is virtually self-sufficient, and it is planning to replace oil with nuclear energy and coal as quickly and completely as possible. South Africa is likely to remain militarily far stronger than its African neighbors, even if the neighbors should combine forces. A credible military threat would either require superpower backing or be based on a greatly augmented internal liberation movement. South Africa's prosperity could probably be curtailed by economic sanctions, but not its viability as a state. Only a direct large-scale military intervention could produce the external leverage needed to overthrow the regime.

- *Mandate.* The mandate to use pressure against South Africa has been expanding steadily over the past 30 years and it is now a strong consensus in favor of censure, which is gradually intensifying in support of an enforcement effort. South Africa's pariah status has preoccupied organs of the UN for many years, culminating in 1977 with a Security Council decision to impose a boycott on arms sales and deliveries to South Africa. The United States and United Kingdom, with their extensive holdings and ties to the present regime, refuse as of 1978 to go farther. But if recent years are any indication, the pressure of Third World opinion will induce even the Americans and British to heighten their antiapartheid posture, although this course of action will also heavily depend on American and British politics. The strength of the mandate, together with the frustrations associated with mounting a coercive response, has led to an emphasis on such symbolic actions as a sports boycott.

The consensus against South Africa is also reinforced by a series of reports by such respected human rights NGOs as Amnesty International and the International Commission of Jurists.[31]

- *Legitimacy*. The intensity and unanimity of the mandate has led the formal organs of the UN to move toward suspension of sovereign rights of the present government in South Africa and to deny it the benefit of the nonintervention norm. In effect, the constraint of the domestic jurisdiction article of the UN Charter has been substantially cast aside by characterizing apartheid as a threat to international peace and security, thus opening the way to the application of sanctions and enforcement measures.

The underlying condemnation of South Africa's racist official policies seems fully justified. The abuses arising from them have been documented and clearly contravene basic prohibitions in international law and morality. An overwhelming consensus of governments and public attitudes supports this view. In addition, many years of negotiation and persuasion have failed to induce South African leaders to abandon or even modify apartheid.

- *Resistance*. Sporadic resistance from the black population has occurred for decades. With the advent of Afrikaaner rule the severity of repression has increased, but in recent years grassroots urban resistance has been rapidly evolving more and more into a movement. Predictably, this domestic challenge has led to a tightening of repressive mechanisms of control and intimidation by the government, which, in turn, escalates the international movement against apartheid. The student uprisings of 1976 and 1977 in Soweto and other black townships led to many excesses in the use of police power, as well as to the arrest, detention, and prison murder of a principal leader, Steve Biko, and a general crackdown on even moderate forms of opposition. The resistance movement seems likely to increase in the course of the next decade, although not without suffering setbacks.

Undoubtedly resistance prospects will be significantly affected by the postures of the front-line government policies and leaders, including especially those that emerge in the next few years in Namibia and Zimbabwe, as well as by the policies toward South Africa that prevail in London, Washington, Moscow, and Peking. In essence, the resistance movement will be influenced by the extent of material and psychic support given to liberation activities and by the degree of success that liberation groups have in building a unified movement that receives support within South Africa.

- *Performance*. South Africa's government has experienced a prosperous period of national development and has generally succeeded in running an efficient, stable state. There is no sign of diminished competence in these respects, but economic performance is down and not expected to recover altogether. In any event, the performance record of the government, however impressive, will not dissipate the political forces arrayed against the apartheid system.

The picture that emerges in the South African case is that despite the strong mandate there is no proximate prospect of a strong nonmilitary antiapartheid campaign without some further developments. These include another dramatic escalatory turn in the resistance/repression cycle of the past three years, the further buildup of an internal liberation movement, and a deepened commitment by critical front-line and Western governments for effective action.

If these developments occur and are not offset by other changes—a prolonged recession, preoccupation with strategic issues, rightward drift in American and British politics, or South African nuclear weaponry—then one can imagine the gradual strengthening of the international sanctions program. This program has been conceptualized in considerable detail, yet stops far short of proposing military measures.[32] Stimulating resistance activities may be sufficient to demoralize segments of the white population. Such a shift in the overall political climate might produce deepening splits in the ruling elite and create an accommodationist faction.

The South African case, like the Ugandan, suggests the limits of what can be done even in the rare situation where all the principal global actors agree on the need to transform an intolerable situation. A determined elite with a firm grip on the governing process can usually exert effective control over the organization of social, political, and cultural life within national boundaries. It is sometimes possible to organize collective security arrangements to deter aggression across boundaries or endorse a geopolitical intervention in internal affairs, but it is far more difficult to mount interventionary operations that have the capabilities and the will required for a humanitarian mission designed to reshape the governing process of a foreign society. International boundaries remain high walls that will be rarely scaled for predominantly human rights objectives.

One general effect, attributable to the strength of the mandate against South Africa, is a tendency for Third World countries to link the overall credibility of Western complaints about human rights to what is done on the South African front. That is, the hue and cry about Amin's barbarism will be viewed as "racist" if it is not coupled with an equivalently credible hue and cry from the same quarters about Pretoria's barbarism. This Third World attitude impedes the development of the mandate in most non-South African contexts and raises the stakes for the West in moving seriously against South Africa.

A NOTE ON BASIC HUMAN NEEDS

Unlike other dimensions of human rights, the official cluster of obligations that characterize basic human needs imposes affirmative duties on governments. Very few societies, including many of the most prosperous, are organized in such a manner as to discharge these duties satisfactorily. Disagreements persist as to what adjustments would be required in a particular society, because vital economic issues relating to capital accumulation and income distribution are at stake. These matters have been traditionally considered to fall completely within the insulated realm of domestic jurisdiction. However, four sets of developments increasingly have "internationalized" this subject:

- Persistent and worsening poverty despite unprecedented rates of national, regional, and global economic growth.

241

- Greater emphasis on the responsibility of governments and international economic institutions to provide for basic human needs.

- An intergovernmental consensus supported by academic validation of claims that the international economy is biased against the Third World, which has produced demands for a new international economic order.

- Increased preference on the part of international lending institutions for development projects directed at satisfying basic human needs.

All governments affirm their commitment to the abolition of poverty as a matter of national policy, just as all governments deny the perpetration of any severe domestic violations of human rights. With basic human needs, however, there are no adequate procedures available to brand a particular government as a violator, although a persuasive consensus can often be obtained by media coverage, NGO reporting, and the activities of governments and international institutions.

Nevertheless, effective responses are possible. The first is an increased emphasis on development assistance programs that are oriented to the satisfaction of human needs in recipient countries. This kind of targeted assistance can be objectionable, however, if it assumes a paternalistic, interventionary, or ideological character that attempts to usurp domestic judgments on development priorities.

The second is international economic restructuring that emphasizes equity. However, a fairer division of global wealth and income among countries does not assure fairer allocations within countries.

The two responses raise complex questions of economic and political feasibility. Some development specialists have suggested that a rechanneling of overseas development assistance and modest increases in aid over a 15–25 year period could do the job if some domestic reforms occurred. Alternatively, others propose that domestic transfers from the upper 10 percent to the bottom 40 percent of 2 percent of annual income would generate sufficient purchasing power among the poor to end poverty.[33]

Such estimates suggest that the task of eliminating poverty is easily manageable in resource terms even without using some of the more than $300 billion or so of the annual expenditures that go for military purposes.

Other approaches have emphasized the feasibility and desirability of needs-oriented development strategies that give a developing society the capability of self-sufficiency in meeting its basic needs over time as well as at a given time.[34] Whether ruling elites in either North or South can be induced to move in these directions seems doubtful for a variety of reasons that cannot be dealt with here.[35] Also, to assess the basic needs challenge in terms of resources is misleading: a variety of bureaucratic and societal rigidities would make it unlikely that a decision to transfer and reallocate resources to eliminate poverty would work efficiently. The United States and other advanced industrial societies have witnessed "trickle-up" phenomena whenever assaults on poverty have been attempted without also transforming underlying societal structures. The point is that unlike the coercive responses associated with other severe deprivations of human rights, persuasive tactics can play a major role in the basic needs context.

A NOTE ON ENVIRONMENTAL HARM AND ECOCIDE

Activities in this category remain in limbo. The grounds for concerted action seem clearest where the causation is clear. If country X impairs health, destroys life, or harms the environment in countries Y and Z, or more widely, in a region, the oceans, or the globe as a whole, then it is obviously at fault. If evidence mounts that cancer arises from increased radiation and a particular government engages in radiation-producing activities, then this is "ecological aggression." If the victims are geographically dispersed far beyond the territory of the country producing the pollutant, then the more traditional premises for recourse to force are present. The appeal to humanitarian impulses can be buttressed in this case by more elemental considerations of self-preservation.

However, no current situation is of sufficient magnitude to allege ecocidal behavior comparable to the severe violations of human rights that have occurred in Uganda or South Africa. The most comparable "case" may be the Chinese nuclear tests, which pose radiation hazards for inhabitants and animals in the Northern Hemisphere. If further medical evidence of harm is established and more Chinese testing takes place, then an international campaign is likely to be mounted, and consideration will be given to the use of coercive measures.

Environmentalists and NGOs can build a greater understanding of environmental rights as a key sector of human rights and generate pressures to translate this understanding into a revised Universal Declaration of Human Rights and a new Covenant on Environmental and Ecological Rights. Such efforts could also focus on specific dangers, such as reactors on space satellites, and seek prohibitions based on the global interest in environmentally sound and sustainable patterns of behavior. At the current stage, fact-finding efforts could make a major contribution. As many individuals now suspect, we may be grossly underestimating the environmental risks and harm associated with various technological innovations.

A NOTE ON WAR CRIMES

This category is also seemingly exotic in the context of human rights. As with ecocide, there is useful work to be done by individuals and NGOs. This includes the articulation of norms, through treaties and international legal customs, that endow the law of war with dimensions that are grounded in the rights of peoples, governments, institutions, and corporations. Especially important in this regard are procedural initiatives and commissions of inquiry that are secure from governmental interference.[36] By and large, governments are too directly implicated to provide effective leadership in this domain.

CONCLUSIONS

On the basis of this discussion some general conclusions can be drawn:

1. The general inability to deal with severe violations of human rights is one of the principal weaknesses of the prevailing system of world order.

2. This weakness is structurally linked to the distribution of power and autonomy among sovereign states and cannot be overcome without the emergence of a new system of world order.[37]

3. However, this structural constraint exhibits considerable variance. It depends on the character of the violator, on how the target regime's survival meshes with geopolitical patterns, and on the orientation of the governments proposing a coercive response to a given human rights challenge.

4. The prevailing world order has a high tolerance for severe violations of human rights, especially if the harmful effects are confined within territorial limits.

5. The prevailing world order, even when significant political actors are aroused by infringements, has a weak potential for effective action against the target polity.

6. Effective international mobilization against a violator usually occurs for reasons largely independent of the denial of human rights.

7. Effective internal mobilization, if it occurs, depends largely on the indigenous will and capabilities of opposition forces, perhaps encouraged and marginally reinforced by international support.

8. The organs of the UN, in the event of a substantial consensus, can contribute to the mobilizing process. But they are limited by geopolitical rivalry and partisanship, and as a consequence, the UN response to severe violations has been mainly symbolic and highly selective.

9. Partly to offset UN weaknesses, human rights and environmental NGOs, as well as a variety of private groups and even individuals can play useful roles, especially by establishing when violations have occurred, mobilizing public opinion, and exerting informal influence.

THREE

Future Prospects
and Speculations

Each severe violation is distinctive, setting its particular constraints on external pressures and suggesting special points of leverage. This quality of distinctiveness, evident in our comparison of the Ugandan and South African cases, makes it seem of dubious value to speculate about the future in more general and systemic terms. However, some trends seem likely to affect the structural dynamics of the state system in ways relevant to human rights.

The "hard state" hypothesis. The "hard state" hypothesis refers to a further buildup of government powers that insulate the state from outside pressures and enable it to maintain internal order in situations of rising internal pressure. Southern demographic growth, together with frustration about the possibilities of achieving domestic or international goals of equity in the distribution of wealth and income, will induce more generalized patterns of severe repression and the neglect of people living at or below subsistence levels. Anomie, together with disintegration of economic growth, will lead to severe stress and the possible decay of democratic polities (the ungovernability hypothesis) in the liberal societies of the industrial North. An era of extreme statism will ensue with no serious will or capability to overcome human rights violations as most governments will feel implicated or preoccupied and thus may restrict NGOs and individuals concerned about human rights.

In such a future there will be an even greater tolerance of

human rights violations than exists in the late 1970s and less of a capacity to respond. The stability of this system will depend on whether it is able to prevent war, economic depression, and ecological breakdown. Such a hard state system has been emerging over the past decade and is likely to establish its preeminence still further in the early 1980s.

The "moderated system" hypothesis. This system depends on a reduction of tensions along both the East-West and North-South axes of conflict, with moderation and liberalization prevailing in the domestic arenas of the most significant states. This process could be reinforced by an increasing permeability of the state to measures that assure the achievement of minimum standards of individual economic, social, and political well-being—a drift, in effect, toward an international welfare state. Such moderation is difficult to envision without several concurrent developments: movement toward a new international economic order; an abatement of the strategic arms race; a loosening of security alliances; successful large-scale international cooperation on issues such as oceans, money, and emergency food reserves; the reduction of unemployment and inflation to "acceptable" levels and the elimination of terrorism in the advanced industrial countries; the spread of needs-oriented development approaches in the Third World; increasing acknowledgment and practice of democratic rights in leading Communist countries; and the rapid growth of feelings of human solidarity as a dimension of increasing interdependence. The mere enumeration of preconditions suggests that this optimistic projection for the 1980s is unlikely to take shape.

However, in the happy event that the improbable should occur, then a more favorable climate for responding to severe violations of human rights would be present; indeed, the more cooperative premises of such a world order evolution would make severe violations less likely to occur. Those that arise would probably not be insulated by superpower rivalries, which we presuppose to be muted in this hypothesis. Thus, it may be easier to shape a consensus and mobilize the international community for appropriate norm-oriented action. In this climate it seems reasonable to assign greater legitimacy, leverage, and capabilities to the UN system. Perhaps a UN policy force could be established that might, under very carefully restricted circumstances, carry out human rights missions. Such a force could, for example, rescue hostages, safeguard tribal minorities, or release unjustly confined prisoners. In addition, human rights NGOs would probably flourish in a wider range of countries. They might be accorded more significant tasks in relation to fact-finding, mediation, and even implementation procedures, and provided with fiscal security and independence.

If the number of governments relying on repressive rule were to decline, then those that engaged in depraved behavior would be easier to isolate. In other words, although an international system with such moderate features could not guarantee the protection of human rights in every instance, it would probably respond more rapidly and effectively to the sorts of challenges posed currently by the Amin regime in Uganda and apartheid in South Africa. Whether it could also deal in an effective manner with severe violations in countries such as Iran and Indonesia is more problematic.

Furthermore, the spread of equity within and among states would provide positive examples of how to cope with modern socioeconomic pressures in a humane way. In a moderated atmosphere where humanistic concerns were more successfully protected, repressive regimes would feel more isolated than they do in the current global setting and would be more inclined to avoid depending so blatantly on cruel repressive tactics.

Also, the shifts in international influences would be important—superpowers and other principal states would generally accept the dynamics of national self-determination and not seek to impose antidemocratic political solutions that promote their geopolitical interests. And aid and capital flows would be contingent on the minimum requirement that the recipient government refrain from any severe violation of human rights.

Regimes with governing styles as deviant as those of Uganda or South Africa are probably not susceptible to major reform despite major changes in the global setting. Even in this highly optimistic projection, the state would remain the dominant organizing entity in international life throughout the 1980s, and thus it would be difficult to change significantly the policy of a medium or large-sized territorial sovereign government without overthrowing it. Powerful states that violate human rights might be more of a pariah minority than is currently the case. But unless they engaged in "aggression" or highly provocative foreign policies, it is unlikely that their domestic policies, however objectionable, would be effectively challenged from without, especially if they were significant participants in the world economy. The fate of certain aboriginal people, such as the Aché Indians in Paraguay, could only be protected against genocidal dangers if human rights NGOs were mobilized in their support and if the strengthening sense of human community embraced in a serious way the fate of such victims.

CONCLUSIONS

There are many possible intermediate variations on the course of the 1980s that could be put forward. It seems to me, however, that there is a polarizing of future possibilities, and that the two projections above represent the most plausible central lines of evolution for the world order system in the next decade. Current trends suggest strongly that the hard state hypothesis is much more likely to characterize the future than the moderate system hypothesis. The balance of available evidence points to the intensification of statism, which means that fewer governments will run their countries in a humane fashion, and a callous form of noninterventionism will inhibit increasingly international responses to human rights violations.

BEYOND MODERATION: THE GROUNDS OF HUMAN GOVERNANCE

As I have argued, even in the most optimistic view of the 1980s, territorial supremacy will insulate severe violations of human rights from international control. The state system imposes structural constraints that set firm limits on global policy. Overcoming these limits presupposes the emergence of a new world order system with enough central guidance capabilities and normative commitment to assure minimum standards of behavior throughout the world. What might this new world order be?

I think that it is most unlikely to suppose that a process of transformation will occur prior to the next century. Change in a world order system is not gradual, but rather occurs in convulsive jolts over a prolonged period, often a matter of several centuries. The "next" world order system is already taking shape within the existing one, although this growth process is obscured by the persistence of the present one. Political ecosystems, like natural ones, tend to maintain their familiar features until the dynamic of transformation has carried so far as to verge on collapse. Hence, system erosion is difficult to identify until long after it occurs.

In world order terms, it seems useful to consider World War I as the time when a new system began to take shape. Because of the destructiveness of that conflict many people were convinced that some reorganization of international society was necessary to avoid another war. Indeed, the creation of the League of Nations, although woefully inadequate to achieve such a goal, was a response to public pressures for some intergovernmental framework devoted to safeguarding world peace. This framework has evolved during the intervening decades. Its contours are indefinite as yet, and likely to remain controversial until a century or so after its dominance becomes evident. This subsidiary evolution has been complemented by the further extension of statism, especially as a consequence of the collapse of colonialism and the effort to build states strong enough to rule effectively and resist outside interferences. Further advances in the technology of war and the global dispersion of sophisticated military equipment has made war even more destructive. Also, the inadequacy of "freedom" as a managerial premise for the oceans has stimulated an expansion of statist control in the form of a massive seaward extension of territorial sovereignty.

The growing constituency for the next world order system is due in part to a deep fear that statism is leading the human race toward a dismal, dangerous future, that it is catastrophe-prone and lacking in the traditions of capabilities needed to safeguard the peoples of the earth and their descendants. The inverse of such dark forebodings is a visionary contemplation of a future that actualizes spiritual ideals of human unity in the arenas of culture, economics, and politics. In effect, this dualistic interpretation of the human situation has been well-embodied in René Dumont's phrase "utopia or else."[38]

In opposition to the "state" as a juristic, territorial center of military and bureaucratic power is the notion of "community" as an experiential, nonterritorial nexus of affinity and value. Whereas the state is set off by boundaries from other states and acts in the field of international relations, the community is bounded by nonterritorial fields of affinity and affection and has no necessary bureaucratic presence. The notion of "global community" is the animating ideal of an alternative world order system, leading to a dialectical emphasis on the unity of the whole and on the dignity of the individual and distinct substatal human groups. This tension between particular and general is, in essence, the proper foundation for the appreciation and protection of human rights. It implies that there would be no territorial enclave that could flout global community norms.

If this positive image of a new world order were ever realized, the occurrence of severe violations of human rights would undoubtedly become an anomaly. Patterns of ethnic, regional, and class domination that are now so characteristic of the way states are structured would be necessarily dissipated in most societies as this new system crystallized. However, new patterns of conflict would undoubtedly arise so long as the scarcity of valued goods—territory, wealth, status, influence—was not handled by a community of perfect equals. To be sure, territorially strong units would persist for decades, and these might govern in ways that violate fundamental norms of human rights. It is difficult to guess how such residual elements of the old world order system would be handled as the balance of energy swung to the new system and the whole context of political relations in the world changed.

This discussion of global transformation seeks only to posit the view that overcoming the constraints of statism requires a drastically altered world order system that rests on a universalistic view of human identity, and generates appropriate forms for the distribution of power and authority. In point of fact, the cumulative historical drift is slowly undermining the present world order, based on territorial states, despite the paradoxical short-term show of strength of statist mechanisms.[39] Whether this process of statist decline will lead to a more humane world order system is quite problematic. The centralization of power, nonterritoriality, and the decline of the state do not necessarily entail any normative promise. The outcome could well be tyrannical, chaotic, exploitative, technocratic, demeaning, and unstable.

What can be said with some confidence, however, is that with regard to world order, the 1980s will be a period of learning and experimentation. The multifaceted struggle to uphold basic human rights will be an important way to convey the image of alternative systems of world order and to test their relative potency.

More specifically, stressing the problems of severe violations of human rights may help mobilize constituencies for varieties of global reform that extend to a wider range of issues including those relating to economic, social, and ecological well-being. Bringing attention to the current situation will underscore how territoriality is serving as a shield for unjust and cruel polities and demonstrate that humane governance can only occur if conditions of security, fairness, and safety can be established at all levels of social organization and in all parts of the planet. Without progress at this fundamental level of human existence there is no way to *prevent* repressive methods of governance and little potential to correct severe violations. Ultimately, global guarantees of human rights are virtually synonymous with the quest for the next world order system.

NOTES

1. See *Amnesty International Report 1977* (London, England: Amnesty International, 1977), p. 9.

2. R. J. Vincent, *Nonintervention and International Order* (Princeton, N.J.: Princeton University Press, 1974), especially pp. 244–249.

3. The conclusion of "purity" is based, in part, on the fact that the French used troops that might have been needed elsewhere during the period. See ibid., p. 11.

4. For a useful discussion of the pros and cons of humanitarian intervention see essays by Ian Brownlie and Richard Lillich in John Norton Moore, ed., *Law and Civil War in the Modern World* (Baltimore: Johns Hopkins University Press, 1974), pp. 217–251.

5. The Charter of the United Nations makes reference to the promotion of human rights in several of its provisions, especially Articles 1, 55, and 56. On December 10, 1946, the UN General Assembly adopted the Universal Declaration of Human Rights by a unanimous vote of 48–0 (with the seven Soviet bloc members abstaining along with South Africa). The Universal Declaration was regarded as an initial step in the process of setting forth more elaborate and authoritative legal instruments in treaty form. The second step was taken when the General Assembly adopted by resolution on December 16, 1966, three human rights covenants: the International Covenant on Civil and Political Rights; the International Covenant on Economic, Social, and Cultural Rights; and the Optional Protocol to the International Covenant on Civil and Political Rights. The first two covenants have been widely ratified and are in force for those parties. President Carter has submitted these two covenants to the U.S. Senate for ratification, but no favorable action is expected in the immediate future. However, even for nonparties these covenants are generally regarded as evidence of widely shared governmental views as to the human rights requirements of international law. For convenient texts of the Universal Declaration and the covenants see Ian Brownlie, ed., *Basic Documents in International Law*, 2d ed. (Oxford, England: Oxford University Press, 1972), pp. 144–186. For a more complete collection of human rights documents see Brownlie, *Basic Documents on Human Rights* (Oxford, England: Oxford University Press, 1971).

6. "Pathological" in the text refers to psychologically deviant behavior on the part of a political leader, and should be distinguished from "structural" repression that is perceived by the leadership as functionally related to maintaining stable rule.

7. See Richard Arens, ed., *Genocide in Paraguay* (Philadelphia: Temple University Press, 1976), especially pp. 132–164.

8. See Shelton H. Davis, *Victims of the Miracle: Development and the Indians of Brazil* (Cambridge, England: Cambridge University Press, 1977).

9. For depiction by an American ambassador and his wife in Uganda from 1972 to 1973 see Thomas and Margaret Melady, *Idi Amin Dada: Hitler in Africa* (Mission, Kansas: Sheed, Andrews and McMeel, 1977). The Meladys contend, for instance, that during Amin's first year in office "about two-thirds of the Langi and Acholi soldiers in the army were killed." Under the prior regime the Ugandan army had been dominated by members of these two tribes.

10. For a fully documented account of the events considered, including the argument that genocide occurred, see Subrata Roy Chowdhury, *The Genesis of Bangladesh: A Study of International Legal Norms and Permissive Conscience* (New York: Asia Publishing House, 1972).

11. Article II(b) of the Genocide Convention defines genocide as extending to serious "mental harm"; also Article II(c) regards as genocide "Deliberately inflicting on the group conditions of life calculated to bring about its physical destruction in whole or in part." In effect, ethnocide is encompassed by genocide to the extent that if the identity of a people can be preserved only under certain conditions, then removing those conditions becomes tantamount to destroying the group.

12. For full account see "The Report of the Mackenzie Valley Pipeline Inquiry," vols. I and II (Ottawa, Canada: Minister of Supply and Services, 1977).

13. At present writing, Rhodesia and South-West Africa are administered by racist regimes, but there is a firm expectation that by the end of the 1970s these societies will be transformed into majority-ruled, multiracial independent states. Their transformed condition will be expressed by the formal adoption of their liberation names, Zimbabwe and Namibia, respectively. Each currently has a different status and each is likely to take a different route away from racism.

14. See Jean-François Revel, *The Totalitarian Temptation* (New York: Doubleday, 1976); see also Michael Crozier, Samuel Huntington, and Jozi Watanuki, *The Crisis of Democracy: Report on the Governability of Democracies to the Trilateral Commission* (New York: New York University Press, 1975).

15. For a systematic inquiry into the scope of human rights see the essay by Jorge Domínguez in this volume.

16. Official conceptions of human rights under the Carter administration have expanded, at least on the rhetorical level, to include "such vital needs as food, shelter, health care, and education," as well as such standard liberal fare as the rights of persons to be free from arbitrary governmental action and the right to enjoy the civil and political liberties necessary for genuine participation in the political life of the state. For a typical formulation of this enlarged conception of human rights see Warren Christopher, "Human Rights: Principle and Realism," *Department of State Bulletin,* vol. 77, no. 1992 (August 29, 1977), pp.269–273, especially pp. 269–270.

17. For impressive results along these lines see Amilcar Herrera and others, *Catastrophe or New Society: A Latin American World Model* (Ottawa: International Development Center, 1976); Graciela Chichilnisky, "Development, Basic Needs, and the International Order," *Journal of International Affairs,* vol. 31, no. 2, pp. 275–304, 1977.

18. See, for example, Simone Weil, *The Need for Roots* (New York: Harper & Row, Colophon edition, 1971; originally pub. 1952), pp. 3–39; see also John

McHale and Magda Cordell McHale, *Basic Human Needs: A Framework for Action* (New Brunswick, N.J.: Transaction Books, 1978).

19. David Morris and Florizelle B. Liser, "The PQLI: Measuring Progress in Meeting Human Needs," *ODC Communique,* no. 32, 1977.

20. Discussed by Johan Galtung in many places. See, for example, his essay in Saul H. Mendlovitz, ed., *On the Creation of a Just World Order* (New York: Free Press, 1975), pp. 152–153.

21. For argument along these lines see Richard Falk, "A World Order Perspective on Authoritarian Tendencies," mimeographed (New York: Institute for World Order, 1978).

22. A. James Gregor gives the figure of 1 to 3 million persons on the basis of "conservative estimates," *The Fascist Persuasion in Radical Politics,* (Princeton, N.J.: Princeton University Press, 1974), p. x.

23. See, for example, Samir Amin, "Self-Reliance and the New International Economic Order," *Monthly Review,* vol. 29, no. 3 (July/August 1977), pp. 1–21, especially pp. 2–3.

24. See Nicos Poulantzas, *Fascism and Dictatorship* (London: New Left Books, 1974), pp. 119, 191, 220–221.

25. More typical, however, has been to regard "humanitarian" rules of the international law of war as an aspect of human rights. These rules, however, are of limited scope. Their concern is to avoid unnecessary suffering for civilians and to confirm the obligation of countries to give medical treatment to all sick and wounded, even if enemy soldiers.

26. Michael Walzer writes in his preface: "I want to suggest that the arguments we make about war are most fully understood . . . as efforts to recognize and respect the rights of individual and associated men and women. The morality I shall expound is in its philosophical form a doctrine of human rights. . . . " See Walzer, *Just and Unjust Wars: A Moral Argument with Historical Illustrations* (New York: Basic Books, 1977), pp xv-xvi.

27. See Gareth Porter, *A Peace Denied: The United States, Vietnam, and the Paris Agreement* (Bloomington, Ind.: Indiana University Press, 1975).

28. For consideration of the extent of U.S. complicity in Trujillo's assassination see "Alleged Assassination Plots Involving Foreign Leaders," Interim Report, Select Senate Committee on Intelligence Activities, November 20, 1975, pp. 191–215.

29. See for example, Richard H. Ullman, "Human Rights and Economic Power: The United States Versus Idi Amin," *Foreign Affairs,* vol. 56, no. 3 (April 1978), pp. 529–543; also James H. Mittelman, "The Amin Phenomenon," unpublished ms., March 1978.

30. Contrary to some popular misconceptions, South African gold and dia-

monds are not "essential" to other countries, and constraints on their export would seriously deprive South Africa of foreign exchange.

31. For a report on the role of NGOs see "Actions of International NGOs in the Implementation of U.N. Resolutions on the Problem of Apartheid and assistance provided by them to the oppressed people of South Africa," Centre Against Apartheid, UN Dep't of Political and Security Council Affairs, March 1978, No. 78–04681; parallel study on role of national NGOs issued at the same time, No. 78–04682.

32. See Clyde Ferguson and William R. Cotter, "South Africa—What Is to Be Done," *Foreign Affairs*, vol. 56, no. 2 (January 1978), pp. 253–274.

33. See Roger D. Hansen, "Major U.S. Options on North-South Relations: A Letter to President Carter," in John W. Sewall and staff, *The United States and World Development: Agenda 1977* (New York: Praeger, 1977), pp. 67–68.

34. For example, see Herrera and others, *Catastrophe or New Society: A Latin American World Model*, and Chichilnisky, "Development, Basic Needs, and the International Order."

35. See Albert Fishlow et al., *Rich and Poor Nations in the World Economy* (New York: McGraw-Hill for the Council on Foreign Relations, 1978).

36. For a populist approach to human rights, see "The Universal Declarations of the Rights of Peoples," approved in Algiers 4 July 1976, International Documentation (IDOC), Bulletin no. 46, September, 1976; also see essays inspired by Algiers Declaration in Antonio Cassese and Edmond Jouve, eds., *Pour un droit des peuples* (Paris: Berger-Levrault, 1978).

37. For extended argument to this effect, see Falk, *A Study of Future Worlds* (New York: Free Press, 1975).

38. Rene Dumont, *Utopia or Else. . .* (New York: Universe Books, 1975).

39. For elaboration, see Falk, "A New Paradigm for International Legal Studies," *Yale Law Journal*, vol. 84, no. 5 (April, 1975), pp. 969–1021.

Selected Bibliography

Archer, Peter: "Action by Unofficial Organizations on Human Rights," in E. Luard (ed.), *The International Protection of Human Rights*, Thames and Hudson, London, 1967.

Arens, Richard (ed.): *Genocide in Paraguay*, Temple University Press, Philadelphia, 1976.

Brownlie, Ian (ed.): *Basic Documents on Human Rights*, Oxford University Press, London, 1971.

Buergenthal, Thomas, and Louis B. Sohn (eds.): *International Protection of Human Rights*, Bobbs-Merrill Co., New York, 1973.

Cantril, Hadley: *The Pattern of Human Concerns*, Rutgers University Press, New Brunswick, N.J., 1965.

Domínguez, Jorge I.: *Cuba: Order and Revolution*, Belknap Press of Harvard University Press, Cambridge, Mass., 1978.

Falk, Richard: *A Global Approach to National Policy*, Harvard University Press, Cambridge, Mass., 1975.

————, Gabriel Kolko, and Robert Jay Lifton (eds.): *Crimes of War*, Random House, New York, 1971.

Held, Virginia, Sidney Morgenbesser, and Thomas Nagle (eds.): *Philosophy, Morality and International Affairs*, Oxford University Press, New York, 1974.

Horowitz, Irving: *Genocide: State Power and Mass Murder*, Transaction Books, New Brunswick, N.J., 1976.

Inter-American Commission on Human Rights: *Handbook of Existing Rules Pertaining to Human Rights*, Organization for American States, Washington, D.C.

International Protection of Human Rights, Hearings Before Subcommittee on International Organizations and Movements, House Committee on Foreign Affairs, 93d Cong., Government Printing Office, Washington, D.C., 1974.

Lasswell, Harold, Daniel Lerner, and John D. Montgomery: *Values in Development,* MIT Press, Cambridge, Mass., 1976.

"The Role of Non-Governmental Organizations in Implementing Human Rights in Latin America," *Georgia Journal of International Law,* vol. 7, no. 477, 1977.

Schwelb, Egon: *Human Rights and the International Community,* Quadrangle Books, New York, 1964.

Scoble, Harry M., and Laurie S. Wiseberg: "Human Rights and Amnesty International," *Annals,* vol. 413, no. 11, 1974.

————: "The International League for Human Rights: The Strategy of Human Rights NGO," *Georgia Journal of International Law,* vol. 7, no. 289, 1977.

Snyder, Richard C., Charles F. Hermann, and Harold Lasswell: "A Global Monitoring System: Appraising the Effects of Government on Human Dignity," *International Studies Quarterly,* vol. 20, no. 2, June 1976.

U.S. Senate, Committee on Foreign Relations: *Foreign Policy Choices for the Seventies and Eighties,* Hearings, October 1975–March 1976, Government Printing Office, Washington, D.C., 1976, 2 vols.

Vincent, R. J.: *Nonintervention and International Order,* Princeton University Press, Princeton, N.J., 1974.

Walzer, Michael: *Just and Unjust Wars: A Moral Argument with Historical Illustrations,* Basic Books, New York, 1977.

Weissbrodt, David: "The Role of International Non-Governmental Organizations in the Implementation of Human Rights," *Texas International Law Journal,* no. 12, 1977.

Wood, Bryce: *Aggression and History: The Case of Ecuador and Peru,* University Microfilms International, Ann Arbor, Mich., 1978.

Interested readers should also look at the publications of Amnesty International, the Minority Rights Group, and Freedom House. A great deal of information is available in the various statistical publications of the United Nations, especially the *Statistical Yearbook.* Other sources include the annual reports of the Agency for International Development, the World Bank, the Inter-American Development Bank, and the Development Coordination Committee; and consult the series of more than 25 documents on human rights issued, principally in the form of hearings, by the Subcommittee on International Organizations of the Committee on International Relations, United States House of Representatives.

Index

Aché Indians (Paraguay), 216, 250
Africa:
  human rights, attitudes toward, 13,
    127, 220, 221, 237–238
    in Uganda, 14–15, 127, 234–236
  human rights in, 94, 96, 98, 218, 221
  (*See also* Organization of African
    Unity; Southern Africa;
    individual countries)
Afro-Asian Peoples' Solidarity
  Organization, 138
Aguilar, Andrés (OAS), 177
Albania, 97, 224
Aleman, Miguel (Mexico), 74
Allende, Salvador/Allende regime
  (Chile), 75, 123, 170, 184, 186
America, Central (*see* Latin America)
America, North, 28, 96
  (*See also* individual countries)
America, South (*see* Latin America)
American Convention on Human Rights,
  173–174, 190
  (*See also* Organization of American
    States)
American Declaration of the Rights and
  Duties of Man, 157, 168, 173
  (*See also* Organization of American
    States)
Amin, Idi:
  policies toward, 14–15, 208, 219,
    234–236, 240, 241, 249
    in Africa, 14–15, 127, 234–236
  regime of, 4, 12, 94, 127, 216, 219, 222,
    254n
  (*See also* Uganda)
Amnesty International (AI), 10, 22,
  139–141, 144–147, 165, 207, 239
  political prisoners and, 10, 101,
    140–141
  on torture, 93, 94, 96
Andean Pact, 164

Angola, 122
Anti-Slavery Society, 91, 120, 139
Arab Lawyers Union, 139
Arab states, 188, 209, 235
  human rights in, 91, 92, 94, 223
  (*See also* individual countries)
Argentina, 4, 14, 162, 170, 174, 180, 194,
  201
  human rights in, 94, 98, 100, 165, 166,
    170, 222, 223
  insurgency in, 4, 163, 165, 169, 171
  military government of, 163–166
  United States and, 182, 186, 187, 194
Asia, 94, 96, 97–98, 126
  (*See also* individual countries)
Association of Southeast Asian Nations
  (ASEAN), 13
Australia, 91, 96

Bahai International, 138
Bangladesh, 97, 100, 219
Banzer, Hugo (Bolivia), 164
Bariloche Institute, 32–33, 42, 43
Basic needs (*see* Needs)
Bejares, Hermán (Chile), 204n
Benavides, Oscar (Peru), 161
Bengalis (Bangladesh/India), 219
Biko, Steven (South Africa), 220, 239
Bolivia, 162, 168, 169, 200
  human rights in, 92, 98, 100, 165
  military government of, 164–165
Bordaberry, Juan M. (Uruguay), 170
Brazil, 3, 75, 162, 170, 174, 178, 186,
  196–197
  human rights in, 91, 94, 99, 100,
    165–167, 175–176
    Catholic Church and, 166, 169,
      171
    repression, 2, 101–102, 161, 169,
      171, 200, 222

Brazil (*Cont.*):
  military government of, 159–161, 163, 165–167, 169, 201
  status of, 160–161, 164, 185, 200
  United States and, 186–187, 190, 194, 201
Brezhnev, Leonid, 12, 224
  (*See also* U.S.S.R.)
British Commonwealth, 28
  (*See also* individual countries)
Bulgaria, 94, 96, 97, 101, 224
Burundi, 94, 218, 221

Cambodia, 219, 222
Cameroon, 91, 92
Canada, 189, 219
  (*See also* America, North)
Cárdenas, Lázaro (Mexico), 75, 77
Carter, Jimmy/Carter administration:
  human rights and, 156, 157, 180, 194, 196, 209–210, 254*n*, 255*n*
  in Latin America, 16, 186, 195
  (*See also* United States)
Castello Branco, Humberto (Brazil), 160
Castro, Fidel, 52, 63, 160
  (*See also* Cuba)
Catholic Church:
  in Latin America, 165–166, 169–171, 174
    Brazil, 166, 169, 171
    Cuba, 54, 59
    Mexico, 72–73, 84
Chad, 91, 98, 100
Chile, 12, 75, 80, 122–123, 162, 171, 175, 186, 193
  human rights in, 30, 94, 99, 100–102, 155–156, 165–166, 168–169, 176, 177
  repression, 102, 167, 169–170, 201, 204*n*
  OAS/IACHR and, 155, 169–170, 175–178, 183–184, 192
  United States and, 155–156, 181–190, 195–196, 199
China, People's Republic of, 14, 126, 238, 240, 244
  human rights in, 93, 226
Christian Democratic World Union, 138

Colombia, 161, 162, 170, 171, 186, 201
  human rights in, 94, 199
  OAS and, 174, 179
Commission on Human Rights (*see*
  Council of Europe; Organization of
  American States; United Nations,
  ECOSOC)
Communist countries:
  human rights in, 94, 96, 101, 248
  (*See also* Europe, East; individual
  countries)
Convention on the Elimination of Racial
  Discrimination, 221
  (*See also* United Nations)
Convention on Human Rights, 4, 124, 155
  (*See also* Council of Europe)
Costa Rica, 174, 202
  human rights in, 96, 128, 199
Council of Europe, 141, 142, 149, 155
  Convention on Human Rights, 4, 124, 155
  Human Rights Commission, 4, 10, 124, 155
  Human Rights Court, 4, 124, 155
  (*See also* Europe, West)
Cuba, 39, 50–66, 82–85, 88, 160, 165, 209
  authoritarianism in, 51–52, 58, 60, 62–63, 65, 85
  Communist Party in, 54, 56, 63–65
  corruption and crime in, 52, 58, 61–62, 63
  economy and labor in, 60–62, 84–85
  education and literacy in, 50–52, 83
  ethnic groups in, 53–55, 83–84
  health and well-being in, 52–53, 55, 83
  political prisoners in, 63–64, 85, 99, 101, 165, 200
    torture, 94, 114–115*n*
  religion in, 54, 59, 84
  United States and, 50, 194, 195, 223
  women, status of, in, 55–57, 83–84

Declaration of Santiago, 174
Dene Indians (Canada), 219
Díaz, Porfirio (Mexico), 163
Dominican Republic, 89, 200, 232
  OAS and, 174, 179
Dumont, René, 252

Ecocide (*see* Environment)
Ecuador, 162, 185, 188
  human rights in, 94, 171
  military government of, 164–165, 199
Egypt, 94
El Salvador, 186, 187
  human rights in, 91, 94, 165
Environment:
  as human rights issue, 227–228,
    243–244
Equatorial Guinea, 91, 94, 219, 222
Eritreans (Ethiopia), 226
Ethiopia, 4, 182, 226
Europe, 45, 93, 96, 189
  East, 44–45, 96, 224
    political prisoners in, 93, 96, 97,
      99–101
  (*See also* Communist countries;
    individual countries)
  West, 28, 44, 234, 236
    human rights, attitudes toward, 4–5,
      13–14, 155
    organizations for, 4, 10, 124, 139,
      140, 155, 157
  (*See also* Council of Europe;
    individual countries)

Faisal (Saudi Arabia), 92
Federation of South Arabia, 91
Ferreira-Aldunate, Wilson (Uruguay),
  187
Ford administration, 184
  (*See also* United States)
France, 14, 208
Franco, Francisco, 4
  (*See also* Spain)
Freedom House, 42
  Comparative Survey of Freedom,
    31–32
Frei, Eduardo (Chile), 75

Galtung, Johan, 226
Gastil, Raymond D. (Freedom House),
  31
Geisel, Ernesto (Brazil), 169, 197
Geneva Conventions, 126, 143
Genocide:
  definitions of, 216, 217, 226, 255*n*

Genocide (*Cont.*):
  incidence of, 216–220, 221, 250
Genocide Convention, 173, 217, 255*n*
Germany, 222, 223, 227
  East, 97, 101, 224
  West, 14
Ghana, 98, 100
Goulart, João (Brazil), 160
Gowon, Yakubu (Nigeria), 102
Great Britain (*see* United Kingdom)
Greece, 4
  human rights in, 94, 96, 155
Grenada, 94
Grunwald, Joseph (U.S.), 189
Guatemala, 160, 187, 194
  human rights in, 91, 165, 199
Guevara, Ernesto Ché, 168

Haiti, 94, 174, 186
Hansen, Olavo (Brazil), 167
Harkin Amendment, 184, 190
Hitler, Adolf, 217, 222, 223, 227
Honduras, 162, 174
  human rights in, 91, 94, 99, 100, 102
Hong Kong, 91
Human rights, action on:
  conditions for, 4, 13–14, 232–234
  obstacles to, 12, 207–210, 231–232
  prospects for, 12, 13, 16–17, 210–213,
    245–253
Human Rights Commission (*see* Council
  of Europe; Organization of
  American States; United Nations,
  ECOSOC)
Human Rights Court (*see* Council of
  Europe)
Human rights, covenants and documents
  on:
  Americas, 157, 168, 173–174, 190
  (*See also* Organization of American
    States)
  Europe, 4, 124
  (*See also* Council of Europe)
  international, 120, 126, 143, 173, 217,
    255*n*
  (*See also* United Nations)
Human rights, criteria for, 8–9, 27–31,
  33–41, 45–46, 87–89, 135

Human rights, data on, 22, 29, 31, 46–47,
    133–135
  restrictions on, 30, 136–138
  sources for, 135–138, 140, 144–146
Human rights, definitions of, 5–6, 8,
    43–45, 129–132, 156–157, 215–217,
    255n
  civil and political, 5, 25, 31, 32, 130–132
  economic and social, 5–7, 26, 32–33,
    130–132, 224–226
Human rights, organizations for:
  governmental:
    Americas (see Organization of
      American States,
      Inter-American Commission on
      Human Rights)
    Europe (see Council of Europe)
    international (see United Nations)
  proposals for, 13, 147–150
  private, 10–11, 22, 31–33, 91, 120,
    138–147, 170, 209–210
  (See also individual organizations)
Human rights, prospects for, 3–4,
    123–129, 207–213, 245–253
  in Africa, 234–241
  in Latin America, 199–202
Human rights, violations of, 1–4
  categories of, 88–96, 217
  (See also individual categories)
Hungary, 97, 100, 101
Hutu tribe (Burundi/Rwanda), 218

Ibo tribe (Nigeria), 226
India, 216, 219
  human rights in, 91–92, 94, 97, 100, 218
Indians, American, 69–71, 83–84, 91,
    216, 218, 219, 250
Indonesia, 94, 98, 99, 101, 249
Infant mortality:
  as human rights issue, 88–90
  rates of, 52, 67, 89–90
Inter-American Bar Association, 170
Inter-American Commission on Human
  Rights (see Organization of
  American States)
Inter-American Development Bank
  (IADB), 180, 183–184, 188–189, 190,
  193

Inter-American Peace Commission (see
  Organization of American States)
Inter-American Press Association, 170
International Alliance of Women, 139
International Association of Democratic
  Lawyers, 139, 141
International Commission of Jurists
  (ICJ), 10, 101, 139, 141–142,
  144–147, 239
  Center for the Independence of
    Lawyers, 142
  Review, 142
International Confederation of Free
  Trade Unions, 138
International Council of Women, 139
International Covenant on Civil and
  Political Rights (see United Nations)
International Covenant on Economic,
  Social and Cultural Rights (see
  United Nations)
International Federation of Human
  Rights, 139
International Labor Organization, 11, 149
International League for Human Rights,
  139
International Peace Bureau, 138
International Youth and Student
  Movement for the United Nations,
  138
Iran, 3
  human rights in, 12, 94, 128, 222, 249
Ireland, North (see United Kingdom,
  Ulster)
Irish Republican Army, 30–31
Israel, 122, 135, 209
Italy, 14, 227
Ivory Coast, 98, 100

Jackson Amendment, 188
Jamaica, 174, 202
Japan, 14, 28
Jews, 217
Jordan, 223

Kaplan, Abraham, 8, 33, 40
Kennedy, John F., 210
Kenya, 235

Kissinger, Henry, 178, 180–182
Korea, South:
    human rights in, 4, 12, 94, 222
    policies toward, 12, 14, 194

Lasswell, Harold, 8, 33, 40
Latin America, 44, 123, 161–162, 173–174
    human rights in, 96, 128, 156–157,
        165–171, 199–202, 218
    religious groups and, 165, 166, 169,
        171, 174
    military governments in, 159–171,
        199–201
    opposition/counteropposition in, 160,
        164, 165–166, 168–170, 195
    United States and, 15–16, 155–157,
        165, 180–190, 194–197, 199, 201,
        203–204n
    (See also Organization of American
        States; individual countries)
Latin American Social Science Council
    (CLACSO), 170
League of Nations, 120, 251
Lebanon, 215, 223
Letelier, Orlando, 200
Libya, 223
Lopez Mateos, Adolfo (Mexico), 77

Malawi, 98, 100
Mali, 91
Mao Tse-tung, 226
Marcos, Ferdinand (Philippines), 12, 94
Masie, Nguema Biyogo (Equatorial
    Guinea), 222
Mexico, 39, 66–85, 88, 94, 170, 174, 180,
    193, 199, 201
    corruption and crime in, 68–69, 72, 79
    economy and labor in, 73–77, 84–85
    education and literacy in, 66–67, 83
    government and politics in, 73, 77–81,
        163
    authority, 79–81, 85, 102
    health and well-being in, 67–69, 83
    Indians in, 69–71, 83–84
    political prisoners in, 80–81, 85, 99, 100
    religion in, 72–73, 84
    United States and, 50, 186
    women, status of, in, 70–71, 83–84

Michelini, Zelmar (Uruguay), 170
Minority Rights Group, 139
Mizo tribe (India), 218
Morocco, 94
Mozambique, 122
Mujibur Rahman (Bangladesh), 219
Mussolini, Benito, 227

Naga tribe (India), 218
Namibia, 122, 240, 255n
    (See also Southern Africa)
Needs, basic:
    as human rights issue, 5–7, 32–33,
        224–227, 241–243
Nepal, 92, 98, 100
New Hebrides, 91
New Zealand, 96
Nicaragua, 171, 185
    human rights in, 91, 99, 100, 102, 165,
        169, 199, 222
Nigeria, 13
    human rights in, 98, 100, 102, 226
Nuremberg Principles, 217

Ongania, Juan Carlos (Argentina), 163
Orfila, Alejandro (OAS), 177–178
Organization of African Unity (OAU), 13,
    141, 209
    Uganda and, 127, 235, 236
    (See also Africa; individual countries)
Organization of American States (OAS),
    141, 178, 179, 188, 197
    American Convention on Human
        Rights, 173–174, 190
    American Declaration of the Rights and
        Duties of Man, 157, 168, 173
    Charter of Bogotá, 192
    Chile and, 155, 169–170, 175–178,
        183–184, 192, 193
    human rights, attitudes toward, 173,
        177–179, 181, 190
    Inter-American Commission on
        Human Rights (IACHR), 10, 149,
        173, 174
    functioning of, 13, 124, 175–182,
        190–193, 202
    reports of, 165, 167, 176, 177, 178,
        200

Organization of American States (OAS)
(*Cont.*):
Inter-American Peace Commission
(IAPC), 192
United States and, 174, 176, 178–182,
190–193
(*See also* Latin America; individual
countries)
Organization for Economic Cooperation
and Development (OECD), 46
Organization of Petroleum Exporting
Countries (OPEC), 185, 188
Overseas Development Council, 226

Pakistan, 94, 216, 218–219, 221
Panama, 94, 178, 179
Paraguay:
Brazil and, 164, 170, 200
human rights in, 91, 94, 99, 100, 165,
188, 216, 250
military government of, 164, 165
Park Chung-Hee (South Korea), 12
Pax Romana, 138
Pérez, Carlos Andrés (Venezuela), 95
Perón, Juan (Argentina), 163
Peru, 161–162, 169, 170, 174
human rights in, 94, 95, 167
military government of, 161–165, 167,
199
United States and, 186, 187
Philippines, 14, 194
human rights in, 12, 91, 92, 94, 98, 100
Physical Quality of Life Index, 226
Pinochet, Augusto (Chile), 12, 166, 184,
193
Poland, 94
Political prisoners, 10, 92–93, 140–141,
165
as human rights issue, 88, 97–102
incidence of, 80–81, 85, 96–102
in Cuba, 63–64, 85, 99, 101, 165, 200
in East Europe, 96, 99, 101
(*See also* individual countries)
Portugal/Iberian peninsula, 96, 122, 224

Qadhafi, Muammar (Libya), 223
Quakers, 138

Racism, governmental, 220–221
Red Cross, 142–143
International Committee of, 139,
142–144, 145, 151n, 183
Revel, Jean-François, 224
Reynolds, Clark, 73
Rhodesia/Zimbabwe, 91, 98, 122, 155,
240, 255n
Roosevelt, Franklin D., 210
Ross, Ian (IDB), 183–184
Ruiz, Hector Gutierrez (Uruguay), 170
Rumania, 97, 101
Rwanda, 91, 94, 218

Saudi Arabia:
slavery in, 91, 92
Shah of Iran, 12
Singapore, 98, 100
Slavery:
as human rights issue, 88, 90–93, 120
incidence of, 91–93
in Saudi Arabia, 91, 92
Socialist International, 138
Somalis (Ethiopia), 226
Somoza, Anastasio (Nicaragua), 222
South Africa, 122, 124, 249, 256–257n
human rights in, 12, 89–90, 94, 127,
220–221, 244
policies toward, 12, 14, 15, 208, 209,
212, 220–221, 236–241
South America (*see* Latin America)
Southern Africa, 122–124, 126, 127, 240,
255n
Namibia, 122, 240, 255n
Soviet Union (*see* Union of Soviet
Socialist Republics)
Spain/Iberian peninsula, 4, 94, 96, 224
Sri Lanka, 94, 98, 100
Stalin, Josef, 222, 223
(*See also* U.S.S.R.)
Stephansky, Ben (U.S.), 166
Stockholm Conference of 1972 on the
Human Environment, 227
Stroessner, Alfredo (Paraguay), 164
Swiss/Switzerland, 142–143
Syria, 94, 208

Tanzania, 128, 235
  Zanzibar, 98, 100
Terrorism, 4
  Arab, 222–223
  governmental, 221–223, 226
  OAS on, 180
Thailand, 222
Third World, 146, 147, 221, 236, 242
  needs of, 193, 225, 248
  South Africa and, 220, 237–238, 241
  (*See also* individual countries)
Torture:
  as human rights issue, 22, 30–31, 88,
    95, 135, 171
  incidence of, 93–96, 101, 155
  (*See also* individual countries)
Totalitarianism, 223–224
Treaty of Rio de Janeiro, 192
Trujillo, Rafael (Dominican Republic),
  89, 232
Tunisia, 94
Tutsi tribe (Burundi/Rwanda), 218

Uganda:
  human rights in, 4, 12, 91, 94, 127, 216,
    218–219, 221, 222, 244, 254n
  policies toward, 14–15, 208, 219,
    234–236, 240, 241, 249
  in Africa, 14–15, 127, 235–236
Ulster (*see* United Kingdom)
Union of Soviet Socialist Republics
  (U.S.S.R.), 3, 14, 85, 126, 134, 139,
  168, 187, 188, 196, 220, 235, 238, 240
  constitution of, 26–27
  human rights in, 4, 12, 93, 94, 96, 97,
    101, 212, 223, 224
United Kingdom (Great Britain), 14, 28,
  91, 136, 138, 219, 238, 240
  Ulster (North Ireland):
    human rights in, 2, 4, 30–31, 94, 95,
      96, 135, 155
United Nations, 11, 141, 142, 149, 155,
  157, 173, 183, 216, 227, 249
  Africa and, 122–124, 127, 235, 238–239
  agencies of, 7, 11, 121–122
  bias and ineffectuality of, 10, 123–124,
    135, 147, 209, 211, 245, 246

United Nations (*Cont.*):
  ECOSOC Commission on Human
    Rights, 121–123, 135, 155
  human rights, documents and
    resolutions on, 13, 121–122, 217,
    221, 227, 254n
  Convention on the Elimination of
    Racial Discrimination, 221
  International Covenant on Civil and
    Political Rights, 44, 121,
    123–124, 131–132, 254n
  International Covenant on
    Economic, Social and Cultural
    Rights, 121, 123, 131, 225,
    254n
  Universal Declaration on Human
    Rights, 5, 25–29, 33–41, 43,
    45–46, 58, 88, 121, 129, 132, 140,
    173, 210, 225, 244, 254n
  International Labor Organization, 11,
    149
  UNESCO, 141, 142, 147, 149
  World Health Organization, 11
United States, 3, 50, 53, 54, 138, 139, 168,
  170, 200, 223, 232, 240, 243
  Agency for International Development
    (AID), 23, 186, 188–189
  human rights, concepts of, 5, 25–26,
    32, 43, 210
  human rights policies, 14, 15, 16,
    46–47, 155–156, 157, 182–183,
    194, 196, 219, 220, 234–236, 238
  Department of State and, 180–185,
    187–188, 191–192, 197
  toward Latin America, 15–16,
    155–156, 157, 165, 180–190,
    194–197, 199, 201, 203–204n
  (*See also* individual countries)
  OAS/IACHR and, 174, 176, 178–182,
    190–193
Universal Declaration on Human Rights
  (*see* United Nations)
Uruguay, 162, 174, 193, 200
  human rights in, 94, 99, 100, 135, 145,
    155–156, 165, 166, 168, 169, 170,
    171
  military government of, 164, 165–166
  United States and, 155–156, 182, 187,
    188

Vance, Cyrus R., 180
Velasco Ibarra, José María (Ecuador), 164
Venezuela, 171, 185, 189, 193, 201
  human rights in, 94, 95, 199
  OAS and, 174, 179, 180
  United States and, 186, 187, 188
Videla, Jorge Rafael (Argentina), 169, 222
Vietnam, 145, 151*n*, 228
Vincent, John, 208
Vorster, John (South Africa), 12

Walzer, Michael, 228, 256*n*
War crimes, 228, 229, 244, 256*n*
War of the Pacific, 162
Watusi tribe (*see* Tutsi)
Wilson, Woodrow, 210
Women, status of, 36–37, 91
  in Cuba, 55–57, 83–84
  in Mexico, 70–71, 83–84
Women's International Democratic Federation, 139

Women's International League for Peace and Freedom, 139
World Assembly of Youth, 138
World Bank, 11, 23, 184, 190, 193, 225
World Confederation of Labour, 138
World Council of Churches, 138, 169
World Federation of Democratic Youth, 138–139
World Federation of Trade Unions, 138
World Federation of U.N. Associations, 138
World Health Organization, 11
World Jewish Congress, 138
World Muslim Congress, 138
World Peace Council, 138
World YMCA-World YWCA, 139

Zaire, 91
Zanzibar (Tanzania), 98, 100
Zimbabwe/Rhodesia, 91, 98, 122, 155, 240, 255*n*

About the Authors

JORGE I. DOMÍNGUEZ is an assistant professor of government and a research fellow at the Center for International Affairs, Harvard University, where he received his Ph.D. in 1972. He is the author of *Governing Cuba: Political Order, Change and Revolution in the Twentieth Century*; he has also written numerous articles and monographs.

NIGEL S. RODLEY is currently Legal Advisor for Amnesty International and part-time lecturer in law at the London School of Economics and Political Science. His past positions include Associate Economic Affairs Officer at the United Nations and Research Fellow at the Center for International Studies at New York University. He is co-editor of *International Law in the Western Hemisphere* and the author of several articles on international law and human rights.

BRYCE WOOD retired in 1973 as Deputy Director for Latin America, Foreign Area Fellowship Program of the American Council of Learned Societies and the Social Science Research Council, where, since 1960, he had been a staff member of the Joint Committee on Latin American Studies. He is the author of *The Making of the Good Neighbor Policy; The United States and Latin American Wars, 1932–1942;* and *Aggression and History: The Case of Ecuador and Peru*, as well as numerous articles.

RICHARD FALK is the author or editor of numerous books and articles dealing with various aspects of international law and world politics, including *This Endangered Planet, A Study of Future Worlds, A Global Approach to National Policy, Crimes of*

War (co-editor), and *The Future of the International Legal Order* (co-editor). He has been a professor at the Center of International Studies, Princeton University, since 1975. Professor Falk is on the board of directors of the Institute for World Order and is a trustee of the Procedural Aspects of International Law Institute; he is on the editorial board of a number of journals, including *Foreign Policy* and the *American Journal of International Law*.

RICHARD ULLMAN, currently the editor of the journal *Foreign Policy*, was Director of the 1980s Project of the Council on Foreign Relations until 1977. Before devoting full time to the Project, he was also Director of Studies at the Council. Richard Ullman has taught government and international affairs at Harvard and Princeton universities and was Associate Dean and Director of the Graduate Program at the Woodrow Wilson School of Public and International Affairs. Richard Ullman's publications include *Anglo-Soviet Relations, 1917–1921* (3 vols.), *Theory and Policy in International Relations* (co-editor), and many articles on international affairs.